BEAT THE PRESS WITH SINGLE & DOUBLE PIVOTS

Build Up Play and Sessions from Flick, Klopp and Emery's Tactics

Written by
Athanasios Terzis

Published by

BEAT THE PRESS WITH SINGLE & DOUBLE PIVOTS

Build Up Play and Sessions from Flick, Klopp and Emery's Tactics

First Published July 2025 by SoccerTutor.com
info@soccertutor.com | www.SoccerTutor.com

UK: 0208 1234 007 | **US:** (305) 767 4443 | **ROTW:** +44 208 1234 007
ISBN: 978-1-910491-79-9

Copyright: SoccerTutor.com Limited © 2025. All Rights Reserved.

All rights reserved. No part of this publication may be reproduced, stored in a retrieval system, or transmitted in any form or by any means, electronic, mechanical, photocopy, recording or otherwise, without prior written permission of the copyright owner. Nor can it be circulated in any form of binding or cover other than that in which it is published and without similar condition including this condition being imposed on a subsequent purchaser.

Author: Athanasios Terzis

Editor: Alex Fitzgerald - SoccerTutor.com

Diagrams designed by SoccerTutor.com
All diagrams in this book have been created using Tactics Manager Software - Available from www.SoccerTutor.com

Note: While every effort has been made to ensure the technical accuracy of the content of this book, neither the author nor publishers can accept any responsibility for any injury or loss sustained as a result of the use of this material.

CONTENTS

Meet the Author: Athanasios Terzis 8
Introduction 9
Coaches Studied to Produce the Tactical Analysis for this Book 10
Diagram Key & Coaching Format 12

Build Up Play Factors: Essential Skills and Opposition Pressing Tactics with Different Formations 13

Build Up Play Factors 14
1. Essential Goalkeeper Skills During Build Up Play 14
2. Essential Defender and Defensive Midfielder Skills During Build Up Play ..15
3. Different Types of High Pressing by Opposition (High or Ultra-Aggressive) ...16
4. Numerical Situation in the Low Area when Opposition Press High 18
5. Different Types of Defending Used by Opposition During High Pressing ...27

Tactical Analysis: Build Up to Beat the Press - Break Lines vs High Press Zonal Defending with a Single Pivot 32

Build Up Play from the Back Principles and Objectives 33
Build Up Play vs High Pressing and Zonal Defending with a Single Pivot (4-3-3) ... 34
Options for Breaking the First and Second Pressing Lines with a Single Pivot (4-3-3) ... 36
Drawing Press with a Pass and Exploit Gaps to Play in Between the Lines ... 39
Goalkeeper Draws Press to Create Space for Centre Backs (4-3-3) 40
Playing Against a Compact Central Block Leaves Space Out Wide (4-3-3) 44

Training Session 1: Build Up to Beat the Press - Break Lines vs High Press Zonal Defending with a Single Pivot 46

1. Passing Decisions to Break Lines Depending on Opposition Pressing 47
2. Breaking Lines Based on Opponent Reactions 6 (+GK) v 2 Functional Practice ... 48
3. Draw the Press and Break Lines Against a High Press 8v6 (+GKs) Positional Game ... 50
4. Break Lines Through Turning, Recycling the Ball, or Dribbling Forward 3 Zone Conditioned Game 52

Contents

Tactical Analysis: Build Up to Beat the Press - Break Lines vs High Press Zonal Defending with a Double Pivot ... 53

Build Up Play from the Back Principles and Objectives with a Double Pivot (4-2-3-1) ... 54
Build Up Play Against High Pressing and Zonal Defending with a Double Pivot (4-2-3-1) ... 55
Drawing Press from Midfielder to Exploit Space Created Between the Lines Behind ... 59
Goalkeeper Draws Press to Create Space Wide ... 60

Training Session 2: Build Up to Beat the Press - Break Lines vs High Press Zonal Defending with a Double Pivot ... 61

1. Passing Decisions to Break Lines Depending on Opposition Pressing ... 62
2. Breaking Lines Based on Opponent Reactions 6 (+GK) v 2 Functional Practice ... 63
3. Draw the Press and Break Lines Against a High Press 10 v 6 (+GKs) Positional Game ... 65
4. Break Lines Through Turning, Recycling the Ball, or Dribbling Forward 3 Zone Conditioned Game ... 67

Tactical Analysis: Build Up to Beat the Press - Goalkeeper's Passing Over Pressing Lines ... 68

Goalkeeper's Passing Over Second Pressing Line ... 69
Goalkeeper's Passing Directly to Players Positioned Between the Lines ... 70

Training Session 3: Build Up to Beat the Press - Goalkeeper's Passing Over Pressing Lines ... 74

1. Goalkeeper's Passing Over Pressing Lines and Decisions to Play in Behind ... 75
2. Goalkeeper's Passing Over Second Pressing Line Functional Practice with Target Zones ... 77
3. Goalkeeper's Passing Over Second Pressing Line 10 v 8 (+GKs) Functional Practice with Target Zones ... 79
4. Goalkeeper's Passing Over Second Pressing Line Conditioned Tactical Game ... 81

Tactical Analysis: Build Up to Beat the Press - Strong Side Advantage vs High Press Zonal Defending ... 82

Numerical Situations Against High Pressing with Zonal Defending (Single Pivot) ... 83
Numerical Situations Against High Pressing with Zonal Defending (Double Pivot) ... 86

Training Session 4: Build Up to Beat the Press - Strong Side Advantage vs High Press Zonal Defending ... 88

1. Exploiting Numerical Advantage to Find Free Player Continuous Possession Game ... 89

Contents

2. Exploiting 4v3 Numerical Advantage 3-Team Small Sided Game 91
3. Build Up with Numerical Advantage on Strong Side Dynamic Split-Pitch Game (Single Pivot) 92
4. Build Up with Numerical Advantage on Strong Side Dynamic Split-Pitch Game (Double Pivot) 93
5. Build Up with Numerical Advantage on Strong Side 11v11 Conditioned Game 94

Tactical Analysis: Build Up to Beat the Press - Strong Side Equality vs High Press Zonal Defending 95

Switching Play from Strong to Weak Side with Single Pivot Midfield (4-3-3) 96

Training Session 5: Build Up to Beat the Press - Strong Side Equality vs High Press Zonal Defending 102

1. Build Up Combinations and Switching Play with Target Areas 103
2. Build Up Play with Equal Numbers and Switch Play in a Dynamic 3-Team Game 105
3. Split-Pitch Build Up Tactical Game to Beat the Press with Equal Numbers (4-3-3).... 107
4. Reading the Game Situation (Advantage or Equal Numbers) 11v11 Conditioned 3 Zone Game 108

Tactical Analysis: Build Up to Beat the Press Against High Press with Zonal Defending and Man Marking 110

Build Up Against High Press with Zonal Defending and Man Marking (Single Pivot) 111
Build Up Against High Press with Zonal Defending and Man Marking (Double Pivot) 114

Training Session 6: Build Up to Beat the Press Against High Press with Zonal Defending and Man Marking 118

1. Exploit 3v2 Numerical Advantage with Single Pivot Midfield Positional Small Sided Game 119
2. Exploit 3v2 Numerical Advantage with Double Pivot Midfield Positional Small Sided Game 121
3. Exploit 3v2 Midfield Advantage Against High Press with Zonal and Man Marking Conditioned Game 123

Tactical Analysis: Build Up to Beat the Press Against Ultra-Aggressive Pressing with Zonal Defending and Man Marking .. 124

Build Up Against Ultra-Aggressive Pressing with Zonal Defending and Man Marking .. 125
Build Up Against Ultra-Aggressive Pressing with Zonal Defending and Man Marking (Single Pivot) 126

Contents

Build Up Against Ultra-Aggressive Pressing with Zonal Defending and Man Marking (Double Pivot) 134

Training Session 7: Build Up to Beat the Press Against Ultra-Aggressive Pressing with Zonal Defending and Man Marking .. 138

1. Functional Build Up Patterns vs Ultra-Aggressive Pressing to Play Through or Over . 139
2. Build Up Patterns with Link Player Principles vs Ultra- Aggressive Pressing and Man Marking 140
3. Using the Link Player to Move the Ball to the Free Player 8v8 (+GKs) Conditioned Game 141
4. Finding Free Player Against Ultra-Aggressive Pressing Half Pitch Game 144
5. Finding the Free Player Against Ultra-Aggressive Pressing 11v11 Game 146

Tactical Analysis: Build Up to Beat the Press - Exploit Space Out Wide to Bypass Midfield Marking 147

Build Up to Exploit Space Out Wide and Bypass Midfield Marking (Single Pivot) 148
Build Up to Exploit Space Out Wide and Bypass Midfield Marking (Double Pivot) 155

Training Session 8: Build Up to Beat the Press - Exploit Space Out Wide to Bypass Midfield Marking 158

1. Decision Making to Break Lines in Wide Areas Depending on Opposition Pressing .. 159
2. Decision Making to Break Lines in Wide Areas Depending on Opposition Pressing Small Sided Game 160
3. Split-Pitch Read the Game Situation Build Up Play Tactical Game to Beat the Press (4-3-3) 161
4. Split-Pitch Read the Game Situation Build Up Play Tactical Game to Beat the Press (4-2-3-1) 162

Tactical Analysis: Build Up to Beat the Press Against Full Pitch Man Marking 163

Build Up Solutions Against Full Pitch Man Marking (Single Pivot) 164
Build Up Solutions Against Full Pitch Man Marking (Double Pivot) 172

Training Session 9: Build Up to Beat the Press Against Full Pitch Man Marking 175

1. Beating a Full Pitch Man Marking Press by Finding Free Player Support Play Zones.. 176
2. Beating a Full Pitch Man Marking Press with a Long Pass and Support Runs Functional Combinations 177

Contents

3. Beating a Full Pitch Man Marking Press with a Single Pivot Build Up Shape in a Half Pitch Game 178

4. Beating a Full Pitch Man Marking Press with the Goalkeeper's Long Pass 6v6 (+GKs) Game 180

5. Reading Tactical Triggers to Beat the Press Against Full Pitch Man Marking Game .. 182

Final Message for Coaches 183

Meet the Author

MEET THE AUTHOR: ATHANASIOS TERZIS

- Football Tactics Expert
- Award Winning Author
- Coach Instructor for German Coaches Association (BDFL) and Scottish FA - UEFA A + Pro
- UEFA Pro Coaching Licence
- Greek Football Federation Instructor
- PAOK U23 Assistant Coach
- Analyst (Pundit) for Cosmote TV
- Former Coach of Professional Teams in Greece
- M.S.C. - Coaching and Conditioning
- Former Technical Director of DOXA Dramas Academy (Greek 2nd division)
- Former Professional Football Player

Athanasios Terzis is a football tactics expert and instructor for many coaching seminars and workshops around the world. Athanasios has written many best selling football coaching books published by **SoccerTutor.com** in multiple languages (English, Spanish, German, Italian, Greek, Japanese, Korean and Chinese) including:

- Beat the Press with a Box Midfield - Build Up Play and Sessions from Guardiola, Alonso and Arteta's Tactics
- Pep Guardiola - Coaching High Pressing Tactics & Sessions Against Different Formations
- Marcelo Bielsa Attacking Tactics and Sessions
- Diego Simeone Attacking and Defending Tactics from Atlético Madrid's 4-4-2
- Pep Guardiola's Attacking Tactics - Tactical Analysis and Sessions from Manchester City's 4-3-3
- Creative Attacking Play - From the Tactics of Conte, Allegri, Simeone, Mourinho, Wenger & Klopp
- Marcelo Bielsa - Coaching Build Up Play Against High Pressing Teams
- Coaching the Juventus 3-5-2 - Tactical Analysis and Sessions: Attacking and Defending
- Jürgen Klopp's Attacking and Defending Tactics from Borussia Dortmund's 4-2-3-1
- FC Barcelona Training Sessions: 160 Practices from 34 Tactical Situations
- Jose Mourinho's Real Madrid - A Tactical Analysis
- FC Barcelona - A Tactical Analysis

INTRODUCTION: BEAT THE PRESS WITH SINGLE & DOUBLE PIVOTS

As football evolves, the **importance of structured build up play from the goalkeeper continues to grow**. More teams are using positional play principles to progress the ball under pressure with single and double midfield pivots, with formations such as the **4-3-3 (single pivot)** and **4-2-3-1 (double pivot)** offering a balance between control, width, and attacking versatility.

This book provides a detailed tactical breakdown of build up play in these formations, with insights drawn from:

- **Hansi Flick** (FC Barcelona)
- **Jürgen Klopp** (Liverpool)
- **Unai Emery** (Aston Villa)

The focus is on how these teams:

- **Create positional advantages**
- **Maintain passing options under pressure**
- **Progress the ball effectively against different pressing structures**

The first sections examine the key factors influencing build up play, starting with an analysis of pressing strategies:

- **High Pressing (on first receiver)**
- **Ultra-Aggressive Pressing (up to GK)**

Following this, we explore the defensive principles used in pressing, including:

- **Zonal Defending**
- **Pressing with Man Marking**
- **Hybrid of Zonal and Man Marking**

We then **outline tactical solutions** to bypass these defensive structures, helping teams effectively build up play from the back under pressure.

For a deeper understanding of build up variations, the **first volume of this series (previous book) focuses on build up play using the box midfield**, featuring tactical insights from **Pep Guardiola** (Manchester City), **Mikel Arteta** (Arsenal) and **Xabi Alonso** (Bayer Leverkusen).

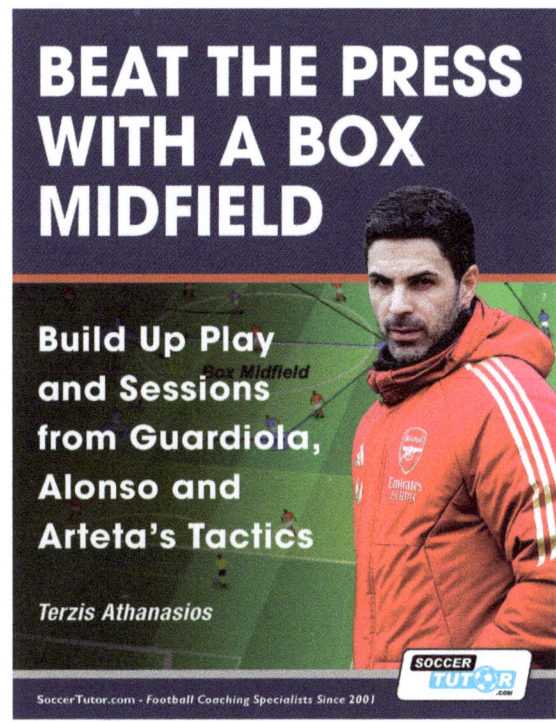

Together, these two volumes provide a comprehensive analysis of how top teams navigate the challenges of build up play across different systems.

COACHES STUDIED TO PRODUCE THE TACTICAL ANALYSIS FOR THIS BOOK

Hansi Flick

FC Barcelona (2024–25 Season):

- Hansi Flick implemented a 4-2-3-1 formation to structure Barcelona's build up and attacking play.
- The double pivot (F. de Jong and Pedri) provided stability and vertical ball progression. The full backs (Balde and Koundé) provided width and supported wide progression. Olmo operated as the Nº10, dropping into deeper areas to create central overloads.
- Flick's balanced and fluid approach improved transitions and positional dominance.
- Barcelona won La Liga, the Copa del Rey, and reached the UEFA Champions League semi-finals.

Bayern Munich (2019–21):

- Flick consistently used a 4-2-3-1, combining structure with attacking intent.
- In 2019–20, Kimmich and Thiago formed a strong double pivot in a standout season. The full backs (Davies and Pavard) stretched play and supported transitions. Müller dropped into midfield to link play and create overloads. Bayern pressed aggressively and dominated through fluid possession.
- Flick's Bayern team won the Bundesliga, DFB-Pokal, Champions League, Super Cup, and Club World Cup.

Impact of 4-2-3-1 Build Up Play:

- 4-2-3-1 offers Flick control, clarity, and fluidity across all phases. It blends stability in the build up phase with dynamic attacking rotations.
- Central overloads and vertical play defined both Bayern Munich and FC Barcelona's success.
- The system remains key to Flick's structured and flexible philosophy.

Coaches Studied to Produce the Tactical Analysis for this Book

Jürgen Klopp

Liverpool (2015–24):

- Jürgen Klopp introduced a high pressing, vertical 4-3-3 system with structured build up play.
- The defensive midfielder dropped into the back line to support the build up. The full backs (Alexander-Arnold and Robertson) advanced high and delivered from wide areas. The narrow front 3 created central threats and opened space for overlapping runs.
- Liverpool won the Premier League, Champions League, FA Cup, League Cup, and Club World Cup.

Impact of 4-3-3 Build Up Play:

- The 4-3-3 gave Liverpool structure, control, and attacking width. It became one of Europe's most recognisable and effective tactical systems. Liverpool consistently competed for major trophies with a clear, defined identity.

Unai Emery

Aston Villa (2022–24):

- Unai Emery uses a 4-2-3-1 system centred on structured build up and positional control.
- The double pivot circulates the ball and helps progress play through the key central areas.
- The Nº10 and wingers drop into pockets to create overloads between the lines.
- Emery's build up play approach prioritises control, compactness, and vertical ball progression.

Impact of 4-2-3-1 Build Up Play:

- The 4-2-3-1 gives Emery structure, control, and attacking fluidity. His tactics have brought consistency and high-level performances from his team.
- Aston Villa qualified for the UEFA Champions League and narrowly lost the quarter-finals to winners PSG.

DIAGRAM KEY & COACHING FORMAT

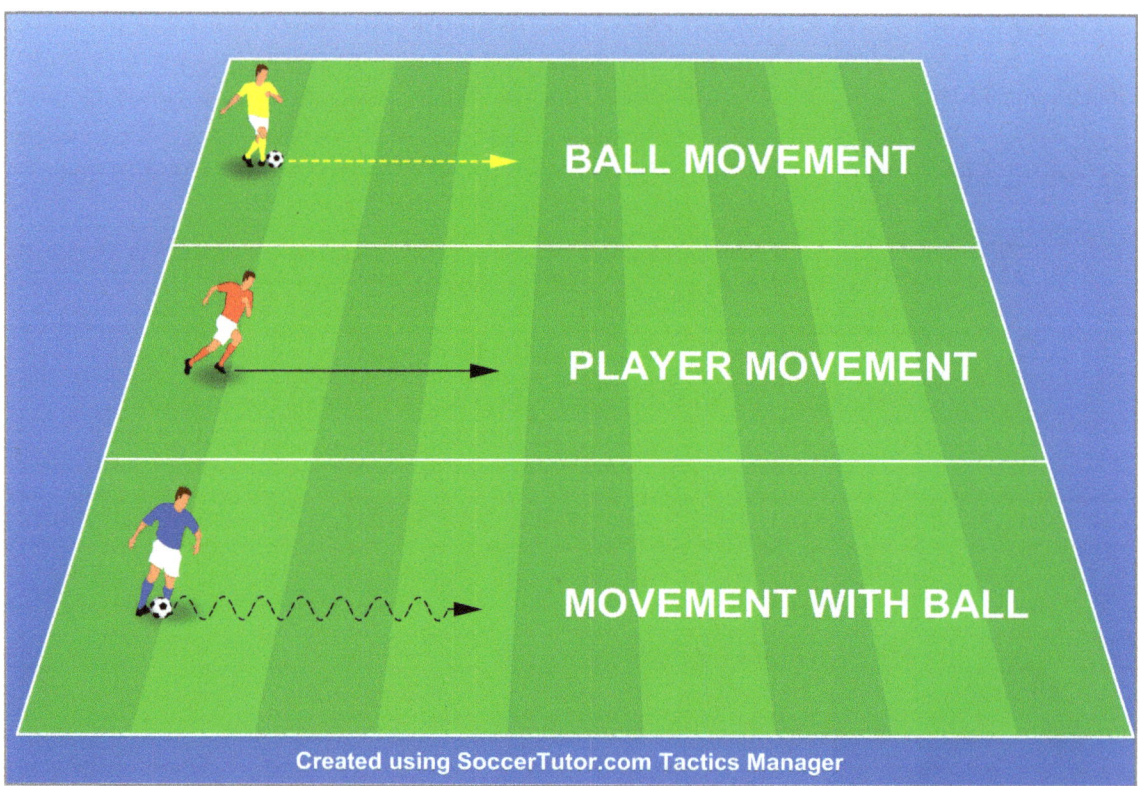

TACTICAL ANALYSIS

- All of the analysis in this book is based on recurring patterns of play observed within **Hansi Flick's Barcelona**, **Jürgen Klopp's Liverpool**, and **Unai Emery's Aston Villa** teams. Once the same phase of play is observed multiple times across many matches, the tactics are seen as a pattern.
- Each action, pass, movement (on or off the ball), and positioning of each player on the pitch, including body shape, is presented with a full description.

TRAINING SESSIONS BASED ON THE TACTICS

- Technical, Functional and Tactical Practices
- Functional Games / Conditioned Games
- Name/Objective, Full Description, Rules/Conditions, Restrictions, Variations, Progressions, and Coaching Points (if applicable)

BUILD UP PLAY FACTORS

Technical Requirements and Opposition Analysis

Essential Skills and Opposition Pressing Tactics with Different Formations

NOTE: *The information is this section also appears in the "Beat the Press with a Box Midfield" book (previous volume in this series).*

It is included again here due to its importance and for the ease of reference for the new content which follows in the subsequent sections of the book.

Build Up Play Factors

There are several factors that affect a team's success when building up play from the goalkeeper and defence:

1. **Essential Goalkeeper Skills During Build Up Play**
2. **Essential Defender and Defensive Midfielder Skills During Build Up Play**
3. **Different Types of High Pressing by Opposition (High or Ultra-Aggressive)**
4. **Numerical Situation in the Low Area when Opposition Press High**
5. **Different Types of Defending Used by Opposition During High Pressing**

1. Essential Goalkeeper Skills During Build Up Play

The goalkeeper plays a crucial role in building up play from the back. If they lack certain technical abilities or the ability to read the game and make good decisions, the team's progression of play is compromised, making build up a high risk strategy for the coach. This is why **coaches who implement these tactics place a strong emphasis on selecting or developing a goalkeeper with the right skill set**. If they do not meet these demands, teams often invest in signing one who does, as seen when Pep Guardiola brought in Ederson from Benfica (replacing Joe Hart) to fit Manchester City's playing style.

A goalkeeper who is proficient in build up play **must be comfortable on the ball and capable of executing various types of passes under pressure**. This includes high level skills in receiving, ball control, and changing direction with the ball when necessary.

The ability to remain composed when pressed allows the team to retain possession and find progressive passing options.

Passing range is another essential trait. A goalkeeper must be able to play:

- **Short passes** with accuracy to defenders, ensuring smooth ball circulation in the first phase of the build up.
- **Through passes** that break at least one and sometimes two lines of pressure, enabling the team to bypass or break through the opposition's press.
- **Medium-range passes** that travel over two lines of pressure, allowing the team to quickly switch play or progress the ball to midfielders in space.
- **Long passes** that are accurately played behind the opposition's defensive line, providing a direct route to goal when necessary.

An effective goalkeeper must now be a **key distributor**, acting as the foundation for the possession phases. Their **technical ability and composure when pressed directly influence the success of a team's build up play**, making them an integral part of modern tactical systems.

2. Essential Defender and Defensive Midfielder Skills During Build Up Play

The defenders play a crucial role in building up play from the back, forming the second line of the team's attacking structure, with the goalkeeper acting as the first line. As the primary receivers of the goalkeeper's initial pass, defenders must be highly competent in:

- **Receiving**
- **Dribbling**
- **Passing the ball with precision**

Their ability to **remain composed under pressure and distribute effectively** is essential for maintaining possession and progressing the play forward. To execute build up play efficiently, defenders must be able to:

- **Comfortably receive the ball in tight spaces while under pressure from pressing opponents**
- **Carry the ball forward when space is available**
- **Draw out opponents to create passing lanes**

Accurate short and medium-range passing skills are crucial, enabling the defenders to connect with teammates and bypass the first line of pressure. Their **decision making must be quick and precise**, ensuring they do not invite unnecessary risk while playing out from the back.

Defensive midfielders must possess similar technical qualities, as they frequently receive the ball in congested areas. In addition to their ability to pass and receive under pressure, they **must excel in scanning their surroundings** before receiving passes. Studies have shown that **elite players scan the pitch 6-8 times in the 10 seconds before receiving the ball**, allowing them to:

- **Anticipate opposition movements**
- **Locate teammates**
- **Identify available space**

This level of awareness enables them to make quick, informed decisions, ensuring smooth ball progression.

Defenders and defensive midfielders must be proactive in possession, **constantly making themselves available to receive the ball**. They should adopt positions that provide passing options for teammates, creating angles that allow for fluid ball circulation. After playing a pass, they must immediately reposition themselves to offer further support, ensuring continuity in possession. This constant movement and awareness helps to **maintain the team's structure and allow the team to advance the ball efficiently while minimising the risk of losing possession**.

The ability to combine technical skills with intelligent movement is fundamental to build up play effectively. Defenders and defensive midfielders who can execute these principles consistently provide their team with greater control in possession, making them less vulnerable to opposition pressing and better equipped to transition into attacking phases.

Build Up Play Factors: Essential Skills and Opposition Pressing Tactics

3. Different Types of High Pressing by Opposition (High or Ultra-Aggressive)

A. High Pressing (On First Receiver) with 4-4-2

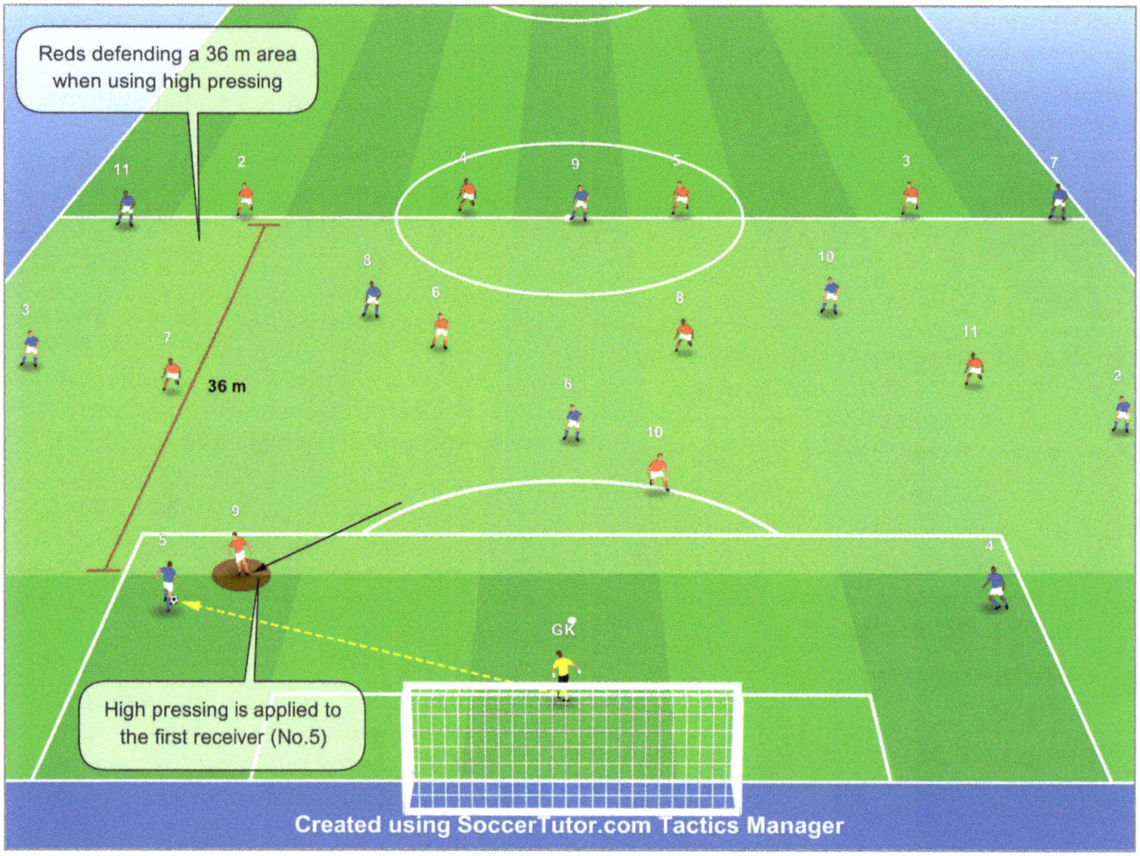

[Diagram: Reds defending a 36 m area when using high pressing. High pressing is applied to the first receiver (No.5)]

The **type of pressing used by the opposition heavily influences how build up play is executed** and the tactics needed to overcome it. Coaches must analyse their next opponent's pressing approach during scouting to prepare effective solutions.

There are **2 types of high pressing** (**high pressing and ultra-aggressive high pressing**). High pressing is applied after the first pass from the goalkeeper to the receiver, which is usually a defender.

Generally, during high pressing, the **defending team has to control less space compared to applying ultra-aggressive high pressing** (up to the goalkeeper).

In the diagram, we show that a team has to defend in an area of approximately 36 metres. This is because the first receiver (blue N°5 in this example) is usually positioned higher than the goalkeeper.

Build Up Play Factors: Essential Skills and Opposition Pressing Tactics

B. Ultra-Aggressive High Pressing (On Goalkeeper) with 4-4-2

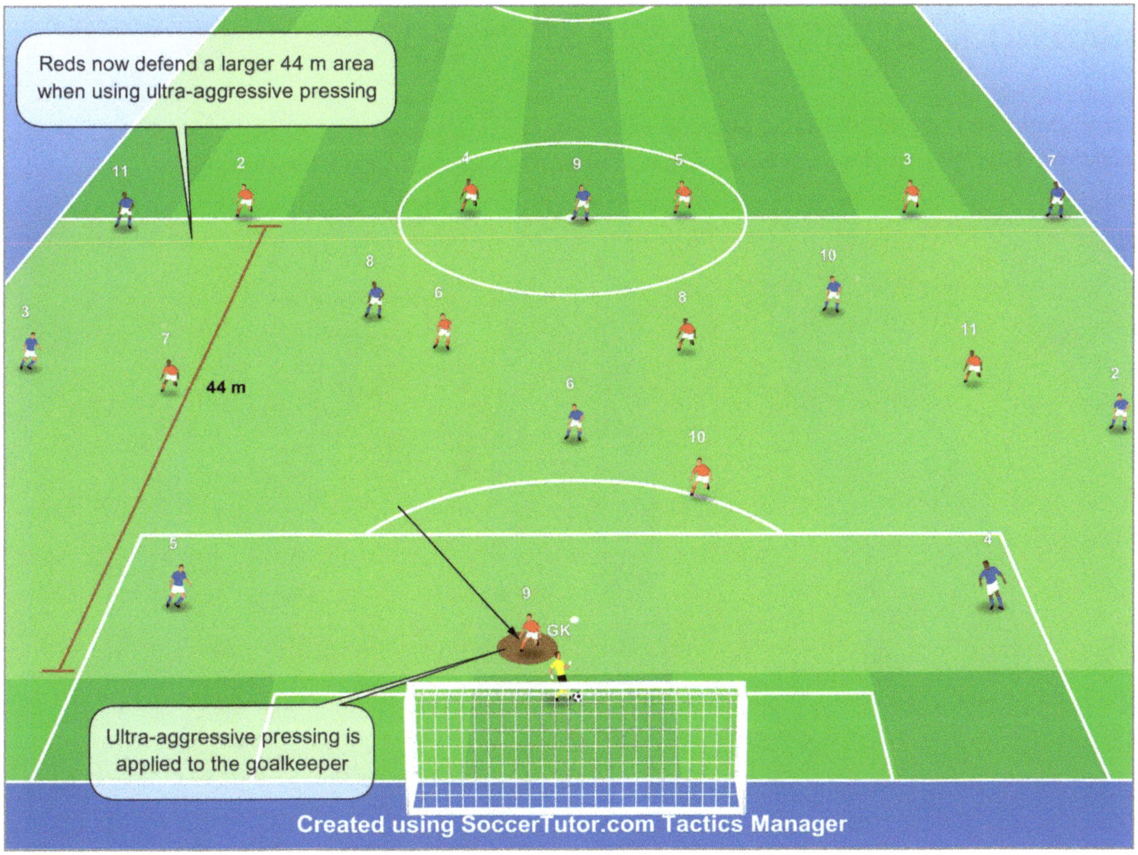

Reds now defend a larger 44 m area when using ultra-aggressive pressing

44 m

Ultra-aggressive pressing is applied to the goalkeeper

Ultra-aggressive high pressing is applied up to the goalkeeper.

As the goalkeeper is most often the deepest positioned player, the **defending team has to control a bigger space compared to when applying high pressing**.

In the diagram, the red defending team has to control and defend an area of approximately 44 metres, compared with 36 metres against high pressing on the first receiver (see previous page).

As each team has 10 outfield players, when the goalkeeper is pressed, there is always **at least 1 outfield player on the attacking team (blues) who will be free of marking**. The defending team has to deal with this free player.

Additionally, with ultra-aggressive high pressing stretching the defensive shape, **more attacking players position themselves between the lines** compared to high pressing.

The extended defensive structure creates gaps and allows attackers more time and space to receive and progress play. As a result, the **defending team must not only manage the free player created by pressing the goalkeeper but also stay compact** to prevent the attacking team from exploiting these spaces.

BEAT THE PRESS WITH SINGLE & DOUBLE PIVOTS

Build Up Play Factors: Essential Skills and Opposition Pressing Tactics

4. Numerical Situation in the Low Area when Opposition Press High

4-2-3-1 (A): Numerical Disadvantage High Up the Pitch (Low Area of Team Building Up) Before Opposition Apply High Pressing

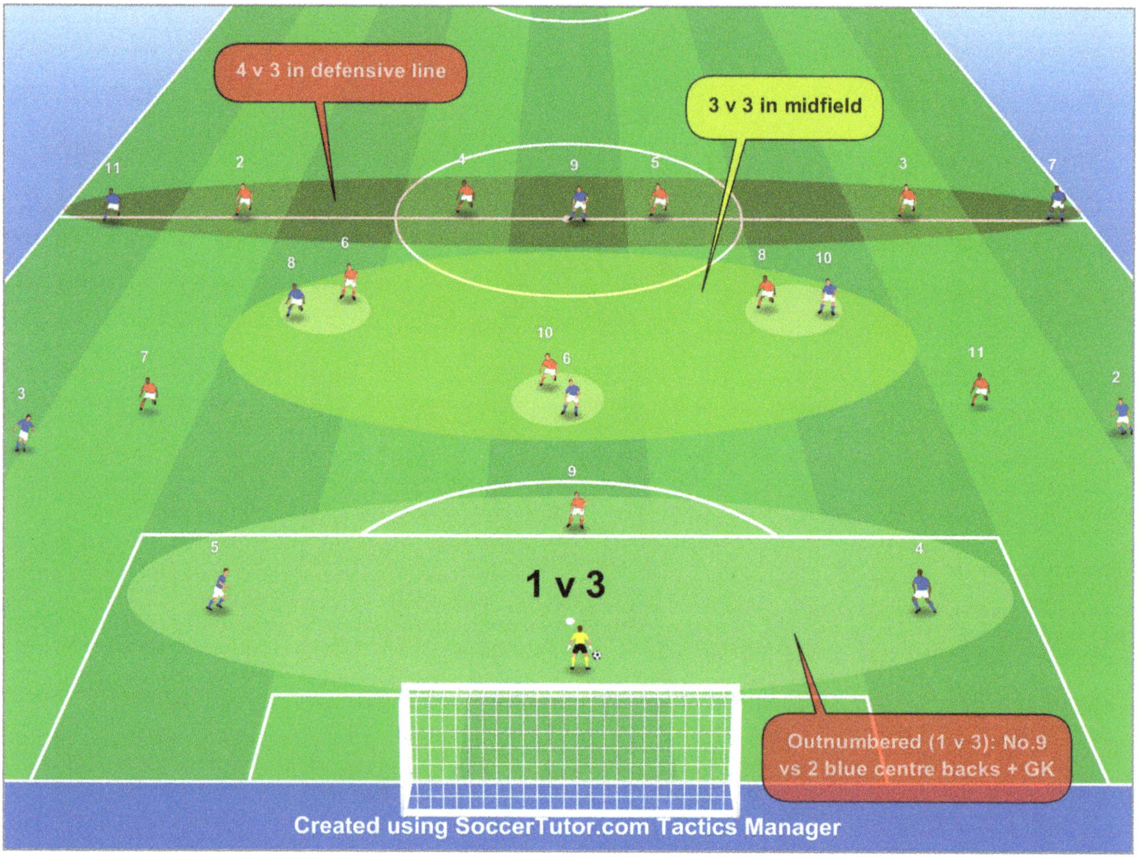

The **numerical situation in the low area is crucial** for the team building up (blues). If the defending team (reds) want to press effectively, the numerical balance should not tilt too much in favour of the blues. Ideally, numbers should be equal (e.g. 2v2 or 3v3), or the **reds should only be 1 player down** (**e.g. 1v2 or 2v3**).

In the diagram, the reds have a 4v3 advantage in the defensive line and 3v3 in midfield.

However, the **blues have a 3v1 advantage against the pressing forward (red Nº9)**.

With only 1 red forward pressing 2 blue centre backs and the goalkeeper, the reds struggle to apply consistent pressure.

This gives the blues more time and space to build up, allowing their centre backs to circulate the ball comfortably, disrupting the press and forcing reactive defending.

©SOCCERTUTOR.COM

BEAT THE PRESS WITH SINGLE & DOUBLE PIVOTS

Build Up Play Factors: Essential Skills and Opposition Pressing Tactics

4-2-3-1 (B): Forward is Unable to Control Both Centre Backs Allowing them to Find Space

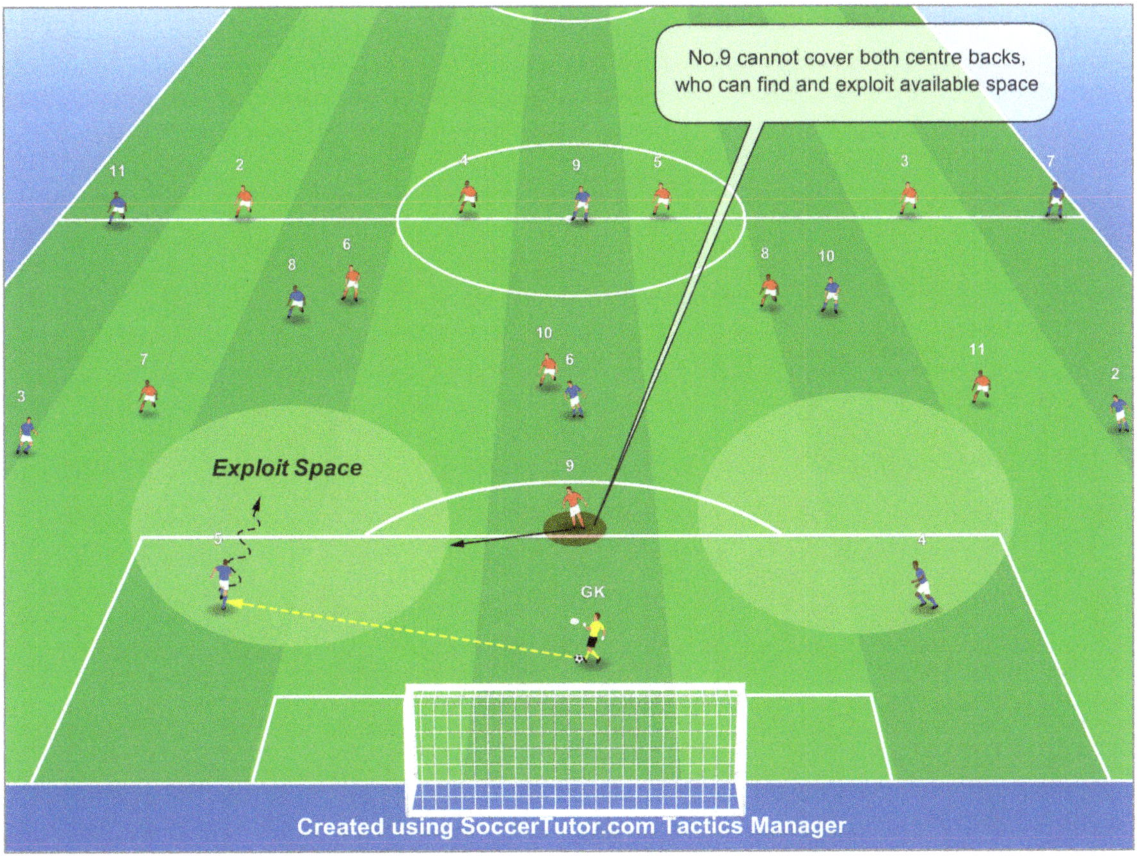

[Diagram: No.9 cannot cover both centre backs, who can find and exploit available space. "Exploit Space" areas marked on both flanks behind the lone forward.]

The key issue when pressing with 1 forward (N°9) is that they cannot effectively cover both centre backs.

With no additional support, the **centre backs are often able to find and exploit available space**, particularly if the forward fails to close down quickly when the goalkeeper plays the first pass.

This **lack of immediate pressure allows the blues to dictate the tempo of their build up**, making it easier to play through the press.

Without defensive adjustments, the blue centre backs have time to receive, turn, and pick out passing options, enabling their team to **bypass the press and progress into midfield** with relative ease.

Note: If the **red forward (N°9)** does not press aggressively or cut off passing lanes, the blue defenders can comfortably shift the ball between themselves, drawing the press before switching play to the weak side, where additional space may be available.

BEAT THE PRESS WITH SINGLE & DOUBLE PIVOTS

Build Up Play Factors: Essential Skills and Opposition Pressing Tactics

4-2-3-1 (C): Forward Presses the Centre Back as Ball is Switched to Free Weak Side Centre Back

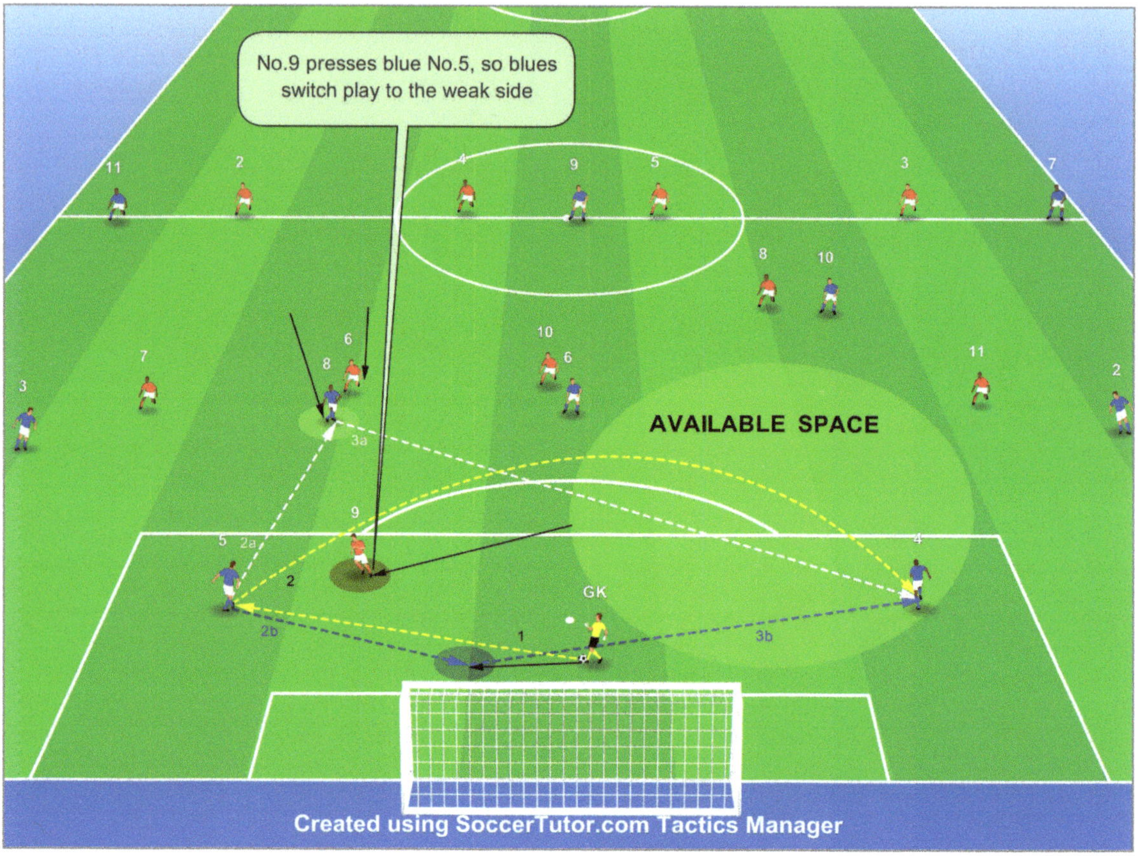

If the pressing **forward (red N°9)** is proactive and moves quickly to press the centre back receiving the first pass from the goalkeeper (N°5 in diagram), the **blue team can still exploit the weak side**.

By shifting the ball across the defensive line, either directly (yellow arrows) or through a link player (blue and white arrows), the weak side centre back (N°4) will be available in a large space and can advance to continue the build up.

If the red defending team does not react quickly, the **blues can take advantage of this open space to progress forward with minimal resistance**.

The **pressing team (reds) must recognise this positional weakness and adjust accordingly to prevent easy switches of play**. This may involve:

- The nearest midfielder shifting across to close down passing lanes.
- The weak side winger adjusting their positioning to anticipate the switch and press the receiving defender.

Note: Without these adjustments, the blue team can comfortably move the ball into dangerous areas with little disruption.

BEAT THE PRESS WITH SINGLE & DOUBLE PIVOTS

Build Up Play Factors: Essential Skills and Opposition Pressing Tactics

4-2-3-1 (D): Adjusting the 4-2-3-1 to a 4-4-2 Defensive Shape to Apply More Effective Pressing

To overcome the numerical disadvantage in the high press, an adjustment is needed. The **red attacking midfielder (N°10) pushes higher and creates a 2v3 situation** against the blue team's 2 centre backs and goalkeeper (highlighted in diagram).

The **red team increase their ability to disrupt the build up phase while limiting the space and time available for the blue defenders** to play forward.

This tactical shift transforms the defensive shape into a **4-4-2, allowing the 2 most advanced players to press both blue centre backs (N°4 and N°5) simultaneously**, reducing their time and space on the ball.

With this structure, more effective pressing can be applied, forcing rushed decisions, inaccurate passes, or long balls when put under pressure.

Note 1: By cutting off passing options and closing down space more efficiently, the **likelihood of forcing the blues into errors in their own defensive third increases**, as does winning possession higher up the pitch, and countering to score.

Note 2: 4-4-2 pressing restricts space for centre backs or full backs (key receivers) effectively. Without this, they could play forward without pressure.

BEAT THE PRESS WITH SINGLE & DOUBLE PIVOTS

Build Up Play Factors: Essential Skills and Opposition Pressing Tactics

4-3-3: Adjusting the 4-3-3 to a 4-4-2 Defensive Shape to Apply More Effective Pressing

Attacking midfielder (No.10) moves into advanced position to help create a new 2 v 3 situation for high pressing

2 v 3

Created using SoccerTutor.com Tactics Manager

The 4-3-3 formation has the same disadvantage as the 4-2-3-1 in regard to the 1v3 situation high up the pitch. This makes it difficult to press effectively. Therefore, there again needs to be an adjustment in the formation/shape of the team.

The **attacking midfielder with the most attacking characteristics (Nº10) should move into a more advanced position** to join the forward and help **create a new 2 v 3 situation** (highlighted).

The **other attacking midfielder (Nº8) should drop deeper close to the defensive midfielder (Nº6)** for defensive security.

Note: Once again, the **formation takes the shape of 4-4-2** and the 2 most advanced players (**Nº9** and **Nº10**) can control the 2 opposing centre backs.

©SOCCERTUTOR.COM

BEAT THE PRESS WITH SINGLE & DOUBLE PIVOTS

Build Up Play Factors: Essential Skills and Opposition Pressing Tactics

3-5-2 (A): Available Spaces for the Opposing Wide Players when Pressing with the 3-5-2 Formation

Unlike the 4-2-3-1 and 4-3-3 formations, the 3-5-2 formation automatically has a 2v3 situation high up the pitch. However, when applied against formations with 4 defenders:

- **Opposing full backs and wingers can find available space** as the wing backs (**N°2** and **N°11**) are positioned between them.

- **The 3 midfielders (N°6, N°7 and N°8) struggle to cover the width** of the pitch.

- If **N°7** and **N°8** moved closer to the blue full backs (N°2 and N°3), it would leave too much space for the blue attacking midfielders (N°8 and N°10) to receive.

Note: With the 3-5-2 shape, the **blue full backs (N°2 and N°3) cannot be controlled**. If a pass is played to one of them, especially if they drop deep to receive, they will find space to exploit before pressure is applied.

BEAT THE PRESS WITH SINGLE & DOUBLE PIVOTS

Build Up Play Factors: Essential Skills and Opposition Pressing Tactics

3-5-2 (B): Adjusting the 3-5-2 to a 4-4-2 Defensive Shape to Apply More Effective Pressing

One wing back (No.2) pushes higher and the other wing back (No.11) drops back

Change from 3-5-2 to 4-4-2 keeps the press compact and makes it harder for blues to progress play forward

2 v 3

Created using SoccerTutor.com Tactics Manager

To press effectively with the **3-5-2**, **tactical adjustments are needed to maintain defensive balance and apply pressure**. Without them, the attacking team can exploit gaps and bypass the press.

Wing Back Movements to Create 4-4-2 Defensive Shape:

1. One of the **wing backs (N°2 in diagram) pushes higher** to close down the blue left back (N°3), restricting passing options and forcing play into congested areas.

2. The **other wing back (N°11) drops deeper** to provide defensive cover and protect against long passes or quick switches.

As **N°2** advances, the **left back and centre backs (N°3, N°4 and N°5) shift across to the right** to maintain structure.

The **3 midfielders (N°6, N°7 and N°8) shift left** to block passing lanes and deny space for the opposing right back (blue N°2).

These **movements keep the press compact and make it harder for the opposition to progress** the play forward.

Note: With these positional adjustments, the press becomes more effective in controlling space, limiting build up play, and increasing the chances of winning the ball higher up the pitch.

©SOCCERTUTOR.COM

BEAT THE PRESS WITH SINGLE & DOUBLE PIVOTS

Build Up Play Factors: Essential Skills and Opposition Pressing Tactics

3-4-3 (A): Numerical Disadvantage High Up the Pitch (Low Area of Team Building Up) Before Applying Pressing

The 3-4-3 formation provides good width with **wing backs (Nº2 and Nº11) and wingers (Nº7 and Nº10) restricting space for the opposing wide players**.

However, the major weakness when pressing is again with the **1v3 numerical disadvantage in the first pressing line**.

With a lone **forward (Nº9)** pressing against 2 centre backs and goalkeeper, the blues can circulate possession easily, making it difficult to disrupt their build up play.

If **Nº9** moves to press a centre back after a pass from the goalkeeper, the **ball can easily be switched to the other (free) centre back, bypassing the press with minimal resistance**.

Note: Without any adjustments, the lack of pressure high up the pitch allows the opposition to progress the ball into midfield easily, forcing a reactive approach rather than an effective press.

BEAT THE PRESS WITH SINGLE & DOUBLE PIVOTS

Build Up Play Factors: Essential Skills and Opposition Pressing Tactics

3-4-3 (B): **Adjusting the 3-4-3 to a 4-4-2 Defensive Shape to Apply More Effective Pressing**

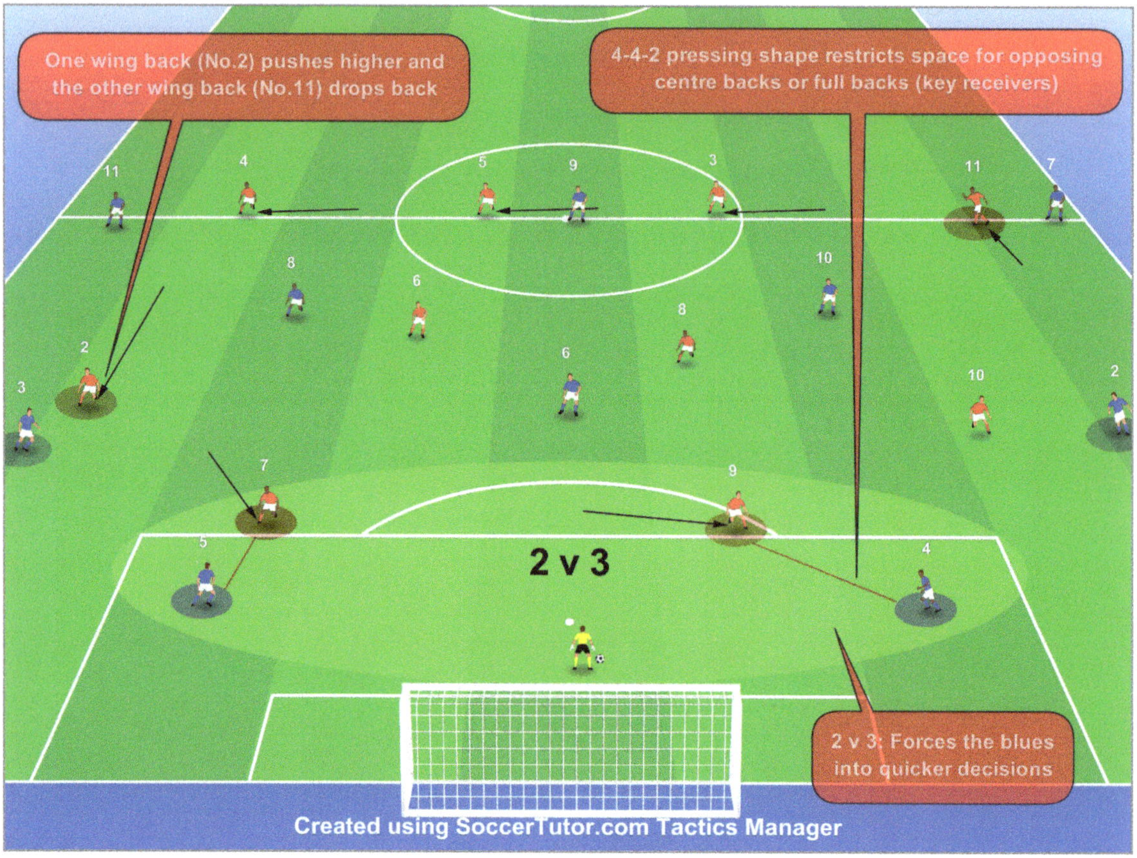

To make the 3-4-3 more effective when pressing, a **2v3 situation must be created high up the pitch**.

Movements to Create 4-4-2 Shape:

- The **winger (N°7) pushes up to mark the blue centre back** (N°5).
- The **forward (N°9) shifts closer to the other centre back** (blue N°4), ensuring both opposing centre backs are under control.
- The **left wing back (N°11) drops back into a left back position** to provide cover.
- The **team adjusts by shifting across** to the right.

These movements compact the shape, limit passing options, and create a 2v3 high press, forcing the opposition into quicker decisions. With these changes, the structure resembles a 4-4-2 and improves the pressing effectiveness.

Note: The **analysis in this section shows that a 4-4-2 pressing shape restricts space for the opposing centre backs or full backs (key receivers)** effectively. Without this, they could play forward without pressure. This makes **4-4-2 one of the most effective formations for pressing**. However, pressing can also be applied by creating 3v3 high up the pitch, which will be analysed later.

Build Up Play Factors: Essential Skills and Opposition Pressing Tactics

5. Different Types of Defending Used by Opposition During High Pressing

A. Zonal Defending: Controlling Space in a Pressing System

Defensive zones of responsibility

Pressing can be applied with different types of defending:

A. **Zonal Defending**

B. **Man Marking with Numerical Advantage at the Back**

C. **Full Pitch Man Marking**

D. **Zonal Defending and Man Marking (Hybrid)**

Each type of defending has advantages and disadvantages. Teams that apply pressing with **zonal defending prioritise controlling space rather than directly marking individual opponents**, aiming to disrupt the opposition's build up while maintaining defensive organisation.

The diagram shows zones of responsibility for players in a 4-4-2 formation with zonal defending. **Each player is responsible for defending a specific area (zone) of the pitch**. The zones of responsibility are dynamic and change according to the position of the ball.

Build Up Play Factors: Essential Skills and Opposition Pressing Tactics

B1. Man Marking with Numerical Advantage at the Back (Option 1)

In this setup, the red team maintain a numerical advantage at the back, where there is a **2v1 situation in the centre of defence**.

As shown, the blue forward (N°9) is covered by **2 red centre backs (N°4 and N°5)**, ensuring control in this zone and minimising the threat of direct play through the centre.

The **red right winger (N°7)** pushes forward to apply pressure on the blue left centre back (N°5), creating a **2v3 situation in the highlighted area for the blue team's initial build up play from the back**.

Across the rest of the pitch, the reds are committed to man marking, resulting in multiple **1v1 duels against the remaining 7 blue outfield players**.

Note: 1 red player (**winger N°7** in diagram) is forced to cover 2 blue players, which creates a weakness in the defensive setup. Also, the blue goalkeeper (GK) is left unmarked, providing a free outlet for the blue team when needed.

BEAT THE PRESS WITH SINGLE & DOUBLE PIVOTS

Build Up Play Factors: Essential Skills and Opposition Pressing Tactics

B2. Man Marking with Numerical Advantage at the Back (Option 2)

The second option retains a numerical advantage at the back while **shifting into a more balanced structure across the rest of the pitch**.

As shown in the diagram, the reds continue to control the blue forward (N°9) with their **2 centre backs (N°4 and N°5)**, preserving the same **2 v 1 situation in the centre of defence**.

In contrast to the first option, there is now a **3 v 3 situation in the highlighted area for the blue team's initial build up play from the back**. This is achieved with the central positioning of the **red forward (N°9)** and the advanced positioning of both **wingers (N°7 and N°11)**.

N°7 and **N°11** mark the 2 blue centre backs (N°5 and N°4), while **N°9** has the role of pressing the goalkeeper (GK). This structure allows the reds to apply **ultra-aggressive pressing (up to the goalkeeper)** with more balance across the pitch.

With all key outfield players marked and pressure being applied to the goalkeeper, the **chances of forcing errors or recovering possession in advanced areas is increased** without creating significant numerical disadvantages elsewhere on the pitch.

Note: 2 red players (**wingers N°7 and N°11**) are forced to cover 2 blue players, which creates 2 points of weakness.

Build Up Play Factors: Essential Skills and Opposition Pressing Tactics

C. Full Pitch Man Marking (Equal Numbers at the Back)

3 v 3 in defensive line

1 v 1 marking of all outfield players (limits options but increases risk if duel is lost)

The second form of man marking creates 1v1 situations for every outfield player including in the defensive line. Every defending team player is matched directly with 1 opponent, as shown.

Unlike structures that retain a spare player at the back, this approach ensures that **every defending player is directly responsible for marking an opponent (1v1)**, leaving no extra cover.

As shown in the diagram, **one of the centre backs (red Nº4) pushes forward to mark an opposing midfielder (blue Nº8)**, maintaining balance while ensuring tight marking throughout the pitch.

This results in a **3 v 3 situation in the defensive line**, where each red defender must track their direct opponent closely.

This setup forces the possession team (blues) into constant individual battles, restricting their space and time on the ball. However, as every defender is occupied, there is an **increased risk if an opponent manages to evade their marker**, as there is no extra cover to provide support.

Note: Defensive discipline, anticipation, and physical duels are essential for successfully applying full pitch man marking.

BEAT THE PRESS WITH SINGLE & DOUBLE PIVOTS

Build Up Play Factors: Essential Skills and Opposition Pressing Tactics

D. Zonal Defending and Man Marking (Hybrid)

This defensive approach combines zonal defending and man marking, requiring players to **mark opponents within their designated zones while adjusting to opposition movement**.

When the **defending team is outnumbered in a specific area** (e.g. **2 v 3 in midfield**), **1 player must adopt a balanced position to cover 2 opponents** instead of marking a single player.

In the diagram example, a **red central midfielder (N°6)** marks a blue attacking midfielder (N°8), while the **other central midfielder (N°8)** is positioned between the other blue attacking midfielder (N°10) and the defensive midfielder (N°6).

This positioning **allows red N°8 to react based on the blue team's movement**, ensuring that the team remains compact while still applying effective pressing.

Note: The success of this approach relies on defensive awareness, communication, and the ability to adjust positioning quickly based on opposition movement.

BEAT THE PRESS WITH SINGLE & DOUBLE PIVOTS

BUILD UP TO BEAT THE PRESS

Tactical Analysis

Break Lines vs High Press Zonal Defending with a Single Pivot

Build up play patterns from Flick, Klopp, and Emery's teams

Build Up Play from the Back Principles and Objectives

Build Up Play from the Back

After analysing the factors that influence build up play, including formations used during pressing and their adjustments, it became clear that the 4-4-2 formation, or formations resembling it, are the most popular and offer the best conditions for effective pressing by restricting space for centre backs and full backs. In this section, we focus on carrying out effective build-up play against the 4-4-2 formation and different types of defending.

Defensive approaches can vary to counter attacking strengths or match pressing intensity. For instance, high pressing is more effective with midfield or full pitch man marking rather than zonal defending. These defensive choices can also lead to adjustments in the opposition's 4-4-2 structure, which will be analysed on the following pages.

Principles of Build Up Play

Effective build-up play from the back relies on key principles to overcome organised pressing:

- **Breaking Lines:** The focus must be on breaking through as many defensive lines as possible.
- **Understanding Defensive Shapes:** Recognising variations of the 4-4-2 and anticipating adjustments.
- **Adaptability:** Adjusting positioning and movement based on the type of pressing and defending encountered.
- **Quick and Accurate Passing:** Executing fast, precise passes to disrupt defensive structures.
- **Creating Passing Options:** Supporting the ball carrier by offering multiple safe and progressive passing lanes.

Objectives of Build Up Play

Main Objective: Break defensive lines, advance play, and create goal scoring opportunities.

To achieve this, teams must:

- **Beat the Press:** Navigate around or through organised high blocks starting from the goalkeeper.
- **Exploit Defensive Adjustments:** Recognise and capitalise on changes in the defensive setup.
- **Progress Safely:** Maintain stability and avoid unnecessary risk while advancing the ball.
- **Set Up Attacks:** Use the successful breaking of pressing lines to transition into goal-scoring opportunities.

Note: By applying these principles, teams can build up effectively from the back even against organised high blocks like the 4-4-2, ensuring progression, control, and opportunities to attack with structure and purpose.

Build Up Play Against High Pressing and Zonal Defending with a Single Pivot (4-3-3)

1. Available Spaces Between the Lines and Players vs High Pressing with Zonal Defending

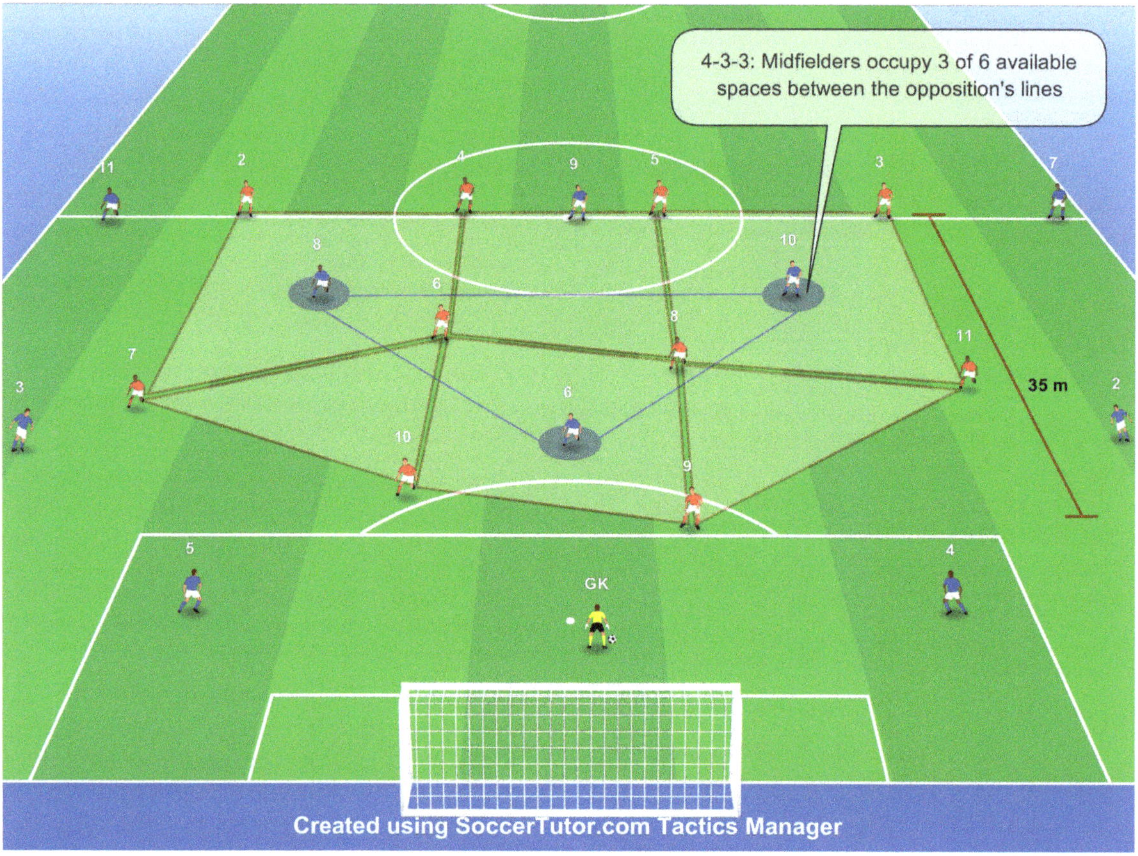

4-3-3: Midfielders occupy 3 of 6 available spaces between the opposition's lines

We will **focus on building up from the back with a 4-3-3 against a 4-4-2 zonal defence**. In this structure, the defending team forms 3 lines: 4 defenders, 4 midfielders, and 2 forwards. Zonal defending makes high pressing (on first receiver) more manageable than ultra-aggressive pressing (up to the goalkeeper), as players defend space rather than man marking. Ultra-aggressive pressing increases the area to control to 50 metres if the GK is deep.

When the opposing forwards wait near the edge of the box for the first pass to be played, it reduces the area to 35 metres. Even then, the team is still not compact, with 17–18 metres often separating lines.

The diagram shows 3 red defensive lines and 6 spaces between them. **The blue midfielders must position themselves intelligently (as shown) to exploit these gaps and support the build up play**.

Build Up to Beat the Press: Break Lines vs High Press Zonal Defending with a Single Pivot

2. Optimal Midfield Positioning to Exploit the Spaces Between the Lines

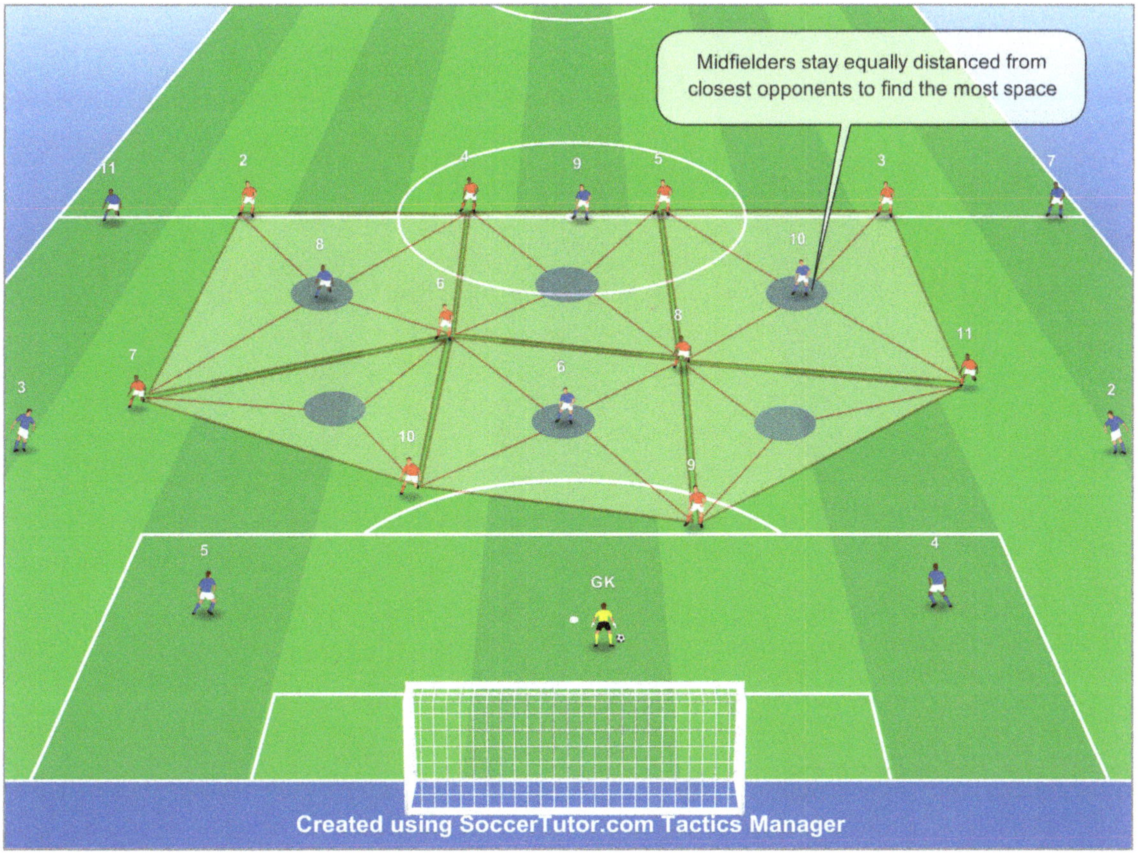

Midfielders stay equally distanced from closest opponents to find the most space

The **central area of the pitch is more important than wide areas** as it offers more passing options.

To exploit available spaces between the opposition's lines:

1. Midfielders position themselves effectively between the lines to maximise space.

2. Midfielders must stay equally distanced from their closest opponents to find the most space.

3. The goalkeeper or defenders attempt to move the ball to one of the midfielders.

Effective positioning requires midfielders to position themselves between the lines and between opponents, maintaining equal distances from nearby defenders to **maximise space**. For example, in the diagram, the **blue defensive midfielder (Nº6)** is positioned equally between red Nº6, Nº8, Nº10 and Nº9. The same principle applies to the other midfielders.

Note: When building up with the 4-3-3, the players naturally occupy these spaces. However, if greater space is identified centrally between the opposition's midfield and centre backs, an attacking midfielder can move into that area to receive.

Build Up to Beat the Press: Break Lines vs High Press Zonal Defending with a Single Pivot

Options for Breaking the First and Second Pressing Lines with a Single Pivot (4-3-3)

1. Goalkeeper's Options to Pass Through or Over Pressing Lines

GK's options to play through or over pressing lines to midfield players

As the blue midfielders take up effective positions and there is no pressure on the goalkeeper, the next step is to move the ball to one of them.

Many coaches wrongly believe that building up from the back only involves short passes. In reality, the **aim is to break as many lines of pressure as possible to neutralise more defenders**. If a medium or long pass is available, it should be used. To improve accuracy, the goalkeeper should step forward with the ball. This reduces the distance to the target and limits the opposition's time to shift and block the pass, increasing the chance of success.

If the first pressing line (red forwards) doesn't shift centrally to block the passing lane, a pass to the **defensive midfielder (N°6)** can be played. **But if a pass to an attacking midfielder (N°8 or N°10) is possible, it's the better option, as it breaks more lines and removes more opponents**.

BEAT THE PRESS WITH SINGLE & DOUBLE PIVOTS

Build Up to Beat the Press: Break Lines vs High Press Zonal Defending with a Single Pivot

2. Free Players Behind the Second Pressing Line to Force Defensive Decisions (Marking vs Balanced Positioning)

If a through pass reaches the **defensive midfielder** (**N°6**) and they can turn, the first line of pressure is broken, neutralising 2 red opponents (N°9 and N°10).

The next step is to break the second line by finding free players behind it who can receive and turn.

Creating these free players depends on positioning. **The blue attacking midfielders (N°8 and N°10) must position themselves between the lines, while the wingers (N°11 and N°7) and forward (N°9) create dilemmas for the opposition's defenders.** This forces the red full backs and centre backs into difficult marking decisions.

For example, red N°2 must track both blue **N°11** and **N°8**, while red **N°4** has to deal with blue **N°8** and **N°9**. If a defender moves to one, the other could be left free.

Typically, defenders mark the more dangerous player, leaving space for the other, or position themselves between 2 opponents. The second option occurs more often in midfield and advanced zones than deeper areas.

Since the wingers and forward pose greater threats, the attacking midfielders often gain extra space.

Build Up to Beat the Press: Break Lines vs High Press Zonal Defending with a Single Pivot

3. Exploiting Passing Lanes to Beat the Second Pressing Line and Play to Attacking Midfielders Between the Lines

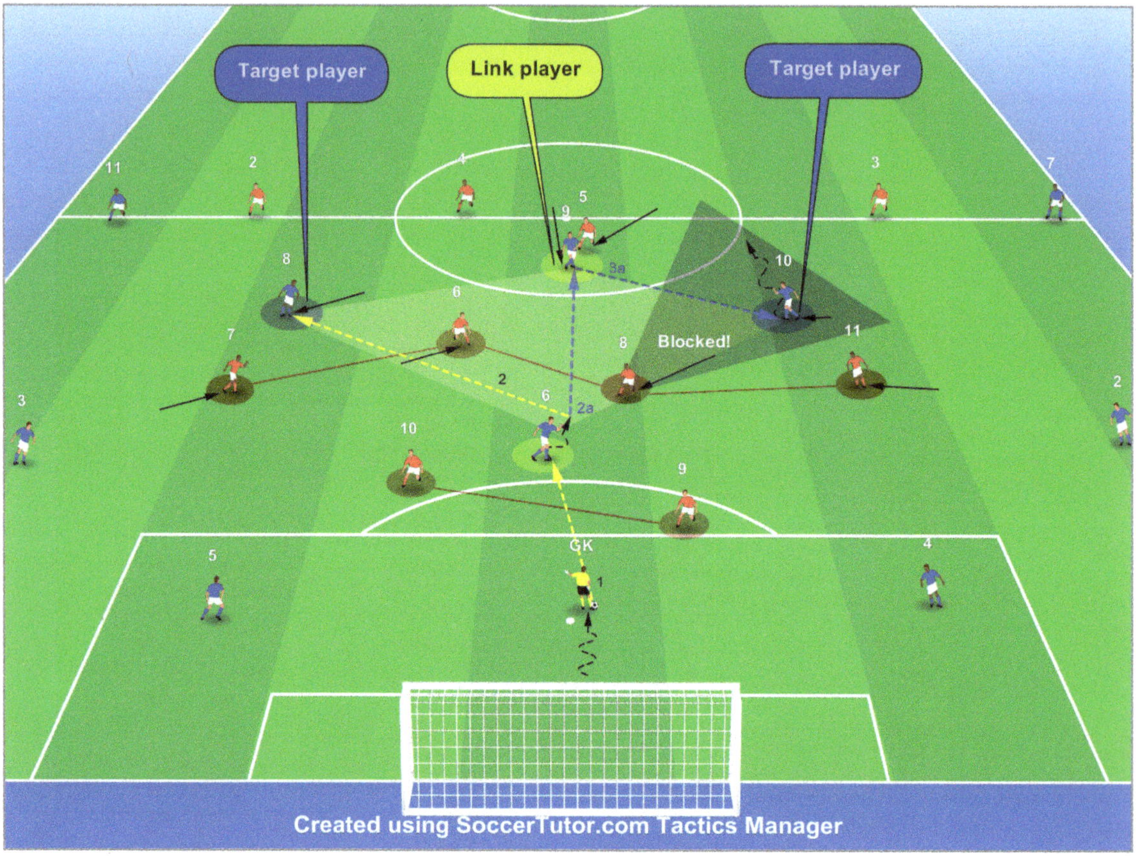

As soon as this situation develops, the next step for the attacking players is to increase passing options for the player in possession. This is done by **players behind the second line moving into different lanes, ensuring there are at least 2 passing options** (**forming a triangle**).

If the **attacking midfielders** and **forward** (**N°8, N°10,** and **N°9**) apply this, it becomes very difficult for the red team to stop the ball reaching a free player.

If a direct pass to **N°8** or **N°10** is blocked, **N°9** can act as a link player to move the ball forward. In the diagram, once the defensive midfielder (**N°6**) receives and turns, the first line of pressure is broken, neutralising red N°9 and N°10. Meanwhile, **N°8** and **N°10** adjust their positions to offer options. **N°8** finds space, while **N°10** is in the shadow of red N°8, who is pressing the ball. However, **N°9** positions himself in a free passing lane, becoming a valuable link player.

The ball can go be played directly to **N°10** or indirectly via **N°9**; the same applies to **N°8**.

Note: If any of these options succeed, the receiver can turn and break the second line of pressure, neutralising 4 more red players (entire second pressing line).

Build Up to Beat the Press: Break Lines vs High Press Zonal Defending with a Single Pivot

Drawing Press with a Pass and Exploit Gaps to Play in Between the Lines

[Diagram: Option 2 — "As red No.8 moves forward, space opens up behind him for blue No.10." Option 1 labeled with yellow arrow.]

A pass to a player positioned behind the first line of pressure can create space behind the second. This forces a second-line defending player to step forward, leaving space in their original position. To exploit this, the attacking team must:

A. **Quickly read which opponent stepped forward and where the available space is.**

B. **Move the ball into this space as quickly as possible.**

Option 1 (Yellow Arrows): When **blue Nº6** receives, red Nº8 steps forward to press, creating space behind. **Nº6** can return the ball to the **GK**, who must react quickly and pass to the **centre back** (**Nº4**).

Option 2 (Blue Arrow): A quicker alternative is for **Nº6** to pass to **Nº4** if there is a safe passing lane.

Note 1: Nº4's pass to Nº10 breaks 2 lines of pressure, neutralising 6 opponents.

Note 2: Nº6 must be aware of red Nº11, as if he is high enough up the pitch, he can get involved and intercept the pass to Nº4.

Note 3: If red Nº6 presses instead, space is created for blue Nº8 to be target player.

BEAT THE PRESS WITH SINGLE & DOUBLE PIVOTS

Goalkeeper Draws Press to Create Space for Centre Backs (4-3-3)

Dribbling the ball forward can create space for a nearby teammate, especially when done between 2 opponents. This movement often forces defenders to shift, leaving space in their original positions.

If the goalkeeper carries the ball forward between the 2 opposing forwards, they may shift to narrow the passing lane, moving away from their initial positions.

This creates space for the defenders to receive from the goalkeeper and progress play.

Note: To break the second line, free players must be created behind it while increasing passing options for the player in possession to find them.

1. Opposing Forwards Narrow the Central Passing Lanes which Creates Space for a Centre Back to Receive and Dribble Forward

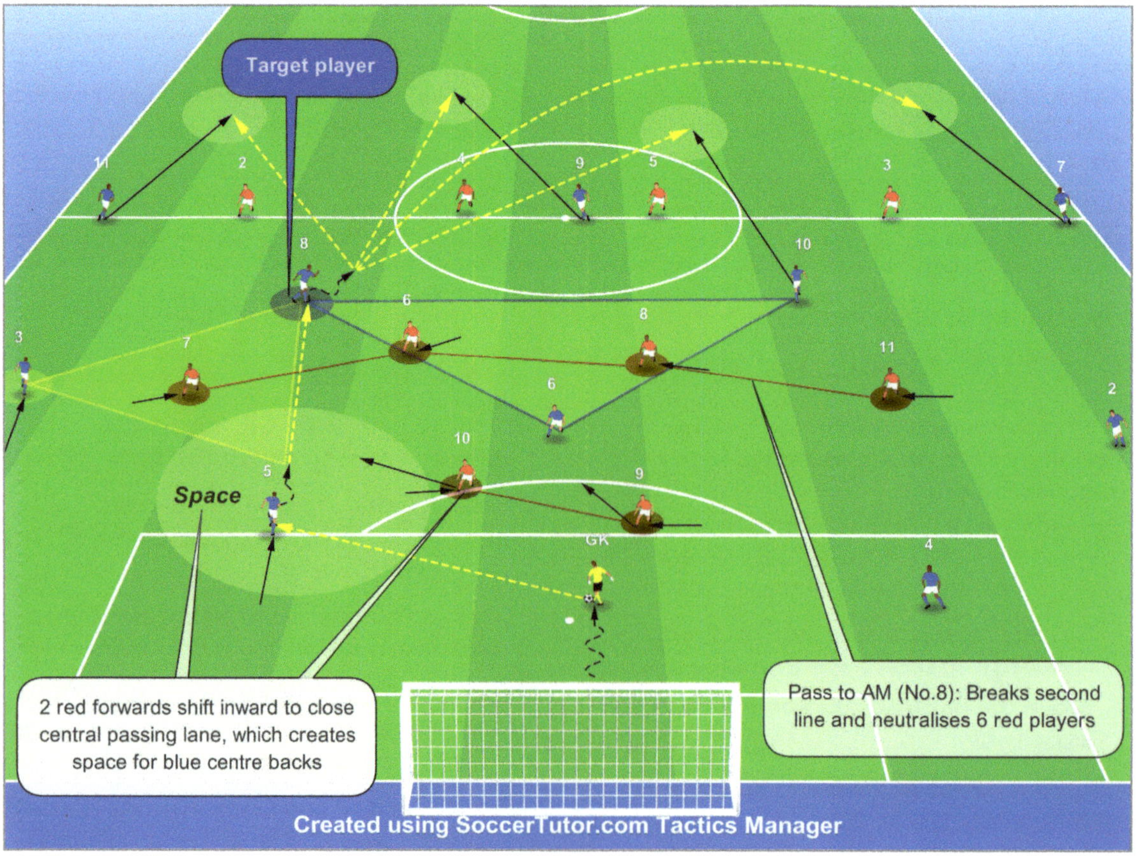

Target player

Space

2 red forwards shift inward to close central passing lane, which creates space for blue centre backs

Pass to AM (No.8): Breaks second line and neutralises 6 red players

Created using SoccerTutor.com Tactics Manager

©SOCCERTUTOR.COM

BEAT THE PRESS WITH SINGLE & DOUBLE PIVOTS

Build Up to Beat the Press: Break Lines vs High Press Zonal Defending with a Single Pivot

Since the receiver is deeper and not fully behind the first line of pressure, he **must drive forward and pass quickly to avoid being closed down by the forwards or blocked by the shifting midfielders**.

It is vital for the **potential receiver (target player - attacking midfielder N°8)** to position himself in the available passing lane while staying equally positioned between red N°2 and N°4 if possible. **This allows N°8 to find space and create doubt over who should mark him**. Both red N°2 and N°4 already have other players (**blue N°11** and **N°9**) in their zones of responsibility, making it harder for them to commit to marking **N°8**.

To increase options behind the second line, the **left back (N°3) pushes forward to create a triangle (highlighted)**, while the **forward (N°9)** must read the play. If the lane to **N°8** is open, he stays high to receive behind the third line. If it's tight, he drops to offer options for **N°5**, forming 2 triangles or a diamond, and acts as a link to move the ball to either **N°8** or **N°10**.

If N°8 receives and turns, the first 2 lines of the opposition's pressure are broken, neutralising 6 opponents and setting up the next phase to play in behind the defensive line.

Note: The success of N°5's pass between red N°7 and N°6 depends on the speed of play between GK and N°5. A firm pass and quick execution are essential. If the ball moves fast enough, the red midfielders will not have time to block the lane.

Build Up to Beat the Press: Break Lines vs High Press Zonal Defending with a Single Pivot

2. Opposing Centre Back Moves Forward to Mark the Attacking Midfielder Between the Lines (CB Plays Long Pass in Behind)

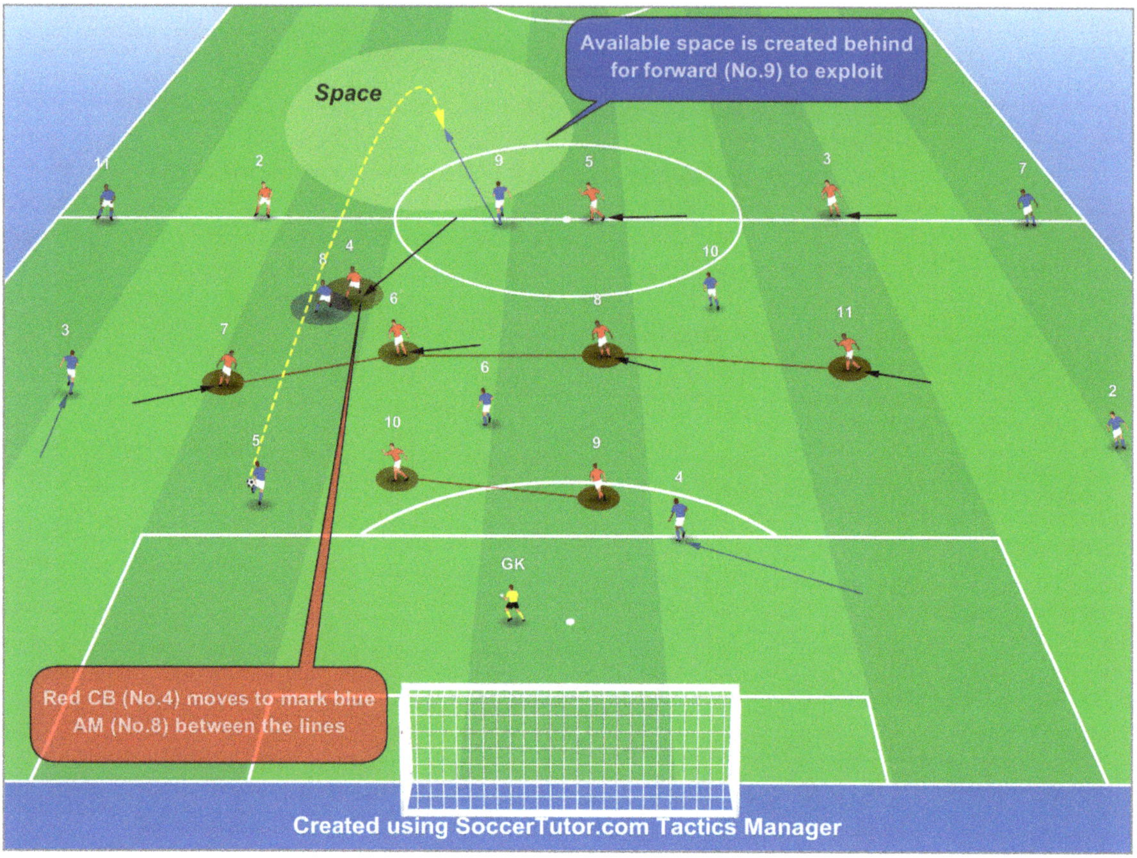

If one of the red defenders who are close to the potential receiver decide to move forward to mark them, **available space will be created behind which can be exploited**.

In the diagram example, the red centre back (N°4) moves forward to mark the **attacking midfielder (N°8)**. This leaves free space behind him, which is exploited by the run of the **forward (N°9)** and the long aerial pass from the **centre back (N°5)** into that space.

With this option, the **blues successfully break all 3 lines of pressure, bypassing the red team's defensive structure and neutralising every outfield player**.

If the red right back (N°2) is the one who steps forward to mark **N°8**, then space opens up on the left side for the winger **(N°11)** to exploit and potentially receive from **N°5** (in behind) instead.

BEAT THE PRESS WITH SINGLE & DOUBLE PIVOTS

Build Up to Beat the Press: Break Lines vs High Press Zonal Defending with a Single Pivot

3. Centre Back's Options to Break Second Pressing Line when the Opposing Winger Narrows the Through Passing Lane

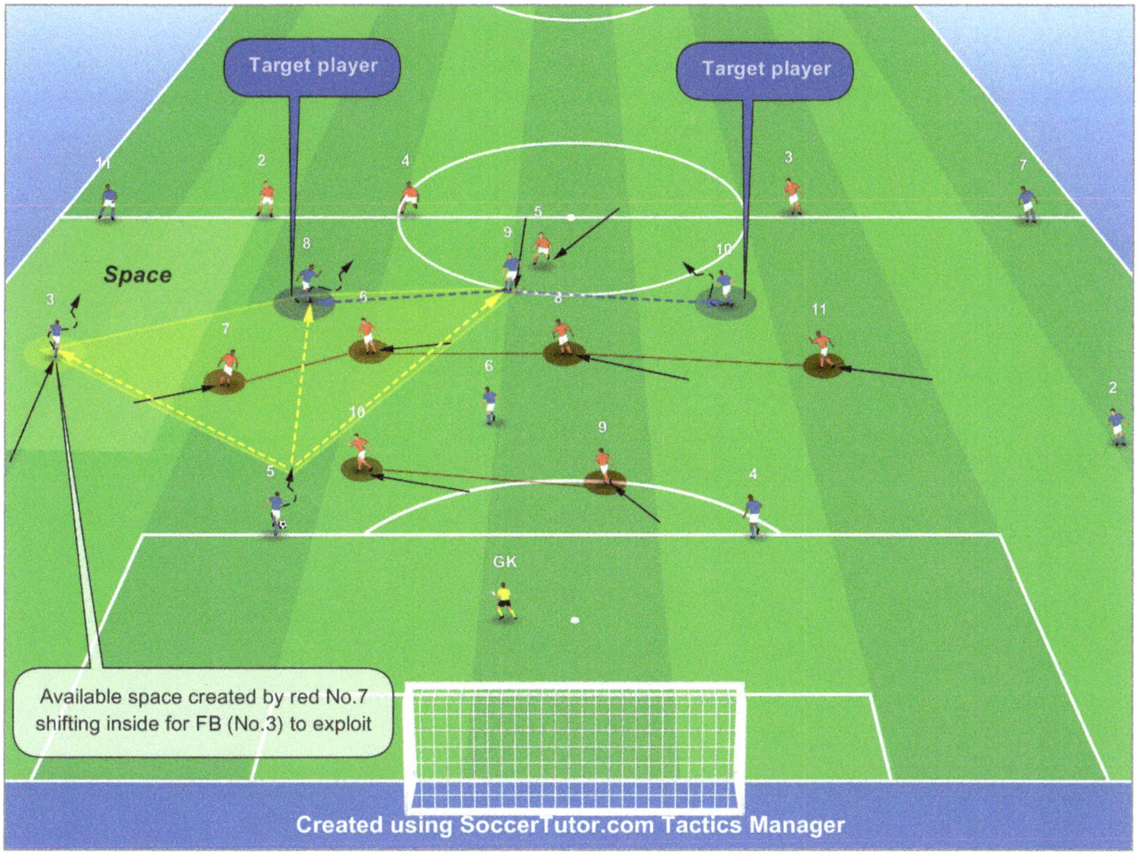

If the red central midfielder N°6 and wide midfielder N°7 have shifted in time and narrowed the passing lane to the **attacking midfielder (N°8)**, then, even though **N°8** is technically free, it becomes difficult for him to receive the ball safely.

In this situation, the pass from the **centre back (N°5)** can be directed towards the **left back (N°3)**, who has more space in a wide position to receive and move forward.

Despite being in a wide area, the pass to N°3 can break the second line of pressure and neutralise 6 red opponents (entire first and second pressing lines).

Additionally, the **forward (N°9)** must read the situation. Since the through pass to **N°8** is difficult due to the narrowed lane, **N°9** should drop into an available passing lane to increase options for **N°5**, helping to form 2 triangles (or diamond shape).

With this positioning, **N°9 can become a link player and help move the ball to N°8 or N°10 (blue arrows), both of whom are free between the lines and serve as key target players**.

BEAT THE PRESS WITH SINGLE & DOUBLE PIVOTS

Playing Against a Compact Central Block Leaves Space Out Wide (4-3-3)

1. Opposing Wide Midfielders Shift Inside for Compact Midfield

If the goalkeeper (GK) is in possession against high pressing opponents and the defending team (reds) shift their wide players inside to restrict the central space, more room will open up in the wide areas (highlighted in the diagram).

This adjustment helps the opposition (reds) compress the pitch horizontally, limiting passing lanes through the middle. However, this does not affect the vertical distances between their defensive lines.

Note: The space between each line remains available and can still be exploited by the blue team with smart positioning and well-timed passes.

Build Up to Beat the Press: Break Lines vs High Press Zonal Defending with a Single Pivot

2. Effective Positioning of Midfielders to Receive from Wide Players After Goalkeeper's Pass to the Flank

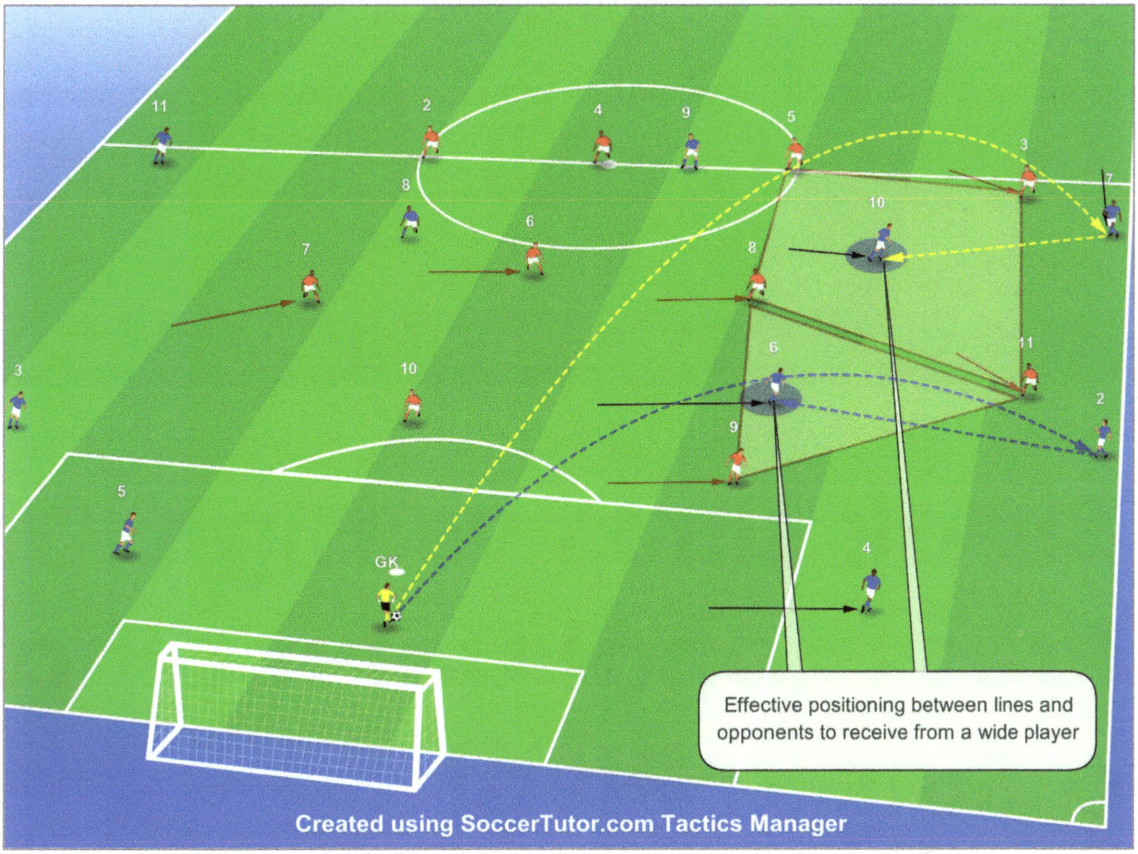

Effective positioning between lines and opponents to receive from a wide player

In this situation, as the **goalkeeper** (**GK**) is in possession, **the wide players can become the targets**, **either to receive, turn, and play forward, or to act as link players to move the ball centrally**.

The effective positioning of the midfielders remains crucial. If they are well positioned between the lines and opponents, they become available to receive the next pass from the wide player following the **GK's** long pass. This directs play into central areas, which are more valuable to exploit and offer more options going forward.

In the diagram example, **GK** can pass to the **winger** (**N°7** - yellow arrow) or the **full back** (**N°2** - blue arrow).

In both options, as the **midfielders N°6 and N°10 have already taken effective positions, they remain free and offer passing options to the receiver of the GK's pass, as shown**.

©SOCCERTUTOR.COM BEAT THE PRESS WITH SINGLE & DOUBLE PIVOTS

BUILD UP TO BEAT THE PRESS

Training Session 1 (4 Practices)

Break Lines vs High Press Zonal Defending a Single Pivot

Based on Flick, Klopp, and Emery build up patterns

Training Session 1: Break Lines vs High Press Zonal Defending with a Single Pivot

TRAINING SESSION (4 PRACTICES)
1. Passing Decisions to Break Lines Depending on Opposition Pressing

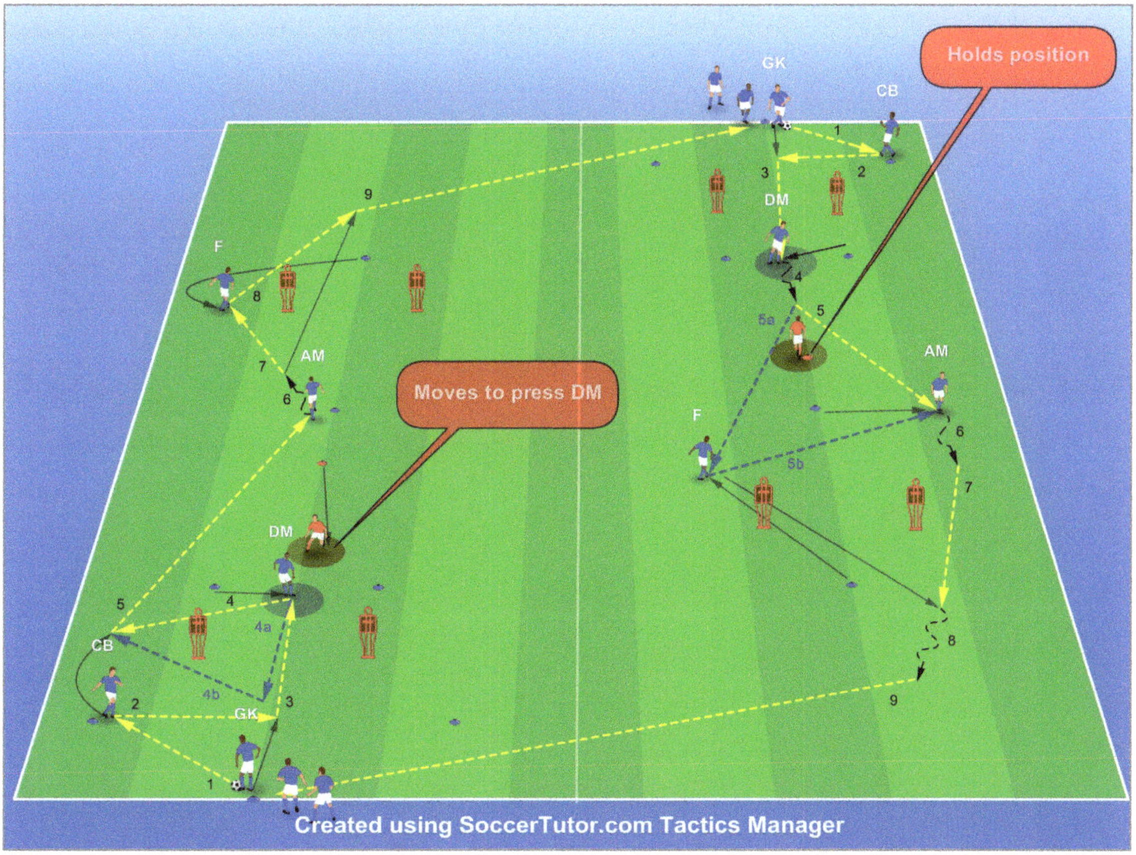

Practice Description

- **Objective:** Decision making for whether to turn or pass back (to exploit space).

- The mannequins mark the first and third pressing lines and the red player is in the second line.

- **Left Side: GK** plays a one-two with **CB**, then passes to **DM**, who must assess the red player's reaction.

- <u>If pressed</u>, **DM** passes to **CB** directly or via link player **GK** (blue arrows) and the ball is quickly played to **AM**.

- **AM** turns and plays a one-two with **F** around the mannequin before passing to the other group.

- **Right Side:** <u>If not pressed</u>, **DM** turns. The ball is either played to **AM** directly or via the **forward (F)** acting as a link player (blue arrows).

- **F** then runs in between the mannequins to receive **AM's** through pass and pass to the other group.

- **Player Rotations:** GK → CB → DM → AM → F → GK (Other Group).

Training Session 1: Break Lines vs High Press Zonal Defending with a Single Pivot

PROGRESSION
2. Breaking Lines Based on Opponent Reactions 6 (+GK) v 2 Functional Practice

Variation 1: Receive + Turn to Break the Second Pressing Line

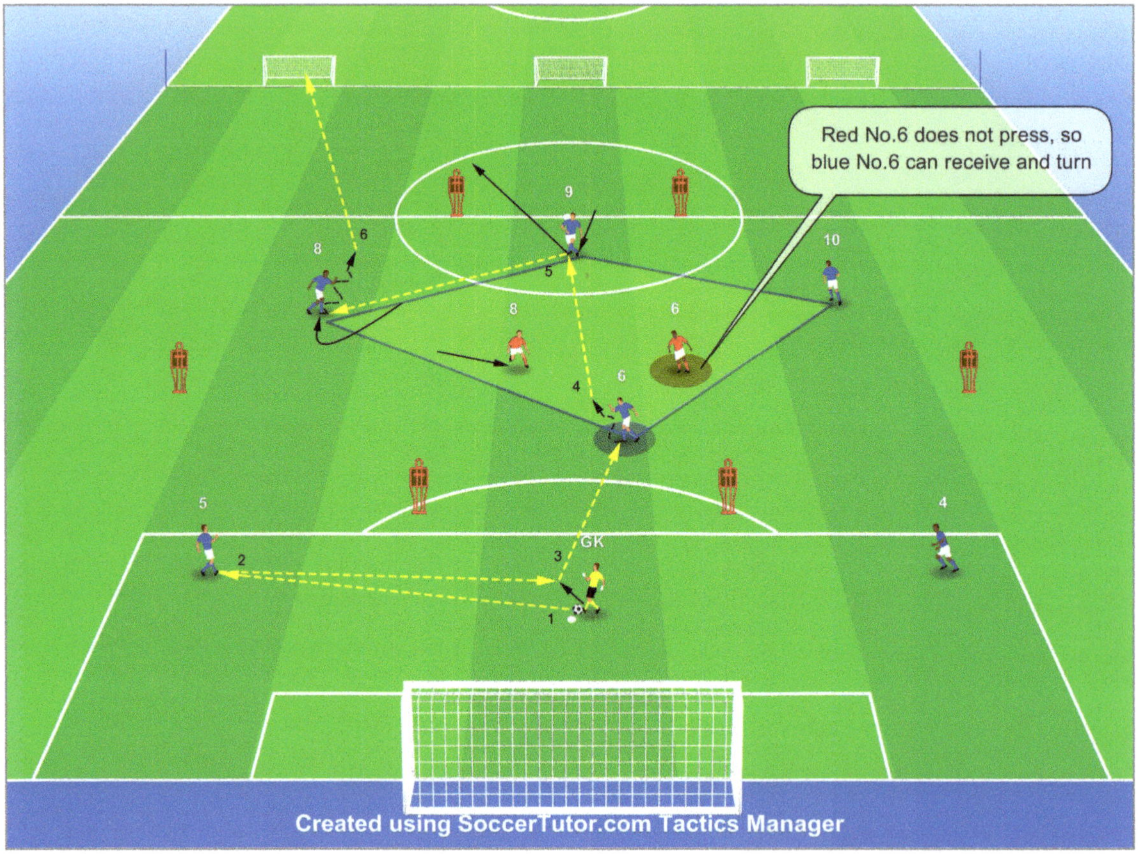

[Diagram: Red No.6 does not press, so blue No.6 can receive and turn]

Practice Description (Variation 1)

- The blues have the goalkeeper, 2 centre backs, 3 midfielders, and the forward.
- The reds have 2 central midfielders and the mannequins form the rest of the defensive formation.
- **GK** starts and circulates the ball with the **centre backs (N°5 and N°4)** before passing to the **defensive midfielder (N°6)** behind the first pressing line, who must scan before receiving.

- If the nearest **red midfielder (N°6) holds their position (Variation 1)**, **blue N°6 receives on the half-turn** and passes forward.
- Nearby teammates quickly offer passing options to progress the attack, ideally forming a triangle or diamond shape.
- In this example, the **forward (N°9)** sets the ball back for the **attacking midfielder (N°8)** to receive, dribble forward and score.

©SOCCERTUTOR.COM　　　BEAT THE PRESS WITH SINGLE & DOUBLE PIVOTS

Training Session 1: Break Lines vs High Press Zonal Defending with a Single Pivot

Variation 2: Pass Back Under Pressure to Switch and Exploit Space

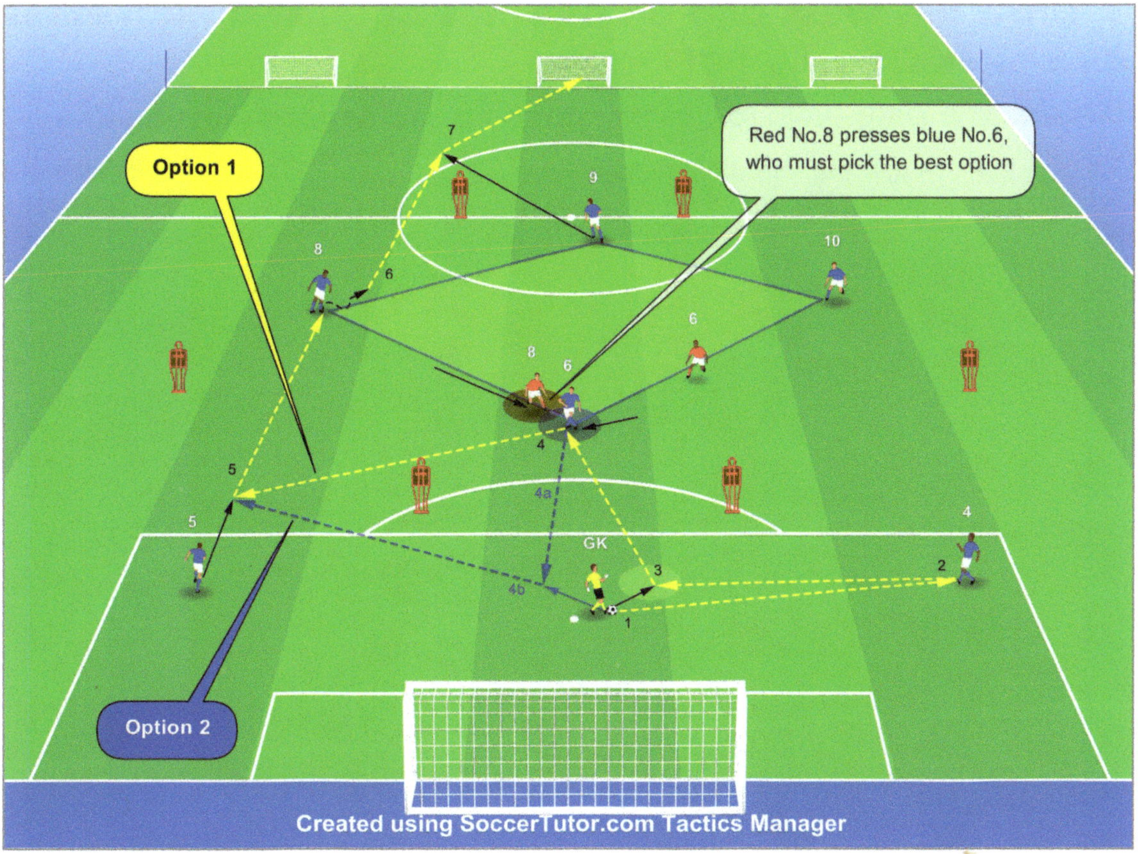

![Diagram showing Option 1 and Option 2 with Red No.8 pressing blue No.6, who must pick the best option]

Practice Description (Variation 2)

- In **Variation 2, the red central midfielder (N°8) presses the blue defensive midfielder (N°6)** as soon as the goalkeeper plays the pass. This means turning is not a good option. He should pass back, triggering a quick switch of play into the available space behind the second pressing line.
- **N°6 must read the situation and make a quick decision whether to pass back to the GK or to a centre back**.
- **Option 1** and **Option 2** (both highlighted) show the different ways to move the ball to the free **centre back (N°5)**, and then to **N°8** who has the most space.

- Quick ball circulation is used to **exploit the space behind red N°8 and move the ball to the blue attacking midfielder (N°8)** in between the lines.
- **N°8** plays in behind for the **forward (N°9)** to score.

Coaching Points

1. **Recognise pressing early** and decide quickly whether to turn or pass.
2. **Move the ball quickly** to exploit space behind the press.
3. **Use sharp combinations** to break through pressing lines.

BEAT THE PRESS WITH SINGLE & DOUBLE PIVOTS

Training Session 1: Break Lines vs High Press Zonal Defending with a Single Pivot

PROGRESSION

3. Draw the Press and Break Lines Against a High Press 8v6 (+GKs) Positional Game

Variation 1: Draw Press to Create Space Behind Second Pressing Line

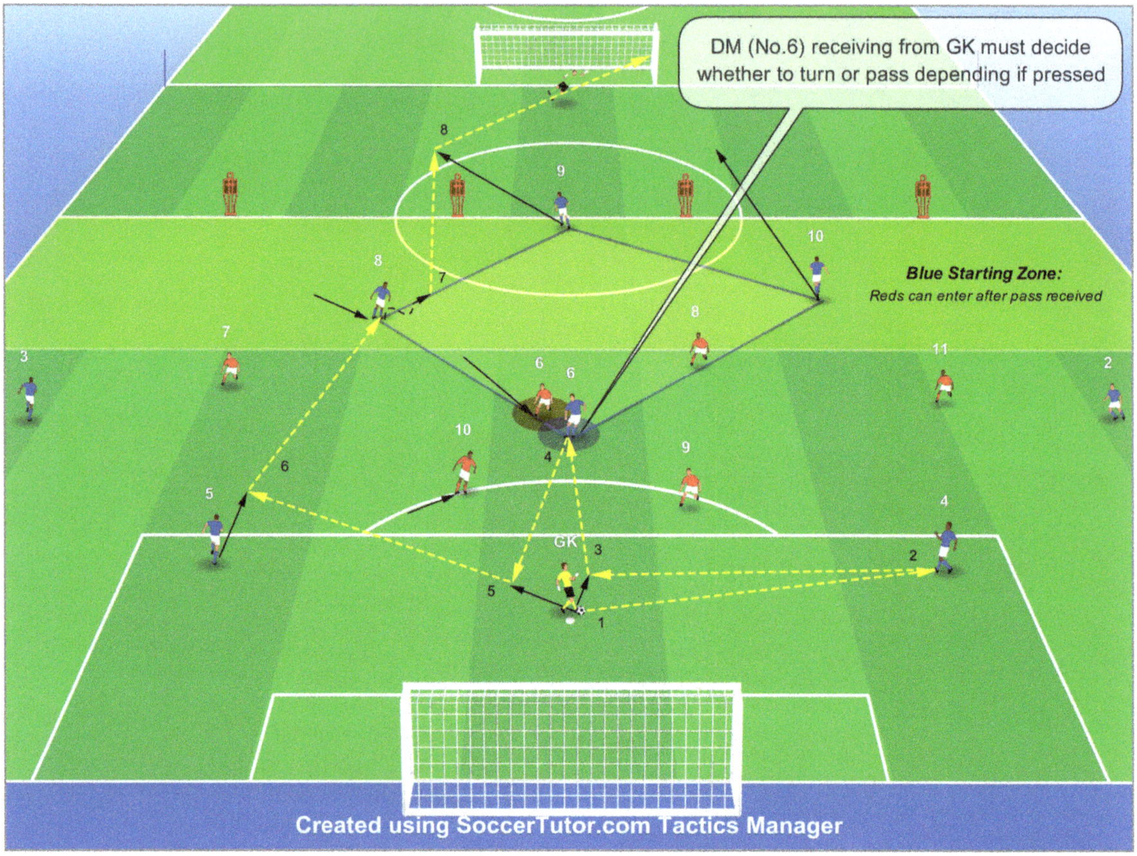

DM (No.6) receiving from GK must decide whether to turn or pass depending if pressed

Blue Starting Zone: Reds can enter after pass received

Practice Description (Variation 1)

- The yellow zone marks where the 3 blue attackers (**N°8, N°10,** and **N°9**) start. The reds can only enter once a blue player receives inside it.
- The reds are in a 4-2 defensive shape.
- The **blue goalkeeper** (**GK**) starts and circulates the ball with the **centre backs** (**N°5 and N°4**) before passing to the **defensive midfielder** (**N°6**) behind the first pressing line.

- **N°6 must decide to turn or pass** based on whether the closest red midfielder (N°6) moves to press or not.
- *Refer to the previous practice variations and analysis pages for more detail.*
- **Blue Objective:** Build up from back, break through the second line, and then the third line (mannequins) to score.
- **Red Objective:** Press to win the ball and counter to score within 8–12 seconds.

BEAT THE PRESS WITH SINGLE & DOUBLE PIVOTS

Training Session 1: Break Lines vs High Press Zonal Defending with a Single Pivot

Variation 2: Goalkeeper Draws Press to Create Space for Centre Back

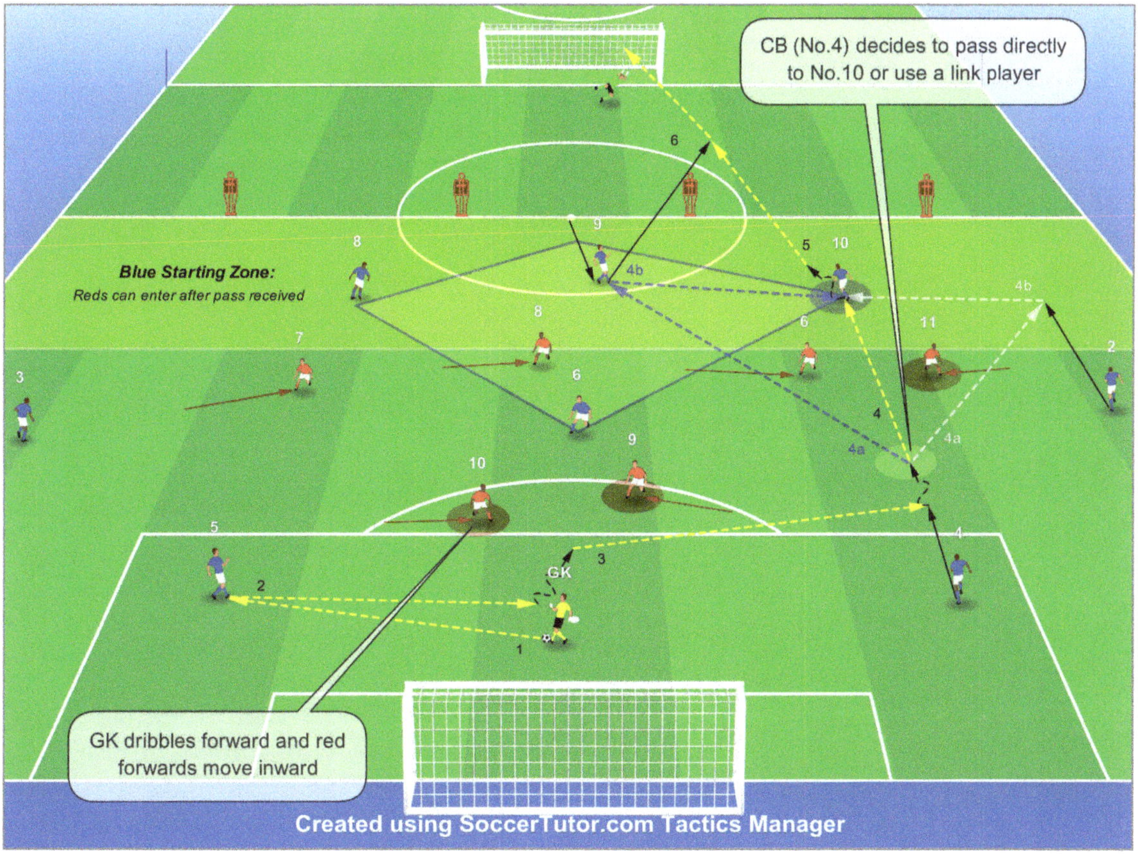

[Diagram: Blue Starting Zone — Reds can enter after pass received. CB (No.4) decides to pass directly to No.10 or use a link player. GK dribbles forward and red forwards move inward.]

Practice Description (Variation 2)

- In this variation, the **goalkeeper (GK)** moves forward with he ball and the red forwards (N°10 and N°9) block the central passing lane. **GK** passes wide to a **centre back (N°4)**. The **full back (N°2)** advances to support.

- **Blue Objective:** N°4 must read the red midfielders' reactions, such as whether the winger (N°11) shifts inside.

- Based on the available passing lanes, **N°4 plays directly to the attacking midfielder N°10 (yellow arrow) or uses link players (blue and white arrows)**.

- Once **N°10** receives, the aim is to play in behind and score.

- In the diagram example, **N°10** passes in behind for the diagonal run of the forward (**N°9**) to score.

- **Red Objective:** Press to win the ball and counter to score within 8–12 seconds.

Coaching Points

1. **Recognise pressure** and decide whether to turn, pass back, or switch play.
2. **Circulate the ball quickly** to exploit space behind pressing lines.

Training Session 1: Break Lines vs High Press Zonal Defending with a Single Pivot

PROGRESSION

4. Break Lines Through Turning, Recycling the Ball, or Dribbling Forward 3 Zone Conditioned Game

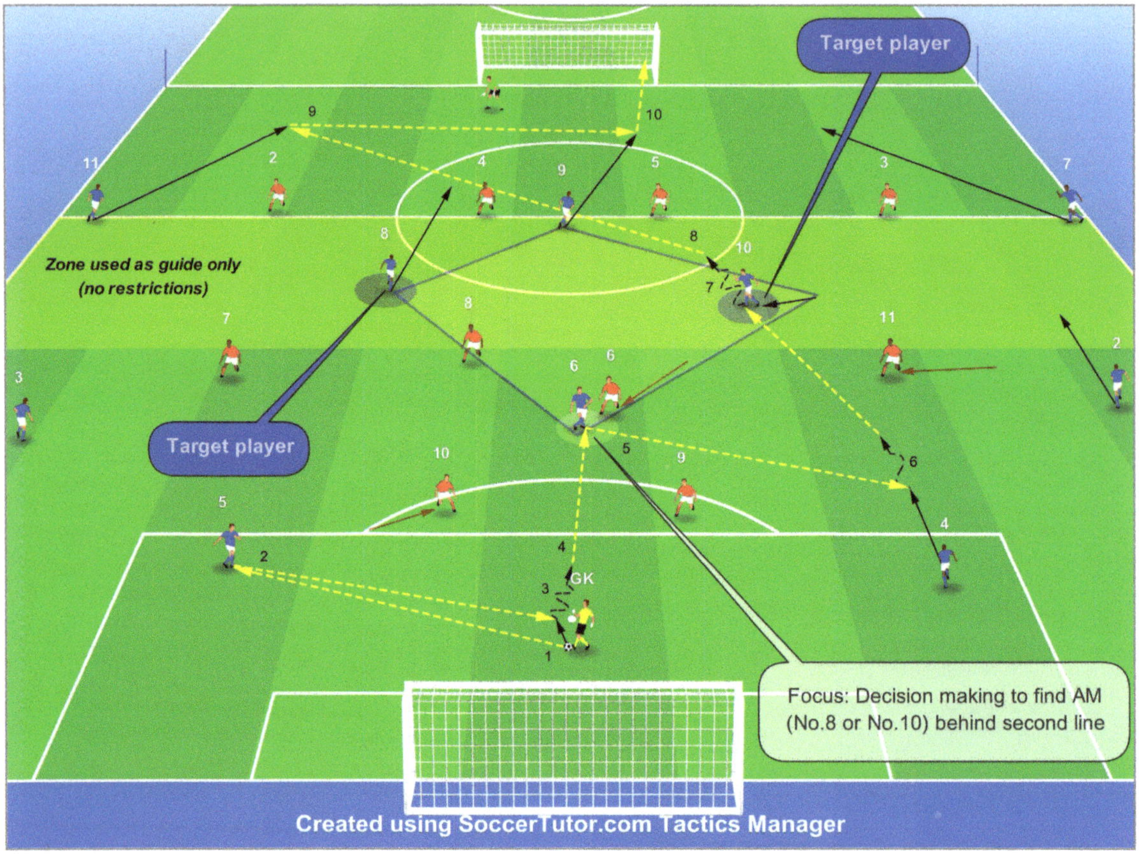

Focus: Decision making to find AM (No.8 or No.10) behind second line

Practice Description

- This final progression of this session is a conditioned 11v11 game in 3/4 of a full pitch. The yellow zone represents space between the lines but has no restrictions.
- **Blue Objective: Focus on decision making when receiving under pressure to find an attacking midfielder (Nº8 or Nº10) behind the second pressing line**.
- From there, progress beyond the third line to score. Note: Awareness is needed if **GK** dribbles forward and creates space for the centre backs to receive.

- **Players must read the reds' defensive actions and decide** to turn, recycle the ball, or dribble forward into space.
- **Red Objective: Press high immediately after the blue GK's first pass**. If they win the ball, they counter to try and score within 12 seconds.
- **Note:** The next section will train the same objectives using the 4-2-3-1 formation.

BEAT THE PRESS WITH SINGLE & DOUBLE PIVOTS

BUILD UP TO BEAT THE PRESS

Tactical Analysis

Break Lines vs High Press Zonal Defending with a Double Pivot

Build up play patterns from Flick, Klopp, and Emery's teams

BEAT THE PRESS WITH SINGLE & DOUBLE PIVOTS

Build Up Play from the Back Principles and Objectives with a Double Pivot (4-2-3-1)

Note: See build up play principles and objectives outlined on page 33.

Having examined how to build up play using a single pivot midfield (4-3-3), we now turn to the double pivot (4-2-3-1) and explore how its structure influences the early phases of build-up play.

Compared to a single pivot formation, the **double pivot (4-2-3-1) provides the goalkeeper with 2 central midfield passing options behind the first line of pressure rather than 1.** This increases the number of immediate short passing choices but introduces a **more advanced and fixed Nº10, who plays an important role between the lines**.

While the 4-2-3-1 supports progression to break the second pressing line, the forward passing options are slightly more limited. With only 4 players positioned beyond the second pressing line compared to 5 in the 4-3-3 (see previous section of book), the **possession team must be more deliberate in how it connects and builds play through the thirds**.

A key objective remains to create a free player between the lines. The **attacking midfielder (Nº10)** plays a central role in this and can shift into any of the 3 spaces behind the second pressing line (left, central, and right), even though the starting position is typically central. **By moving horizontally across the vertical channels, the Nº10 causes dilemmas for the defending team and increases the chance of evading pressure and remaining unmarked.**

Equally important is the ability to create multiple passing lanes behind the second pressing line when a defensive midfielder receives the ball. For instance, If the attacking midfielder stays in the same vertical lane as the forward and a defensive midfielder receives and turns, the forward options become narrow and predictable. To solve this, the players ahead of the ball must reposition themselves into different lanes, creating triangle shapes as discussed in the previous single pivot (4-3-3) section. When the attacking midfielder moves away from the forward's lane, he creates a new angle and gives the defensive midfielder a clearer path to progress the attack with greater flexibility.

Build Up to Beat the Press: Break Lines vs High Press Zonal Defending with a Double Pivot

Build Up Play Against High Pressing and Zonal Defending with a Double Pivot (4-2-3-1)

1. Available Spaces Between the Lines and Players vs High Pressing with Zonal Defending

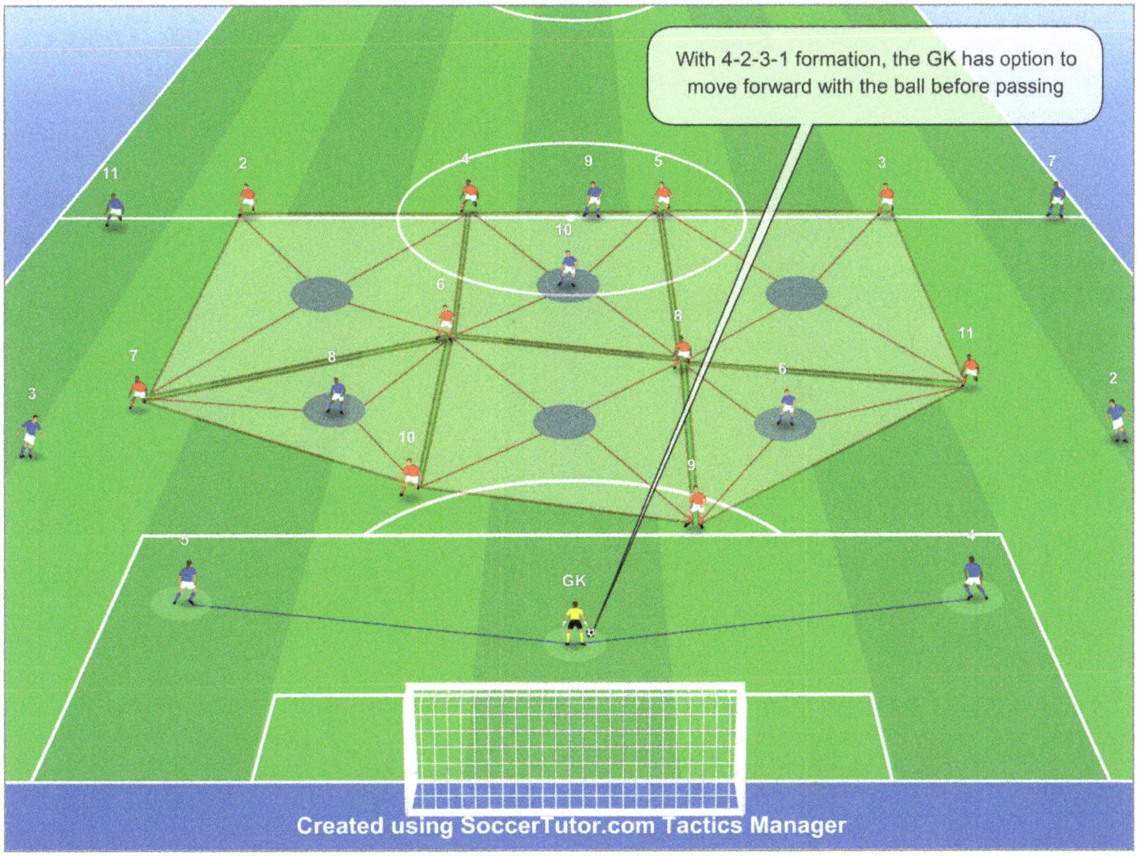

With 4-2-3-1 formation, the GK has option to move forward with the ball before passing

The objectives are similar when using a double pivot midfield (4-2-3-1) compared with a single pivot 4-3-3 (previous section of the book).

The main difference lies in the positioning of the midfielders, who typically occupy different spaces compared to those in a 4-3-3. However, they can shift into nearby areas if they identify more space to receive the ball.

Once again, **effective positioning by the midfielders is essential** for receiving passes unmarked between the lines.

With the 4-2-3-1 formation, **3 of the 6 available spaces between the opposition's lines are usually occupied, creating a structure that supports build up play through central areas**.

©SOCCERTUTOR.COM

BEAT THE PRESS WITH SINGLE & DOUBLE PIVOTS

Build Up to Beat the Press: Break Lines vs High Press Zonal Defending with a Double Pivot

2. Goalkeeper's Options to Pass Through or Over Pressing Lines

In this example, the **goalkeeper (GK) moves forward with the ball** to reduce the distance between himself and both the first pressing line and the potential target players. This movement **increases the chance of playing through (breaking lines) and improves the likelihood of delivering an accurate pass**.

The **defensive midfielder (Nº6)** positions himself centrally between the 2 red forwards and central midfielders, where he can find space to exploit.

At the same time, the other **defensive midfielder (Nº8)** shifts wider to receive between red Nº7 and Nº6.

Both passing options (especially to Nº6) will break the first pressing line and neutralise 2 red players.

Alternatively, the **GK** can target the **attacking midfielder (Nº10)**, who is positioned between the red centre backs and central midfielders.

If the aerial pass is accurate and Nº10 can turn with the ball, it breaks 2 lines of pressure and neutralises 6 opponents. For this to be effective, **Nº10** must find the most available space between lines and opponents.

BEAT THE PRESS WITH SINGLE & DOUBLE PIVOTS

Build Up to Beat the Press: Break Lines vs High Press Zonal Defending with a Double Pivot

3. Exploiting Passing Lanes to Beat the Second Pressing Line and Play to Attacking Midfielder Between the Lines

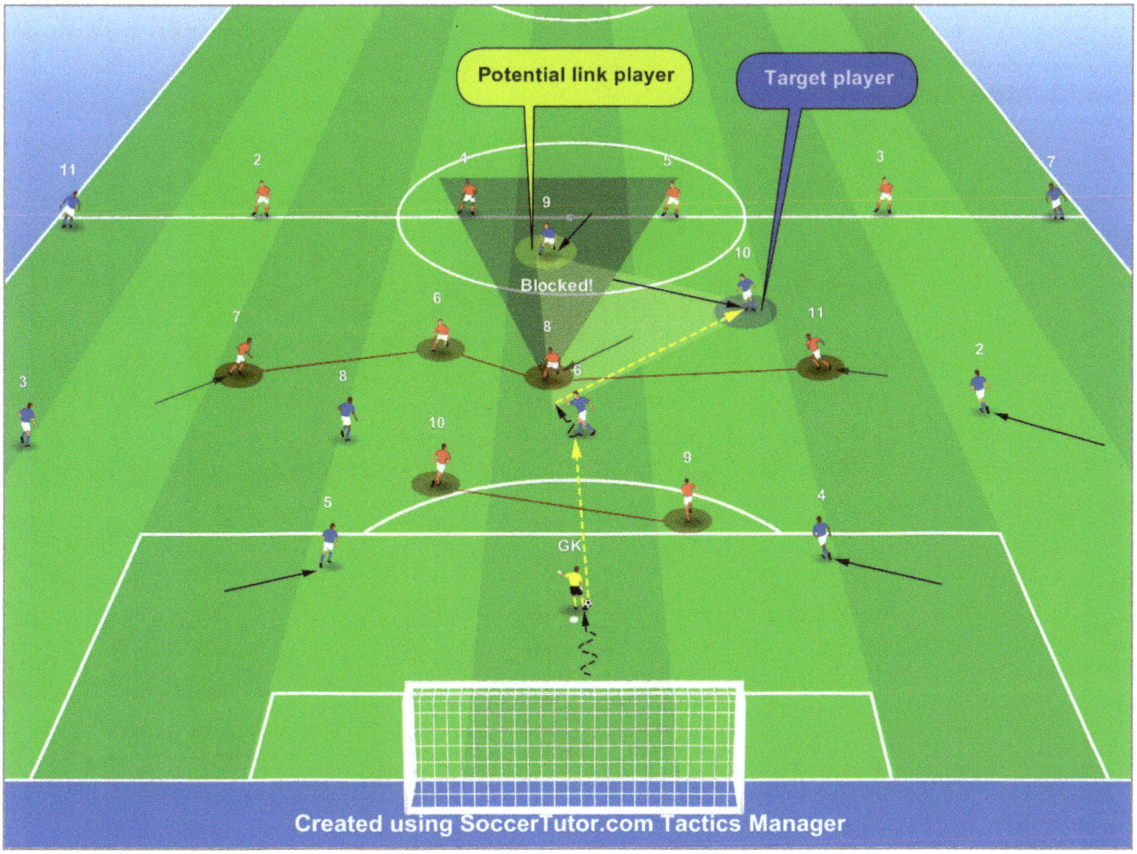

In this example, as soon as the **defensive midfielder (N°6)** receives the ball, the **attacking midfielder (N°10)** initially occupies the same passing lane as the **forward (N°9)**. This positioning creates a problem if an opponent positions themselves to block the pass to **N°10**, as they can effectively block the passing lane to both players at once.

To solve this, **N°10 shifts into a different passing lane**. This adjustment gives the player in possession **2 distinct passing options**. Even if the pressing opponent successfully blocks one of the passing lanes, the second remains available.

In this situation, **red N°8 blocks the pass towards blue N°9, which leaves N°10 free to receive the ball**.

Note: This movement by N°10 not only restores passing variety but also helps maintain tempo and progression.

Once **N°10** receives, the next step is to move the ball behind the third pressing line and continue the build up into more advanced areas.

Build Up to Beat the Press: Break Lines vs High Press Zonal Defending with a Double Pivot

4. Build Up Play on Side and Moving the Ball to the Free Attacking Midfielder Behind the Second Pressing Line

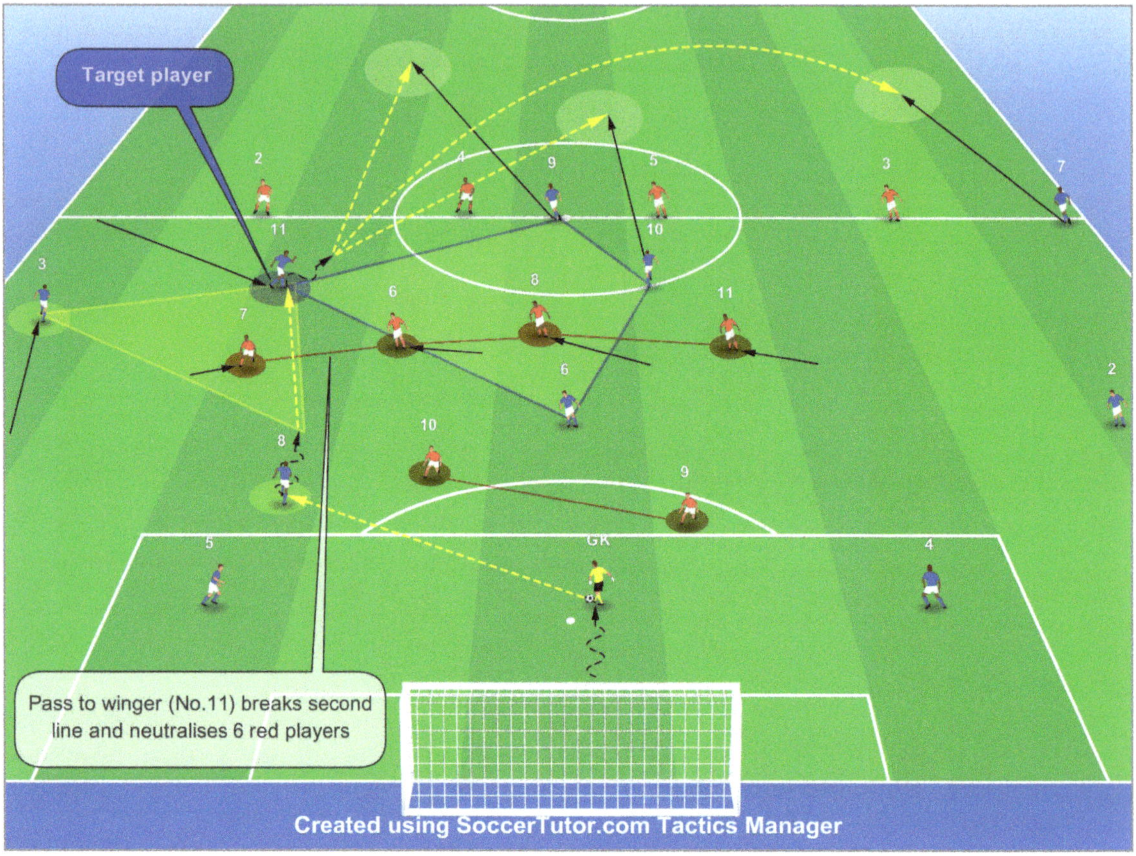

Pass to winger (No.11) breaks second line and neutralises 6 red players

If the ball is played to the **defensive midfielder (N°8)** on the left, the blues must apply the same build up principles. **The first priority is to create a free player between the lines**.

Since the **attacking midfielder (N°10)** is positioned away from the ball, the nearby teammates to **N°8** must take the initiative. **The left winger (N°11) makes an inside movement to offer a passing option and potentially become the free player between the lines**. At the same time, the **left back (N°3)** moves forward and a dilemma is created for the red right back (N°2), who is now uncertain whether to follow **N°11** or hold his position.

These coordinated movements achieve 2 goals for the blues. If red N°2 does not follow **N°11**, he can receive unmarked. If red N°2 does track him, space is created for **N°3** to advance. Either way, the **actions generate a triangle around the ball (highlighted) and increase passing options for N°8**.

In the diagram example, as **N°11 and N°3 move in sync**, red N°2 chooses to stay in position to deny space for **N°3**. As a result, **N°11 receives the ball unmarked behind the second line**, turns, and plays the next pass in behind the defensive line (3 options).

BEAT THE PRESS WITH SINGLE & DOUBLE PIVOTS

Build Up to Beat the Press: Break Lines vs High Press Zonal Defending with a Double Pivot

Drawing Press from Midfielder to Exploit Space Created Between the Lines Behind

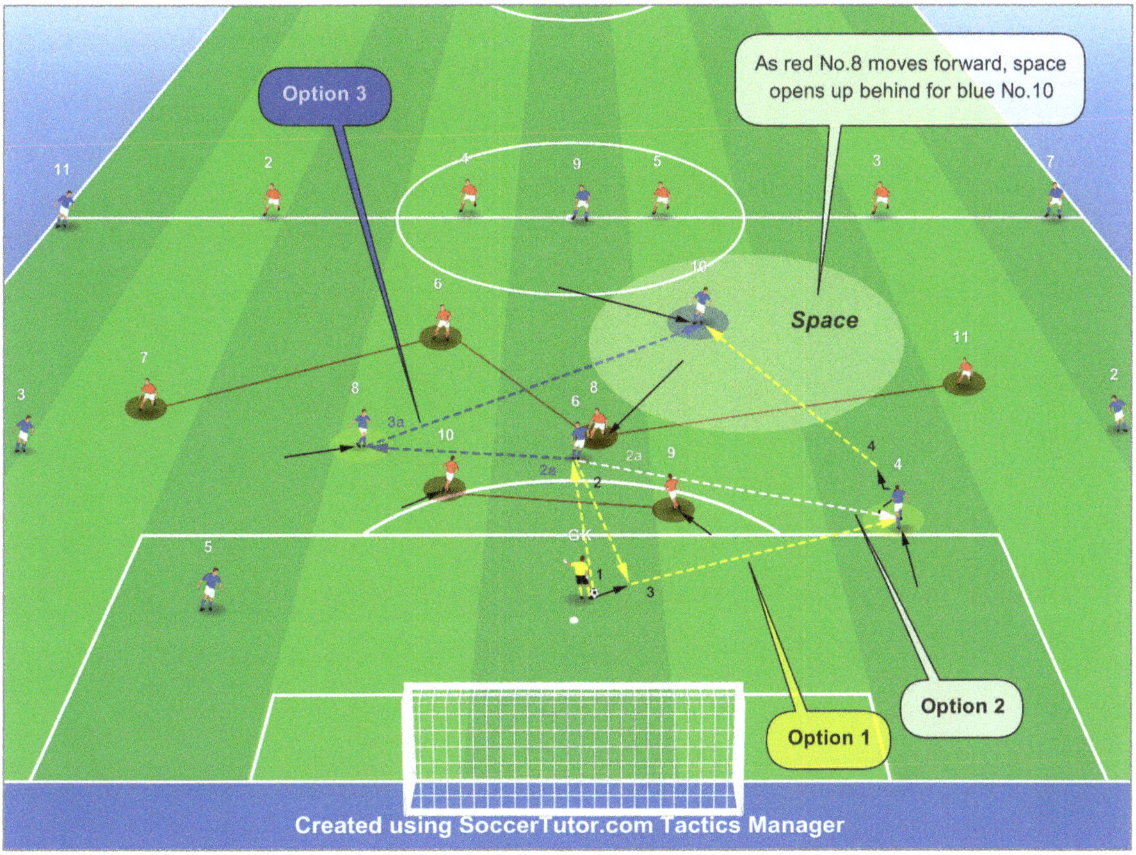

The **goalkeeper** (**GK**) is positioned between 2 pressing forwards and can play through the first line. As the potential receiver usually has their back to goal, the **through pass typically draws pressure**. This is guided with these principles:

A. **Quick read of the situation and where the available space is**.

B. **Move the ball into this space as quickly as possible**.

GK plays a through pass to **N°6**. As red **N°8** moves to press, space opens up behind for blue **N°10** to receive behind.

Option 1: **N°6** passes back to **GK**, who passes to the **centre back** (**N°4**) or passes directly (**Option 2**) - **N°4** finds **N°10** before the opposition shifts back into shape.

Option 3: A quicker but riskier option is **N°6's** to pass to **N°8**, who then finds **N°10**.

Note 1: If red N°6 is drawn out of position, N°10 should move into the space behind him, and the ball should be directed there.

Note 2: The awareness and scanning of the area by blue N°6 is important for success and avoiding any mistakes.

BEAT THE PRESS WITH SINGLE & DOUBLE PIVOTS

Build Up to Beat the Press: Break Lines vs High Press Zonal Defending with a Double Pivot

Goalkeeper Draws Press to Create Space Wide

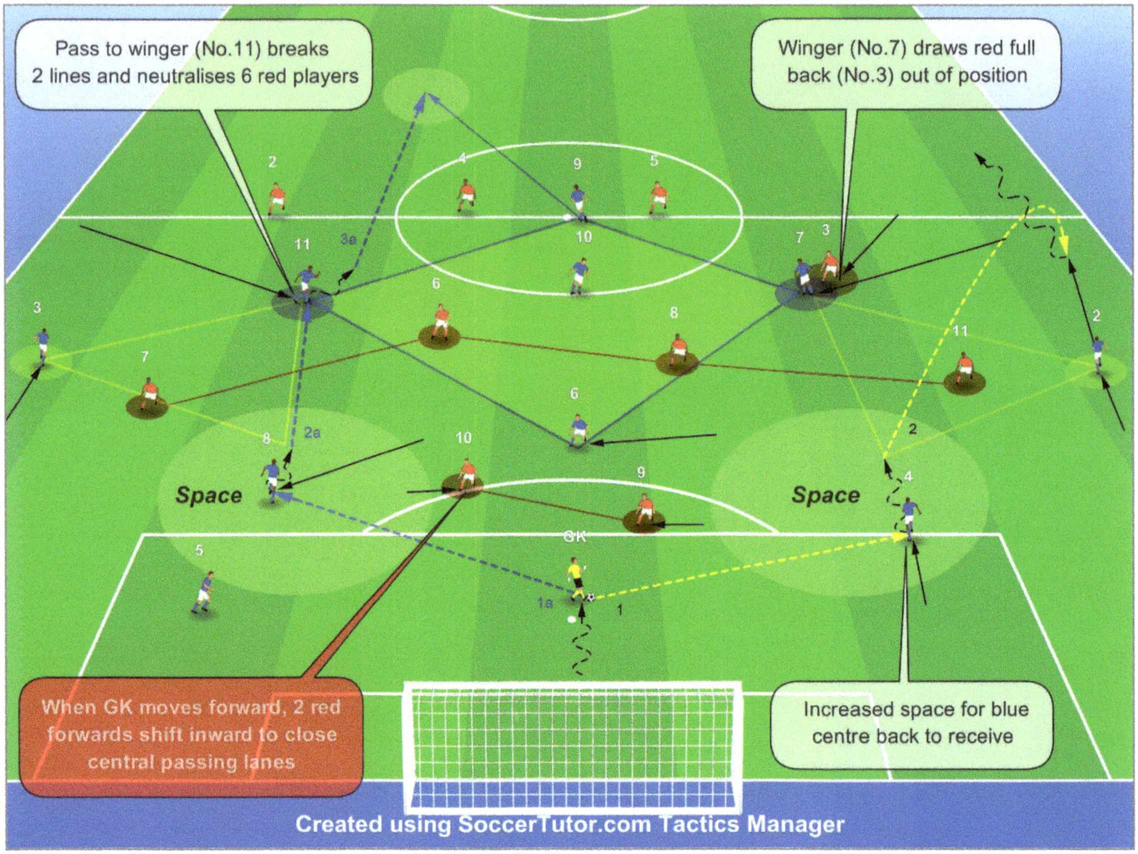

Pass to winger (No.11) breaks 2 lines and neutralises 6 red players

Winger (No.7) draws red full back (No.3) out of position

When GK moves forward, 2 red forwards shift inward to close central passing lanes

Increased space for blue centre back to receive

When the **goalkeeper** (**GK**) drives forward between 2 red forwards, they naturally shift inside to block central passing lanes. This creates space either side of them, which can be exploited by the **blue centre back (N°4)** or **defensive midfielder (N°8)** depending on which lane opens.

As the first pressing line collapses centrally, the centre backs become viable passing options, and the **full backs (N°3 & N°2)** push forward. **The next task is to create a free player between the lines.** With **N°10** central, a **winger (e.g. N°11) can move inside** while the full back pushes forward.

This coordinated movement forces the red full back into a decision to follow the winger or stay and allow space for the full back. These actions form a triangle and give the receiver multiple passing options. If the red wide midfielders shift inside to block through passes, the full backs can exploit the wide spaces. If a pass in between the lines is available, it can break 2 lines and neutralise 6 red players.

Note: If N°8 is central, N°5 can use space on the left. If N°10 is wider between the centre back and full back, the respective winger does not need to move inside.

©SOCCERTUTOR.COM

BEAT THE PRESS WITH SINGLE & DOUBLE PIVOTS

BUILD UP TO BEAT THE PRESS

Training Session 2 (4 Practices)

Break Lines vs High Press Zonal Defending with a Double Pivot

Based on Flick, Klopp, and Emery build up patterns

Training Session 2: Break Lines vs High Press Zonal Defending with a Double Pivot

TRAINING SESSION (4 PRACTICES)
1. Passing Decisions to Break Lines Depending on Opposition Pressing

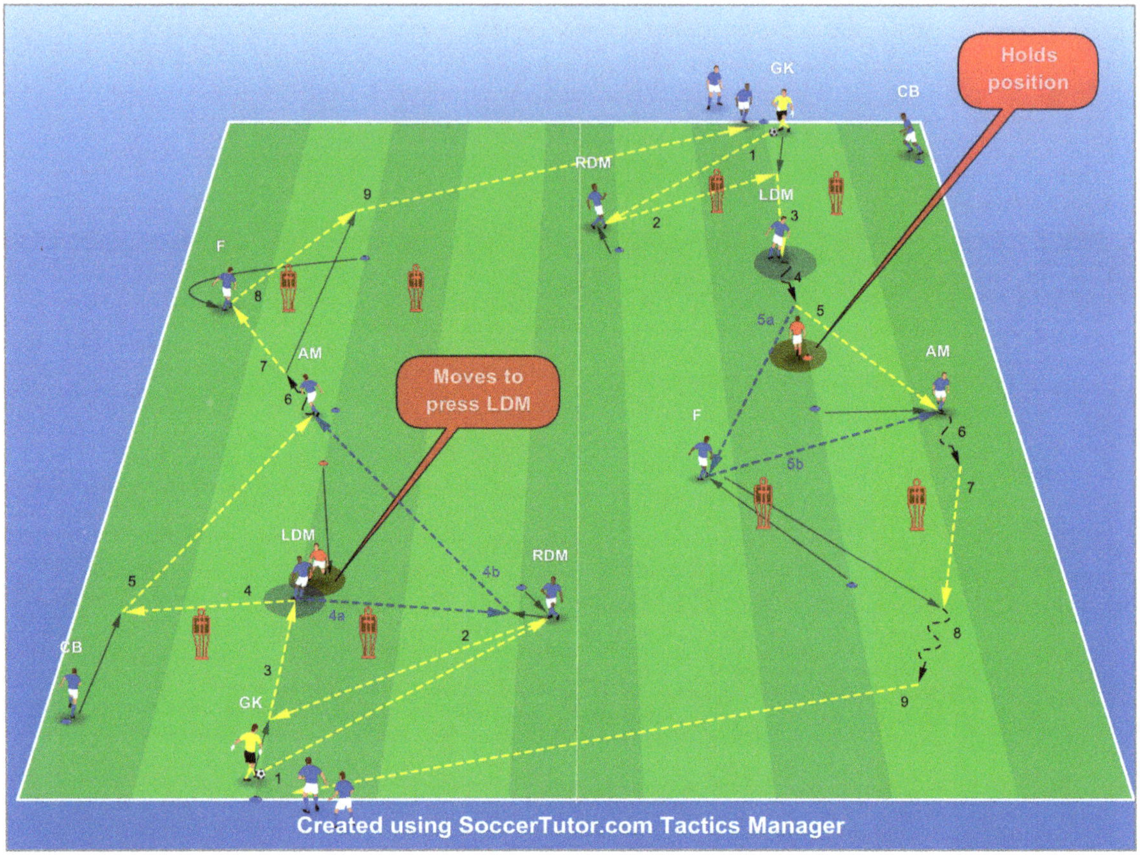

Practice Description

- **Objective:** Decision making for whether to turn or pass back (to exploit space).

- The mannequins mark the first and third pressing lines and the red player is in the second line.

- **Left Side: GK** plays a one-two with **RDM** and then passes to **LDM**, who must assess the red player's reaction.

- If pressed, **LDM** passes to **CB** (or **RDM**) and the ball is quickly played to **AM** behind the red player.

- **AM** turns and plays a one-two with **F** around the mannequin before passing to the other group.

- **Right Side:** If not pressed, **LDM** turns. The ball is either played to **AM** directly or via the **forward (F)** acting as a link player (blue arrows).

- **F** then runs in between the mannequins to receive **AM's** through pass and pass to the other group.

- **Player Rotations:** GK → CB → LDM → RDM → AM → F → GK (Other Group).

Training Session 2: Break Lines vs High Press Zonal Defending with a Double Pivot

PROGRESSION

2. Breaking Lines Based on Opponent Reactions 6 (+GK) v 2 Functional Practice

Variation 1: Receive + Turn to Break the Second Pressing Line

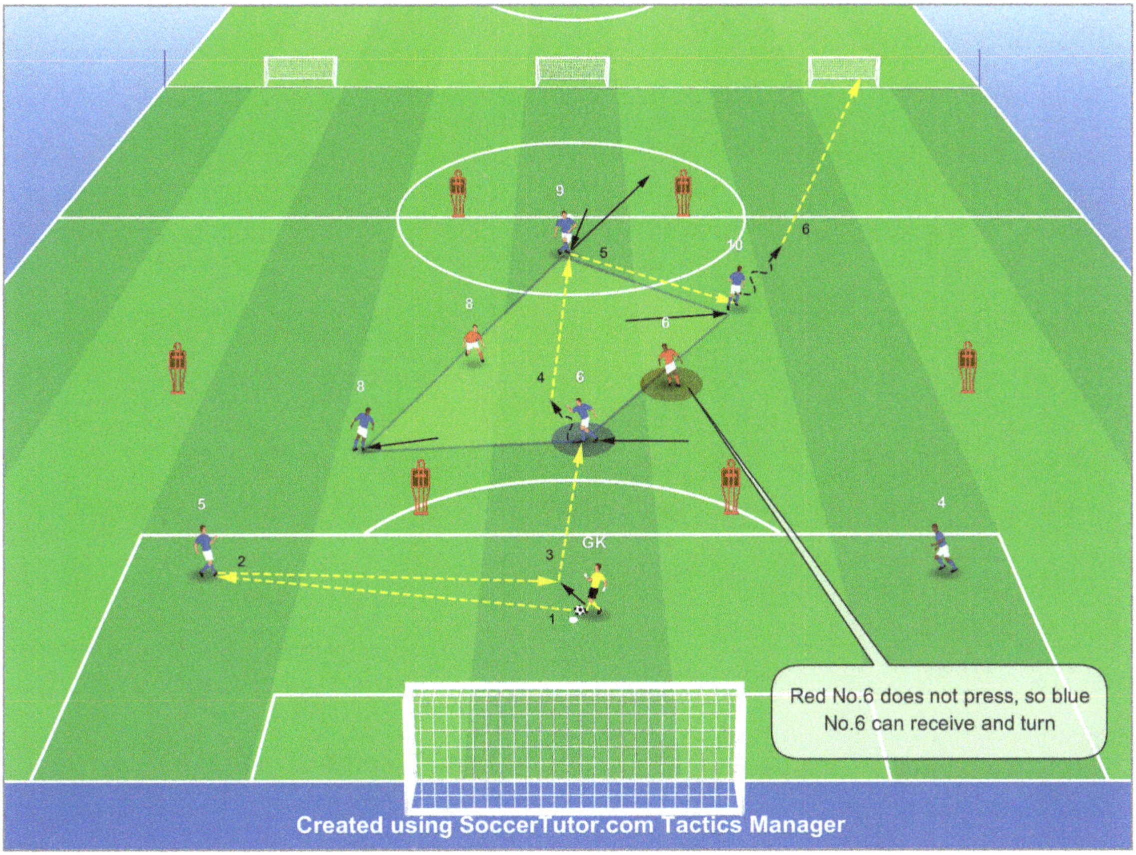

Red No.6 does not press, so blue No.6 can receive and turn

Practice Description (Variation 1)

- The blues have the goalkeeper, 2 centre backs, 3 midfielders, and the forward.
- The reds have 2 central midfielders and the mannequins form the rest of the defensive formation.
- **GK** starts and circulates the ball with the **centre backs (N°5 and N°4)** before passing to a **defensive midfielder (N°6 in diagram)** behind the first pressing line, who must scan before receiving.

- The objective is to move the ball to the **attacking midfielder (N°10)** after reading the defensive reactions.
- If the nearest **red midfielder holds their position (Variation 1)**, **N°6 receives on the half-turn** and passes forward.
- Teammates offer options to progress the attack, ideally forming a triangle or diamond shape. In this example, the **forward (N°9)** sets the ball back for **N°10** to receive, dribble forward, and score.

BEAT THE PRESS WITH SINGLE & DOUBLE PIVOTS

Training Session 2: Break Lines vs High Press Zonal Defending with a Double Pivot

Variation 2: Pass Back Under Pressure to Move the Ball into Free Space

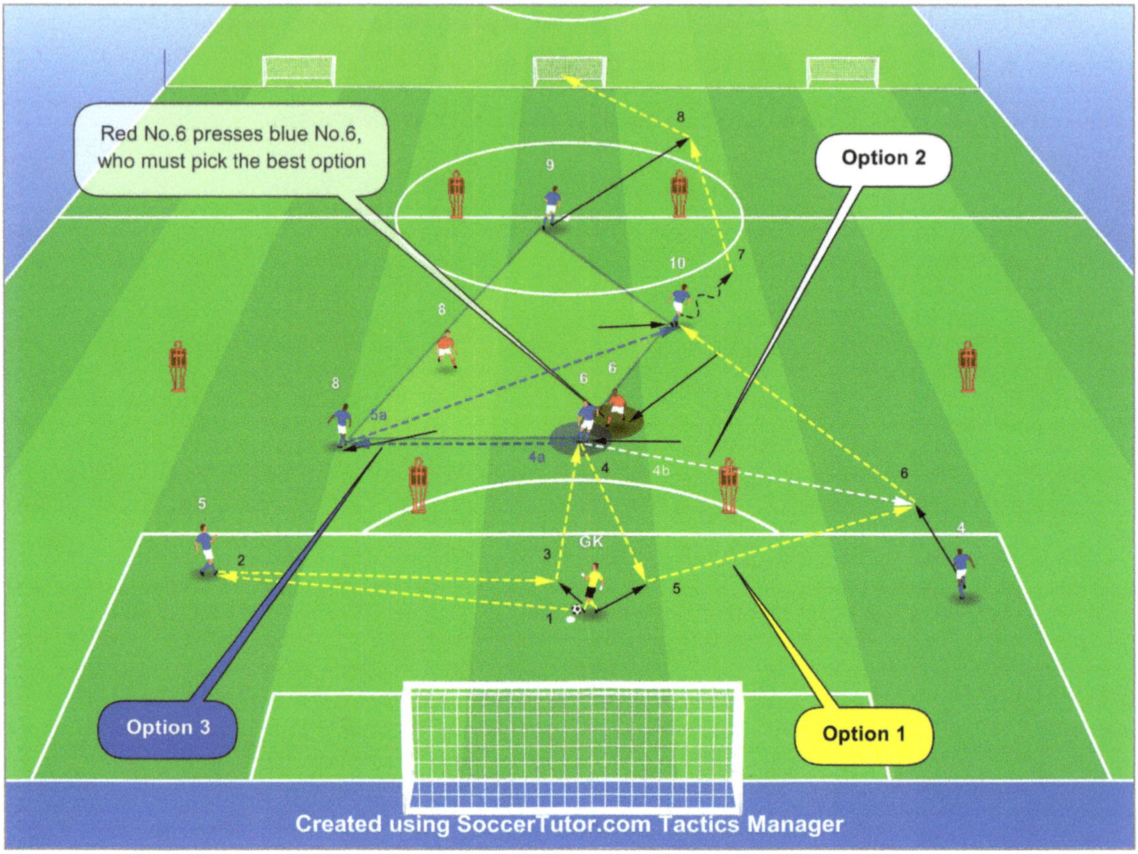

Red No.6 presses blue No.6, who must pick the best option

Option 2

Option 3

Option 1

Created using SoccerTutor.com Tactics Manager

Practice Description (Variation 2)

- In **Variation 2, the red midfielder presses blue Nº6** as soon as the goalkeeper plays the pass to him. This means turning is not a good option as it was in Variation 1. **Nº6 should instead pass back, triggering an aim to find the free the attacking midfielder (Nº10)** in available space behind the second pressing line.

- The **defensive midfielder (Nº6)** must read the situation and make a **quick decision whether to pass back to the GK or to a centre back.**

- Quick ball circulation is used to **exploit the space behind red Nº6 and move the ball to Nº10.**

- **Option 1** and **Option 2** use the **right centre back (Nº4)** as the link player.

- **Option 3** uses the other defensive midfielder (**Nº8**) as the link player.

- **Nº10** plays in behind for the **forward (Nº9)** to score.

Coaching Points

1. **Recognise pressing early and access the defensive reaction** to decide quickly whether to turn or pass.
2. **Move the ball quickly** when space opens up behind the second pressing line.
3. **Use sharp combinations** to break pressing lines and progress play forward.

©SOCCERTUTOR.COM

BEAT THE PRESS WITH SINGLE & DOUBLE PIVOTS

Training Session 2: Break Lines vs High Press Zonal Defending with a Double Pivot

PROGRESSION

3. Draw the Press and Break Lines Against a High Press 10v6 (+GKs) Positional Game

Variation 1: Draw Press to Create Space Behind Second Pressing Line

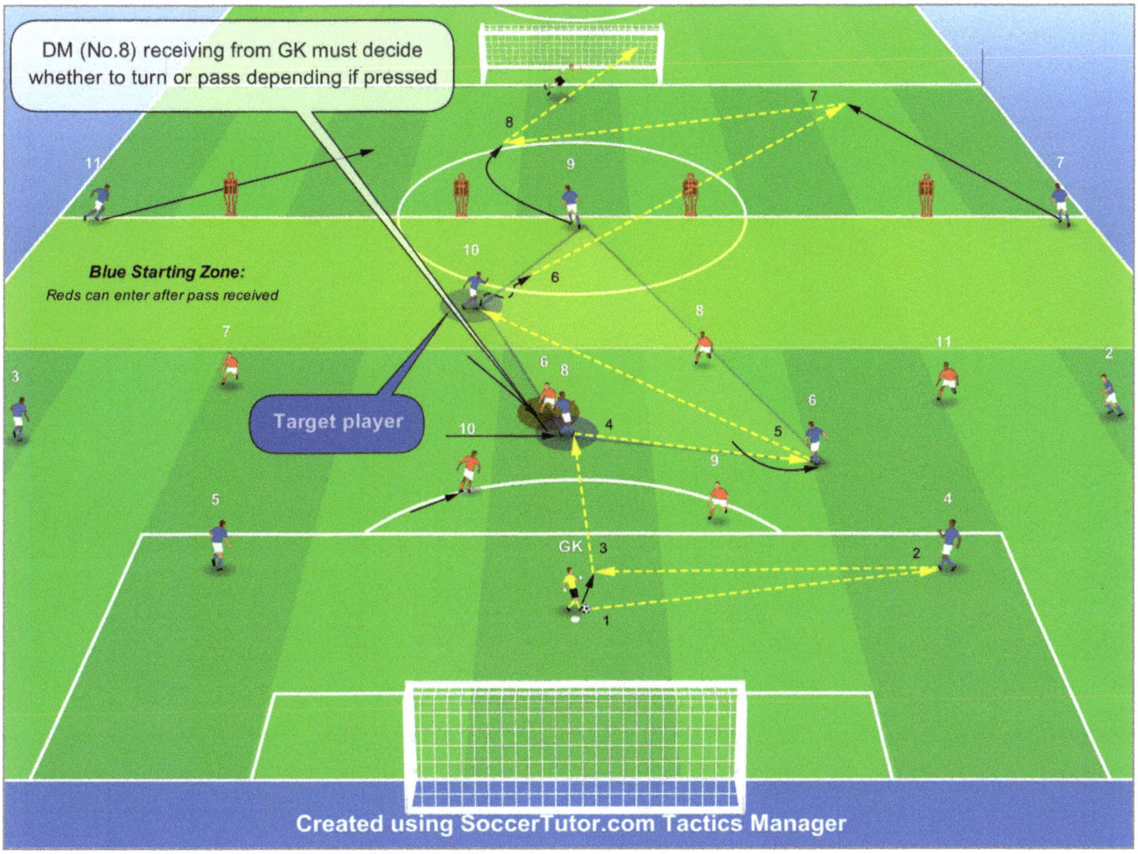

DM (No.8) receiving from GK must decide whether to turn or pass depending if pressed

Blue Starting Zone: Reds can enter after pass received

Target player

Practice Description (Variation 1)

- The yellow zone marks where the 4 blue attackers (**N°10, N°11, N°9,** and **N°7**) start. The reds can only enter once a blue player receives inside it.
- The reds are in a 4-2 defensive shape.
- The goalkeeper (**GK**) starts and circulates the ball with the **centre backs** (**N°5 and N°4**) before passing to a **defensive midfielder** (**N°8 in diagram**) behind the first pressing line.

- **N°8 must decide to turn or pass** based on whether the closest red midfielder (N°6) moves to press or not.
- *Refer to the previous practice variations and analysis pages for more detail*.
- **Blue Objective:** Build up from back, break through the second line, and then the third line (mannequins) to score.
- **Red Objective:** Press to win the ball and counter to score within 8–12 seconds.

Training Session 2: Break Lines vs High Press Zonal Defending with a Double Pivot

Variation 2: Goalkeeper Draws Press to Create Space for Centre Back

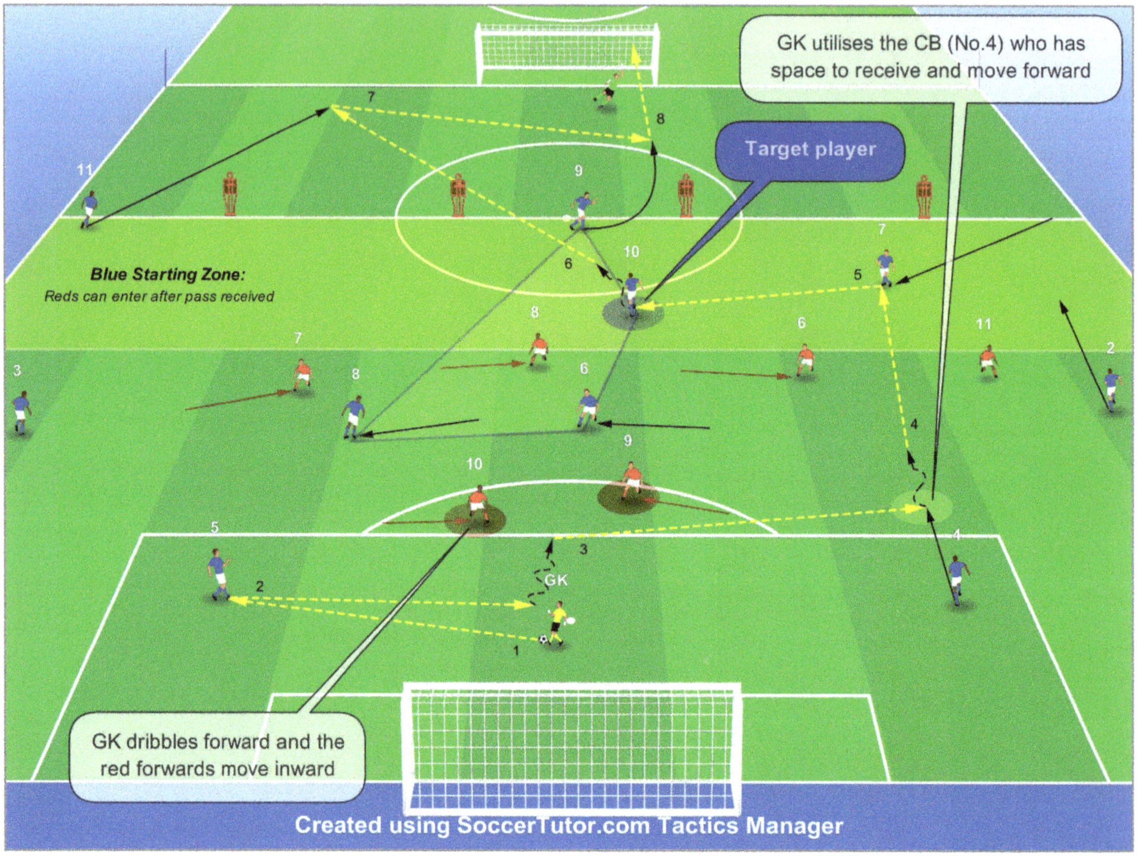

Practice Description (Variation 2)

- In this variation, the **goalkeeper** (**GK**) moves forward with he ball and the red forwards (N°10 and N°9) block the central passing lane. **GK** passes wide to a **centre back** (**N°4**). The **full back** (**N°2**) advances forward to support.

- **Blue Objective:** **N°4 must read the red midfielders' reactions**, such as whether the red winger (N°11) shifts inside (he doesn't in the diagram). Based on the available passing lanes, **N°4** plays to the **winger N°7**, who acts as a link player to move the ball to the target player (**attacking midfielder N°10**). The aim from there is to play in behind and finish.

- **Red Objective:** Press to win the ball and counter to score within 8–12 seconds.

- **Restriction:** Red players cannot enter the yellow zone until a blue player receives inside it.

Coaching Points

1. **Recognise pressure** and decide whether to turn, pass back, or exploit space.
2. **Communicate clearly** using key phrases.
3. **Move the ball quickly** when space opens wide or behind the second pressing line.
4. **Sharp combination play** to progress play and break the lines.

Training Session 2: Break Lines vs High Press Zonal Defending with a Double Pivot

PROGRESSION

4. Break Lines Through Turning, Recycling the Ball, or Dribbling Forward 3 Zone Conditioned Game

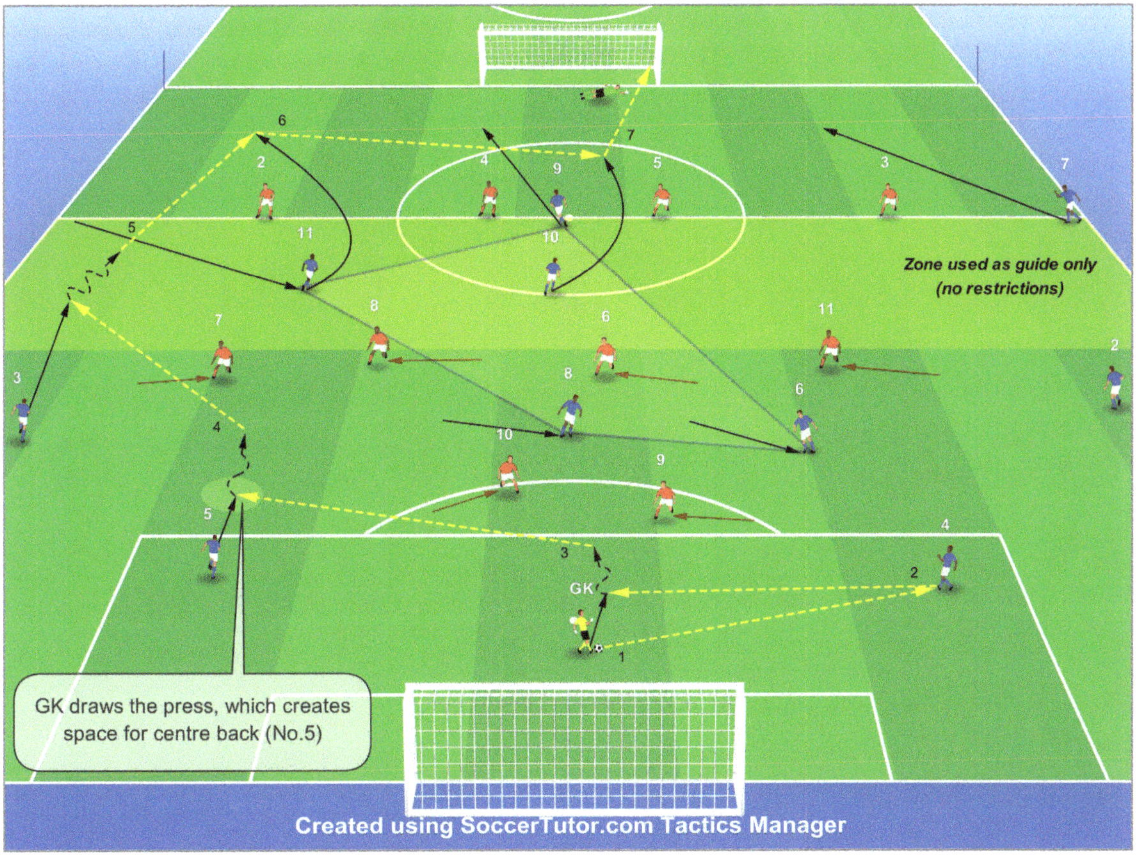

Zone used as guide only (no restrictions)

GK draws the press, which creates space for centre back (No.5)

Practice Description

- This final progression of this session is a conditioned 11v11 game in 3/4 of a full pitch. The yellow zone represents space between the lines but has no restrictions.
- **Blue Objective: Decision making to find the free player behind the second pressing line - attacking midfielder (Nº10) or strong side winger (Nº11), then progress beyond the third line to score.**
- Players must **read the reds' defensive actions** and decide to turn, recycle the ball, or dribble forward into space.

- Note 1: As shown in the diagram, awareness is needed if the **goalkeeper (GK)** dribbles forward and creates space for the centre backs to receive.
- Note 2: The blue must read the situation and the reactions of the defending players so that the appropriate solution is used.
- **Red Objective: Press high immediately after the GK's first pass.** If they win the ball, they counter to try and score within 12 seconds.

BUILD UP TO BEAT THE PRESS

Tactical Analysis

Goalkeeper's Passing Over Pressing Lines

Build up play patterns from Flick, Klopp, and Emery's teams

Goalkeeper's Passing Over Second Pressing Line

The goalkeeper can play the ball directly to the players positioned behind the second line of pressing, **bypassing the opposition's midfield press in a single pass**. This method allows the team to **progress quickly while avoiding the risks associated with building up through shorter passes under pressure**. However, for this approach to be successful, 3 key elements must be present:

1. **The receiver must be positioned effectively between lines and opponents**, ensuring they have enough space to control and progress the ball. **The ability to receive on the half-turn and scan the pitch before receiving is crucial**, as it allows them to make a quick decision on the next action.

2. **Teammates must position themselves strategically to challenge the defenders' decision making and make it difficult for them to press without leaving gaps**. By stretching the defensive line and adjusting their positioning, they can force defenders into reactive decision making, which can be exploited with quick ball movement.

3. **Awareness and communication** between the receiver and nearby teammates is essential. **The receiver must anticipate pressure from opponents and recognise when to release the ball quickly or dribble the ball forward into space**. Teammates must also signal their availability and adjust their movements to ensure they provide the best possible passing options, continually adapting to the opposition's positioning, pressing actions, and the overall flow of play.

Specifically, there has been an analysis of what is considered effective positioning. Players who are positioned behind the second pressing line should be positioned between lines and opponents to create options and unsettle the defensive structure.

Nearby teammates should take up positions in areas that create a tactical dilemma for their opponents. This means positioning themselves in such a way that forces opposing players into difficult decisions about who to mark.

During the build up, the **wingers must stay as wide as possible**:

- **If the opposing full backs decide to stay back** (close to the wingers), they are away from the attacking midfielders, who will then find more space to operate.

- **If the opposing full backs choose instead to mark the attacking midfielders**, then the wingers will have more space.

- **If the opposing full backs position themselves between the wingers and attacking midfielders**, both sets of players will likely find space to exploit.

The forward should be positioned as high as possible between the 2 opposing centre backs to remain unmarked and pose a dilemma about who should take responsibility for their marking. Additionally, the **opposing centre backs will be unsure whether to track the attacking midfielder close to them or the forward**, which increases attacking options for the team in possession.

Build Up to Beat the Press: Goalkeeper's Passing Over Pressing Lines

Goalkeeper's Passing Directly to Players Positioned Between the Lines

1a. Attacking Midfielder Receives Goalkeeper's Aerial Pass in Space Behind the Second Pressing Line (Single Pivot - 4-3-3)

In the diagram, after the **goalkeeper (GK)** moves forward with the ball to decrease his distance from potential target players, he delivers an aerial pass to the **left attacking midfielder (N°8)**, who finds space between the lines.

The red full back (N°2) is caught in an in-between position, having to cover **N°8** and the **left winger (N°11)**.

By not stepping forward to press, **red N°2 leaves N°8 unmarked**, allowing him to receive freely and turn.

This positioning opens a clear opportunity to progress the attack. Once turned, **N°8 can play a through pass in behind the red team's defensive line** to find a teammate making a run in behind - 3 options are shown in the diagram (white, yellow, and blue arrows).

BEAT THE PRESS WITH SINGLE & DOUBLE PIVOTS

Build Up to Beat the Press: Goalkeeper's Passing Over Pressing Lines

1b. Exploiting Space Created in Behind by the Opposing Full Back Moving Forward to Press Receiver (Single Pivot - 4-3-3)

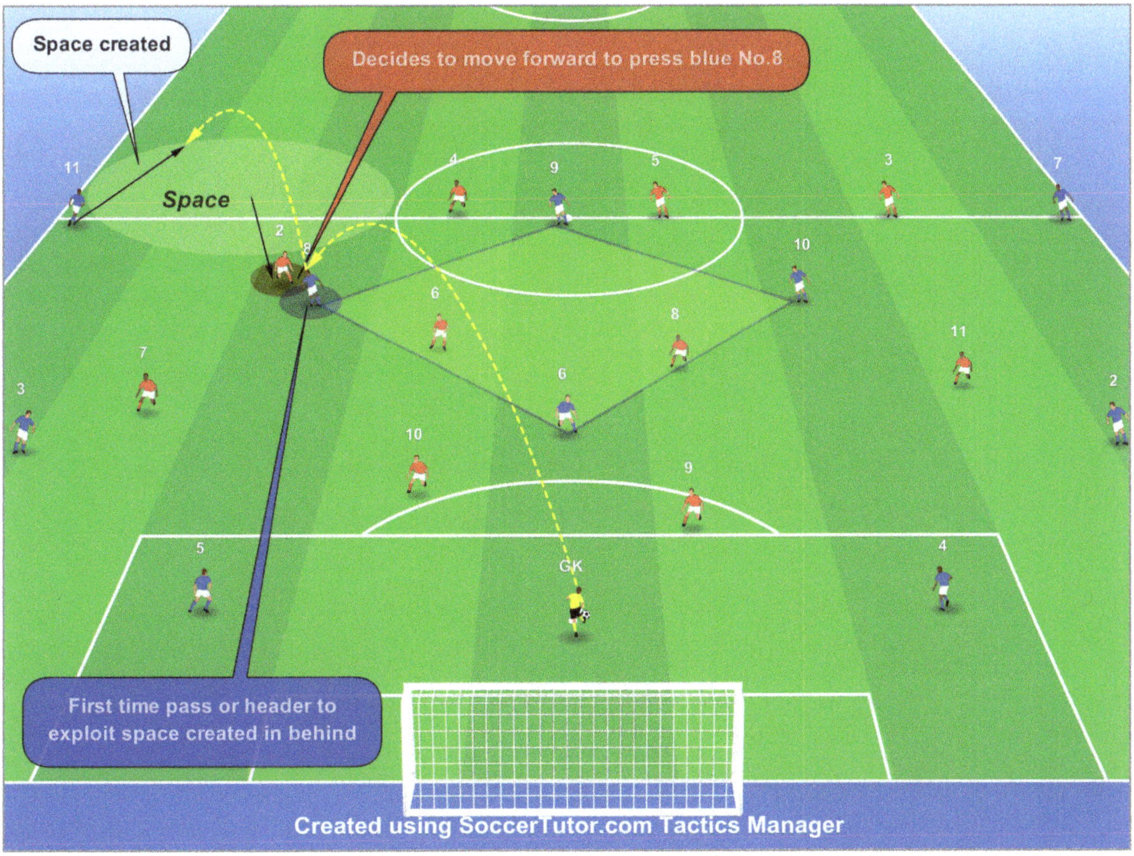

In this variation of the previous example, the **opposing red full back (Nº2) decides to step forward and press the receiving blue attacking midfielder (Nº8)**, attempting to prevent him from turning between the lines.

However, this pressing action by red Nº2 **creates available space in behind which can be exploited**.

If Nº8 recognises the movement early through scanning or is alerted by a teammate (**Nº11** or **Nº9**), he **can play a first-time pass or header into the space** left by red Nº2.

This allows the **left winger (Nº11)** to run in behind and receive in an advanced position.

The success of this move relies on **Nº8's** awareness, the timing of **Nº11's** run, and clear communication between teammates. If executed well, the **team can bypass the pressing lines and progress quickly into the attacking phase**.

Build Up to Beat the Press: Goalkeeper's Passing Over Pressing Lines

1c. Exploiting Space Created in Behind by the Opposing Centre Back Moving Forward to Press Receiver (Single Pivot - 4-3-3)

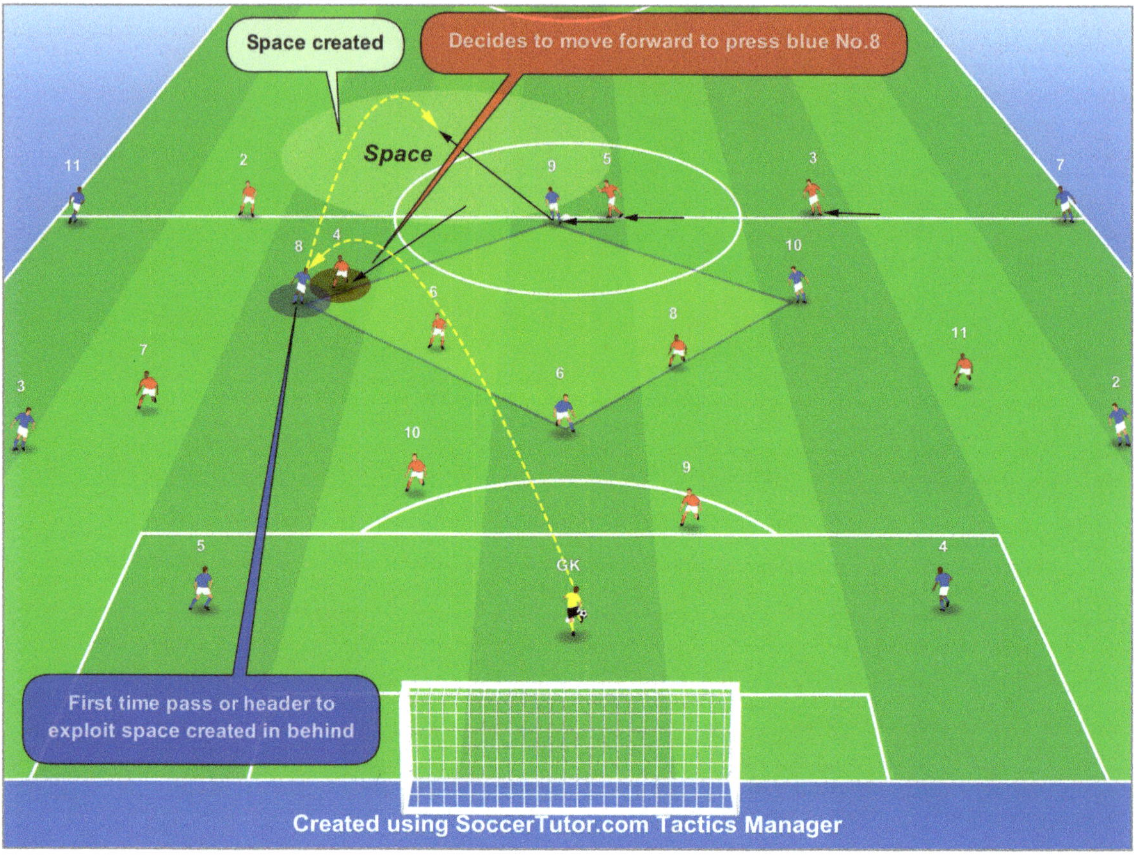

If an **opposing centre back** (red Nº4 in the diagram) **steps out to press the blue attacking midfielder (Nº8)**, it leaves a gap in the centre of the opposition's defence, disrupts the shape of their back line, and **creates space behind that can be exploited**.

The **forward** (Nº9) is positioned effectively between the 2 red centre backs, allowing him to remain unmarked, ready to move into the open space as soon as the opportunity arises.

If **Nº8** sees red Nº4's movement or is alerted by a teammate (**Nº11** or **Nº9**), he can play a **first-time pass or header into the created space**.

Nº9 has a clear opportunity to receive and carry the ball towards goal.

BEAT THE PRESS WITH SINGLE & DOUBLE PIVOTS

Build Up to Beat the Press: Goalkeeper's Passing Over Pressing Lines

2. Exploiting Space Created in Behind by the Opposing Centre Back Moving Forward to Press Receiver (Double Pivot - 4-2-3-1)

In this variation, we show a situation when **building up play from the goalkeeper (GK) with a double pivot (4-2-3-1 formation)**.

If an **opposing centre back** (red N°5 in the diagram) **steps out to press the blue attacking midfielder (N°10)**, it again leaves a gap in the centre of the opposition's defence, disrupts the shape of their back line, and **creates space behind that can be exploited**.

As shown with the single pivot (4-3-3) example on the previous page, the **forward (N°9)** is positioned effectively between the 2 red centre backs, allowing him to remain unmarked, ready to move into the open space as soon as the opportunity arises. If **N°10** sees red N°5's movement or is alerted by a teammate (**N°9** or **N°7**), he can play a **first-time pass or header into the created space**.

Again, as with the previous 4-3-3 example, **N°9** then has a clear chance to receive and carry the ball towards goal for a scoring opportunity.

BEAT THE PRESS WITH SINGLE & DOUBLE PIVOTS

BUILD UP TO BEAT THE PRESS

Training Session 3 (4 Practices)

Goalkeeper's Passing Over Pressing Lines

Based on Flick, Klopp, and Emery build up patterns

BEAT THE PRESS WITH THE 4-3-3 AND 4-2-3-1

Training Session 3: Goalkeeper's Passing Over Pressing Lines

TRAINING SESSION (4 PRACTICES)
1. Goalkeeper's Passing Over Pressing Lines and Decisions to Play in Behind

Variation 1: Single Pivot (4-3-3)

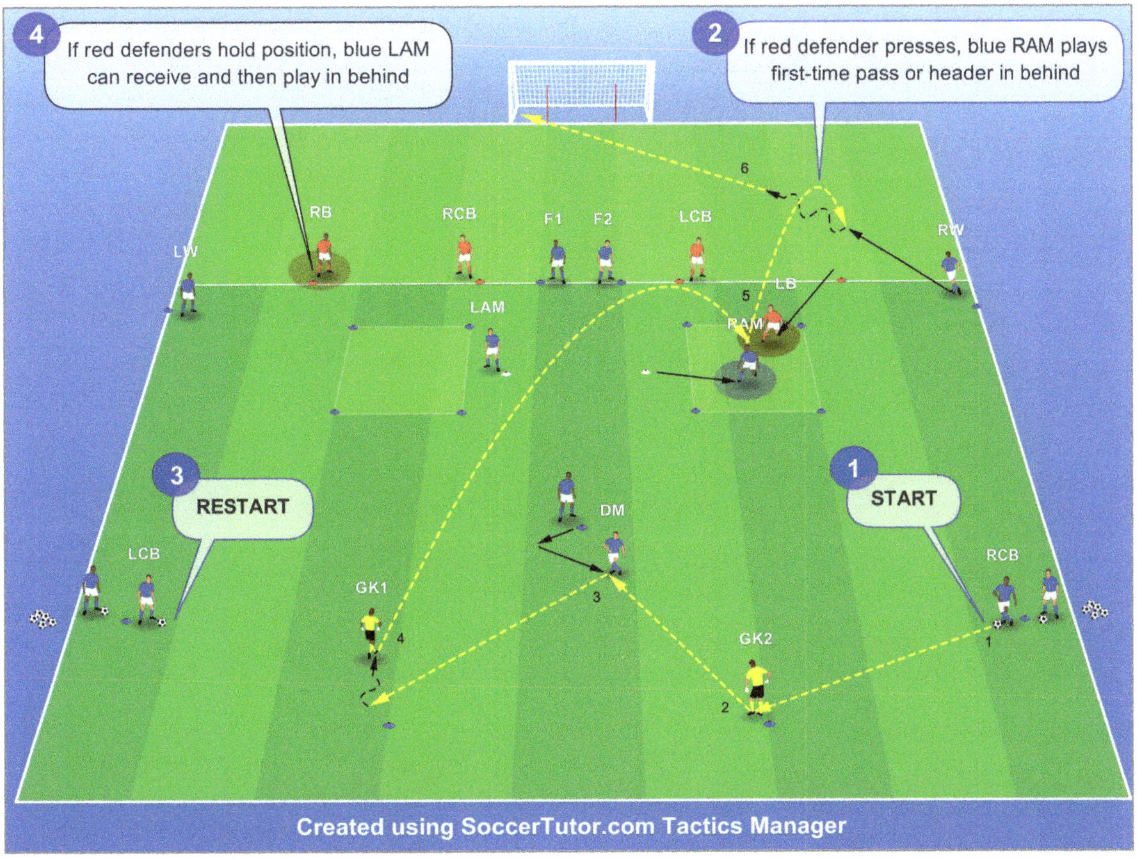

4 If red defenders hold position, blue LAM can receive and then play in behind

2 If red defender presses, blue RAM plays first-time pass or header in behind

3 RESTART

1 START

Practice Description (Variation 1)

- **Repetition 1:** The practice starts with **RCB's** pass to **GK2**. **GK2** passes to the defensive midfielder (**DM**), who plays back to **GK1**. **GK1** plays a long diagonal pass to the attacking midfielder (**RAM**) in the target area (25-35m distance).

- **If the red full back (LB) presses RAM as the ball travels, RAM must play a first-time pass into space for RW**, who runs to receive in behind and score (aiming for the corners marked by poles).

- **Repetition 2:** LCB → GK1 → DM → GK2 → LAM → React to red full back's (RB) decision to hold or press.

- **Repetition 3:** RCB → GK2 → DM → GK1 → RAM → React to red centre back's (LCB) decision to hold or press.

- **Repetition 4:** LCB → GK1 → DM → GK2 → LAM → React to red centre back's (RCB) decision to hold or press.

- *After each repetition, the blue outfield players rotate positions.*

BEAT THE PRESS WITH SINGLE & DOUBLE PIVOTS

Training Session 3: Goalkeeper's Passing Over Pressing Lines

Variation 2: Double Pivot (4-2-3-1)

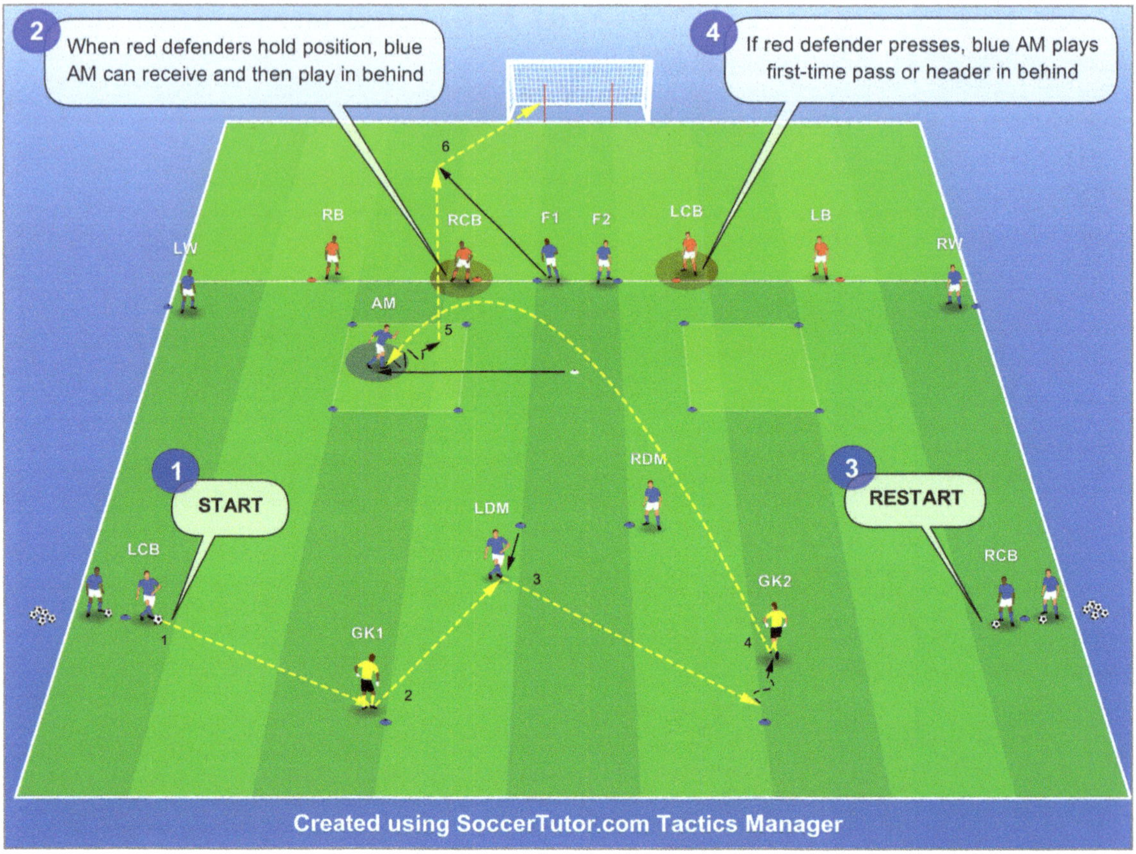

2 When red defenders hold position, blue AM can receive and then play in behind

4 If red defender presses, blue AM plays first-time pass or header in behind

1 START

3 RESTART

Practice Description (Variation 2)

- In <u>Variation 2</u>, we now have 2 defensive midfielders (**LDM** & **RDM** - **double pivot**) and only 1 attacking midfielder (**AM**).

- **Repetition 1: LCB → GK1 → LDM → GK2 → AM →** React to red centre back's (RCB) decision to hold or press.

- **Repetition 2: RCB → GK2 → RDM → GK1 → AM →** React to red centre back's (LCB) decision to hold or press.

- **Repetition 2: LCB → GK1 → LDM → GK2 → AM →** React to red full back's (RB) decision to hold or press.

- **Repetition 4: RCB → GK2 → RDM → GK1 → AM →** React to red full back's (LB) decision to hold or press.

- **KEY NOTE: First-time headers/passes are delivered into available spaces left by a red defender moving to press** e.g. Red LB presses on previous page, so the header is directed to blue RW.

Coaching Points

1. **Pass accuracy:** The goalkeepers must deliver precise passes into target areas.

2. **Shot accuracy:** The wingers or forwards focus on finishing in the corners which are marked out by poles.

3. **Decision making:** Players must scan to see position of defenders and react quickly under pressure to maintain fluidity.

BEAT THE PRESS WITH SINGLE & DOUBLE PIVOTS

©SOCCERTUTOR.COM

Training Session 3: Goalkeeper's Passing Over Pressing Lines

PROGRESSION

2. Goalkeeper's Passing Over Second Pressing Line Functional Practice with Target Zones

Variation 1: 4-3-3 with 2 Attacking Midfielders (7v4 +GKs)

AM: Scan to see if there is pressure from a red defender

Practice Description (Variation 1)

- The practice starts with the coach and 3 players circulating the ball until the **goalkeeper (GK)** plays forward.
- **GK's aim is to find an attacking midfielder (N°8 or N°10)** arriving in a 5x5m target zones at the right moment.
- **Main Blue Objective:** The attacking midfielder's decision to turn or pass first-time in behind depends on whether a red defender moves forward to press.

- If N°10 is free to turn (as in Variation 1 diagram), it triggers a **5v4 attack** with the aim to **score within 8 seconds**.
- **Red Objective:** Win the ball and counter to score in the 2 small goals within 8 seconds.
- *On the following page, the second variation shows the same situation with only 1 attacking midfielder, based on the 4-2-3-1 formation.*

©SOCCERTUTOR.COM   BEAT THE PRESS WITH SINGLE & DOUBLE PIVOTS

Training Session 3: Goalkeeper's Passing Over Pressing Lines

Variation 2: 4-2-3-1 with 1 Attacking Midfielder (6v4 +GKs)

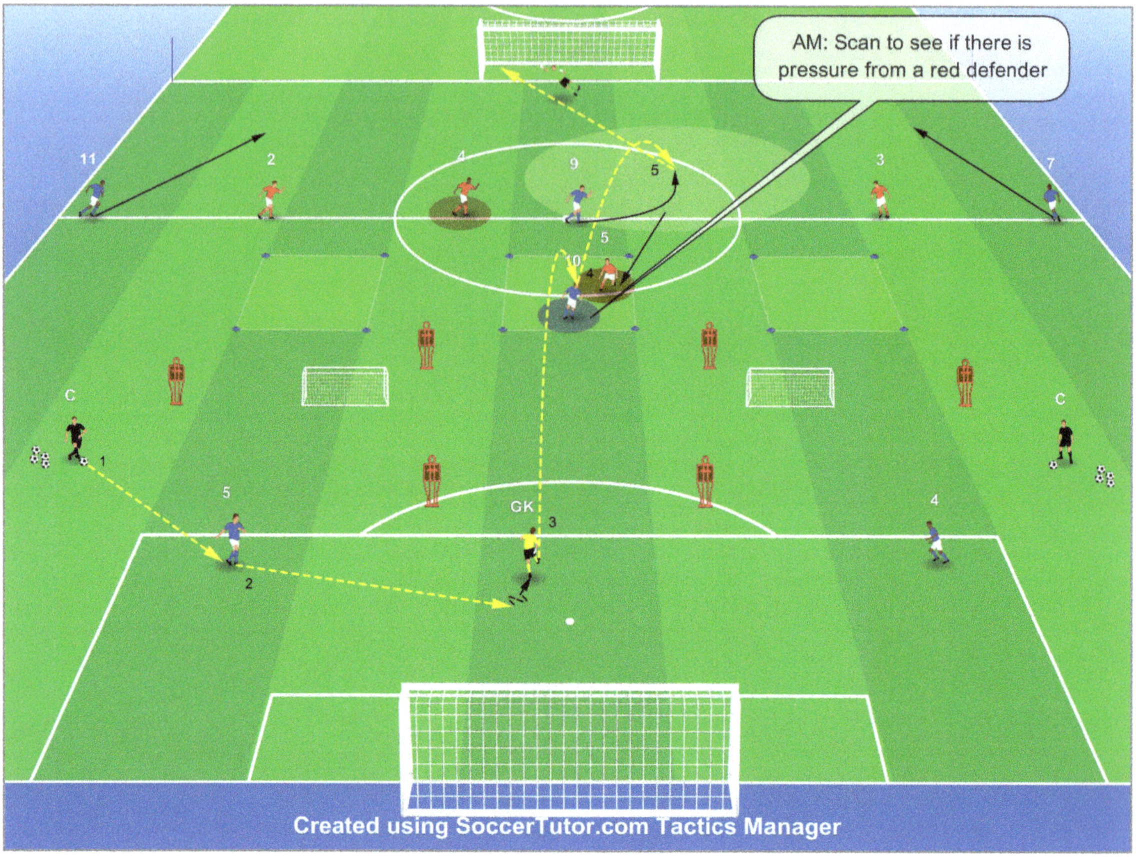

AM: Scan to see if there is pressure from a red defender

Created using SoccerTutor.com Tactics Manager

Practice Description (Variation 2)

- In Variation 2, the **shape is adjusted based on the 4-2-3-1 formation with only 1 attacking midfielder** positioned in the centre, but he can also move into the other zones too.
- Apart from the blue team's shape with 1 less player, the practice setup remains identical to the previous variation.
- **The only other difference is the numerical situation for the attack (4v4).**
- If **N°10** receives within the target area, he should read the situation or be coached by his teammates to make the correct decision (turn or pass/header).
- If **N°10 is pressed (diagram example)**, he plays a first time pass or header into the available space for the forward (**N°9**).
- If **N°10 receives free of marking**, he should turn and play in behind.

Coaching Points

1. **The goalkeeper must play accurately** into the target zones.
2. **Quick decision making** when receiving.
3. **Scanning before receiving** and communication are key to deciding whether to turn or play first-time.
4. **Fast and accurate finishing.**

©SOCCERTUTOR.COM — BEAT THE PRESS WITH SINGLE & DOUBLE PIVOTS

Training Session 3: Goalkeeper's Passing Over Pressing Lines

PROGRESSION

3. Goalkeeper's Passing Over Second Pressing Line 10 v 8 (+GKs) Functional Practice with Target Zones

Variation 1: 4-3-3 with 2 Attacking Midfielders (Single Pivot)

Red CB (4) presses, so blue AM (8) uses first-time header into created space

Practice Description (Variation 1)

- This progression has the same main objective as the previous practice.
- The blues build up from the back against 4 red defenders and 4 pressing midfielders.
- **The players at the back circulate the ball until the GK plays forward.** If the ball is passed short behind the first pressing line (2 mannequins), the player turns, passes forward, or recycles possession.

- If GK plays an aerial pass over the second **pressing line (diagram example)** into a target zone to an attacking midfielder, the **receiver (N°8 in diagram) must read the situation and either receive and turn or pass first-time in behind** for a runner (**N°9** in diagram example).
- **Red Objective:** Press to win the ball and counter to score by dribbling through the red line, receiving beyond it, or by scoring in the goal.

BEAT THE PRESS WITH SINGLE & DOUBLE PIVOTS

Training Session 3: Goalkeeper's Passing Over Pressing Lines

Variation 2: 4-2-3-1 with 1 Attacking Midfielder (Double Pivot)

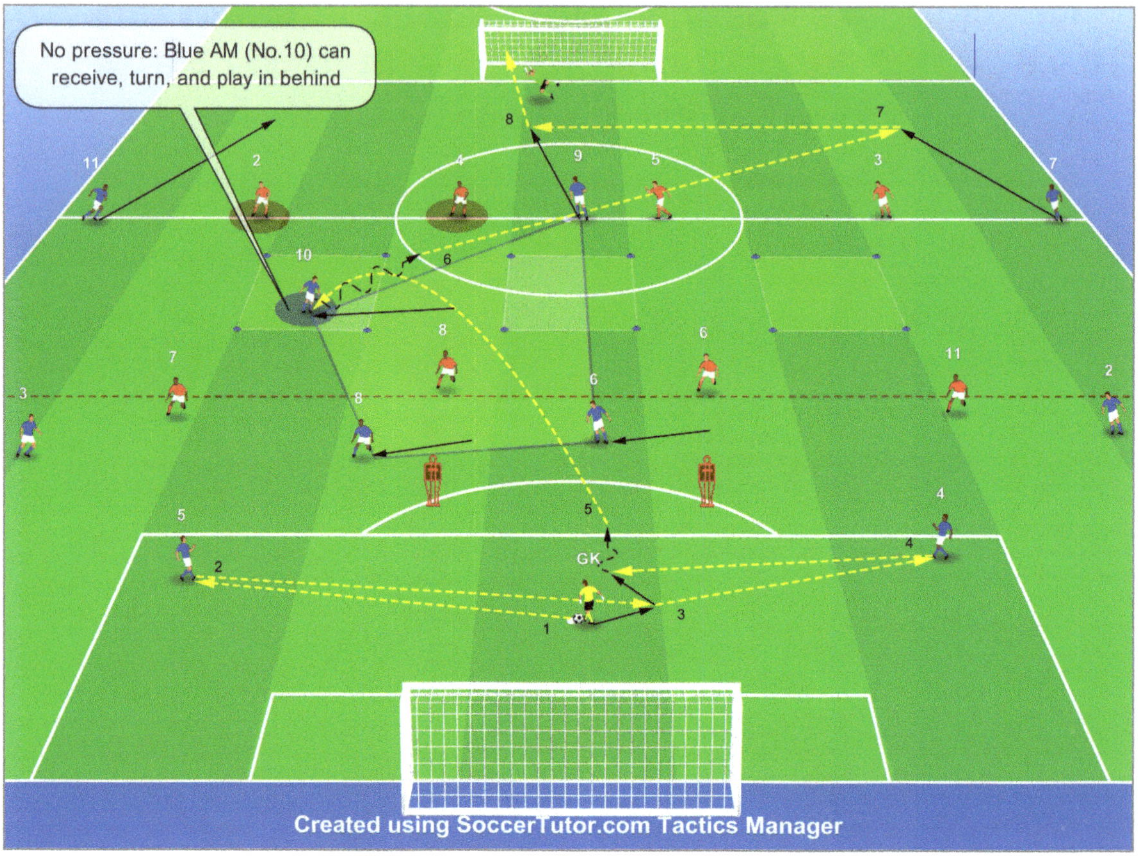

No pressure: Blue AM (No.10) can receive, turn, and play in behind

Practice Description (Variation 2)

- In <u>Variation 2</u>, **adjust the shape to the 4-2-3-1 formation with only 1 attacking midfielder/target player**, who can move into any of the 3 target zones.
- Apart from the blue team's shape, the practice setup remains identical to the previous variation.
- **The main objective of the practice still focuses on the attacking midfielder's (Nº10) decision** to turn or pass first-time in behind, depending on if a red defender moves forward to press.
- In the diagram example, **Nº10 is left unmarked**, so receives and turns.

- From there, the aim is to play in behind and score. In this example, **Nº10** dribbles towards goal and passes in between the 2 red centre backs for the run of the **right winger (Nº7)**, who delivers a low cross for the **forward (Nº9)** to score.

Coaching Points

1. The **goalkeeper must play accurately** into the target zones.
2. **Quick decision making** when receiving.
3. **Scanning before receiving** and communication are key to deciding whether to turn or play first-time.
4. Fast and **accurate finishing**.

BEAT THE PRESS WITH SINGLE & DOUBLE PIVOTS

Training Session 3: Goalkeeper's Passing Over Pressing Lines

PROGRESSION

4. Goalkeeper's Passing Over Second Pressing Line Conditioned Tactical Game

[Diagram: 11v11 conditioned tactical game with blue team building up from goalkeeper against red pressing team. Callout: "No pressure: Blue AM (No.10) can receive, turn, and play in behind"]

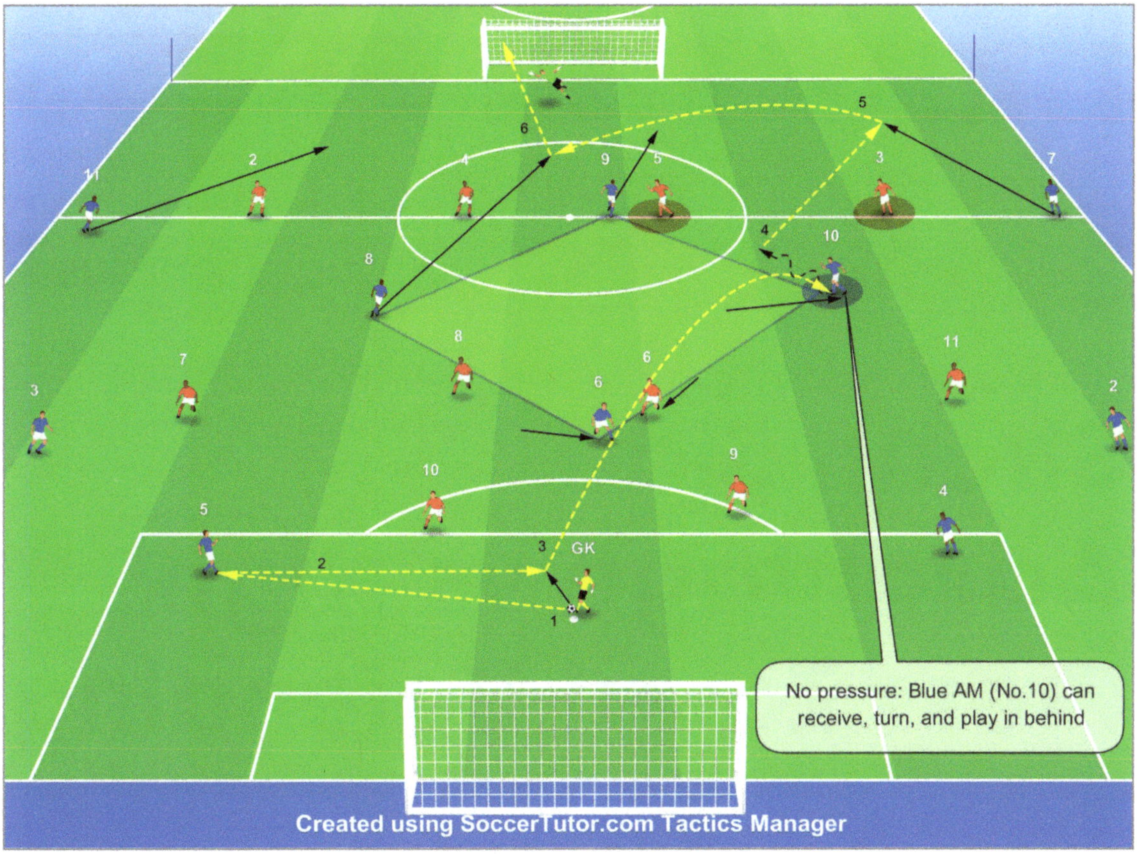

Practice Description

- This final practice of this session is an 11v11 game. Starting with the blue **goalkeeper (GK), the reds press aggressively after the first pass** and the blues build up play from the back.
- **GK decides how to progress play** by passing behind the first pressing line, over, or through the second line.
- **Main Blue Objective:** Attacking midfielder's decision to turn or pass first-time in behind, depending on if a red defender moves forward to press.

- *If a goal is scored after a long pass to an attacking midfielder, it counts double*.
- In this example, **N°10 is not marked and is able to receive**, turn, and play in behind for **N°7** to cross into the box.
- **Red Objective:** Press to win the ball and counter to score within 10–12 seconds.
- **Coaching Points:** Same as previous practices in this session.
- **Note:** This practice is presented with a 4-3-3 build up shape but can easily be adapted to 4-2-3-1 (see previous page).

BUILD UP TO BEAT THE PRESS

Tactical Analysis

Strong Side Advantage vs High Press Zonal Defending

Build up play patterns from Flick, Klopp, and Emery's teams

Build Up to Beat the Press: Strong Side Advantage vs High Press Zonal Defending

Numerical Situations Against High Pressing with Zonal Defending (Single Pivot)

1. Numerical Advantage in Defence and Midfield Areas when Building Up Play from the Back (4-3-3)

With the GK, the blues have 8 v 6 for build up in defence and midfield = +2 players

7 (+GK) v 6

Numerical superiorities, when properly exploited, can play a crucial role in building up from the back. **Creating and using a numerical advantage is one of the fundamental objectives of effective positional play.**

With a 4-3-3 formation against a 4-4-2 defensive shape during the build up phase, there is a **7 (+GK) v 6 situation in the middle and lower thirds of the pitch.**

As previously mentioned, when the opposition apply high pressing, the pressing starts after the goalkeeper plays the first pass (on the first receiver).

At that moment, the situation becomes 7 v 6 in favour of the possession team in terms of outfield players, giving them a clear numerical advantage in that zone. **The extra outfield player provides a valuable outlet for progressing play under pressure.**

BEAT THE PRESS WITH SINGLE & DOUBLE PIVOTS

Build Up to Beat the Press: Strong Side Advantage vs High Press Zonal Defending

2. Defensive Midfielder is the Key Player to Create a Strong Side Against 4-4-2 Zonal Defending (4-3-3)

Certain formations can help **create a numerical advantage near the ball area**. If this advantage is exploited effectively, it can break through the opposition's pressing structure.

In this section, we continue analysing build up play against zonal high pressing systems, with a specific focus on numerical situations. When using a single pivot midfield (e.g. 4-3-3 formation), several positional options become available after the first pass is made.

The diagram shows the starting positions when the **goalkeeper** (**GK**) has possession of the ball.

This setup creates a **3 v 3 situation on both sides of the pitch, with the defensive midfielder (Nº6) being the key player**.

If Nº6 shifts quickly towards one side, he can create a numerical advantage on that side, giving the possession team an edge in progressing the play during their build up phase.

BEAT THE PRESS WITH SINGLE & DOUBLE PIVOTS

Build Up to Beat the Press: Strong Side Advantage vs High Press Zonal Defending

3. Build Up to Bypass Press on the Strong Side by Creating and Exploiting a Numerical Advantage Around the Ball Area (4-3-3)

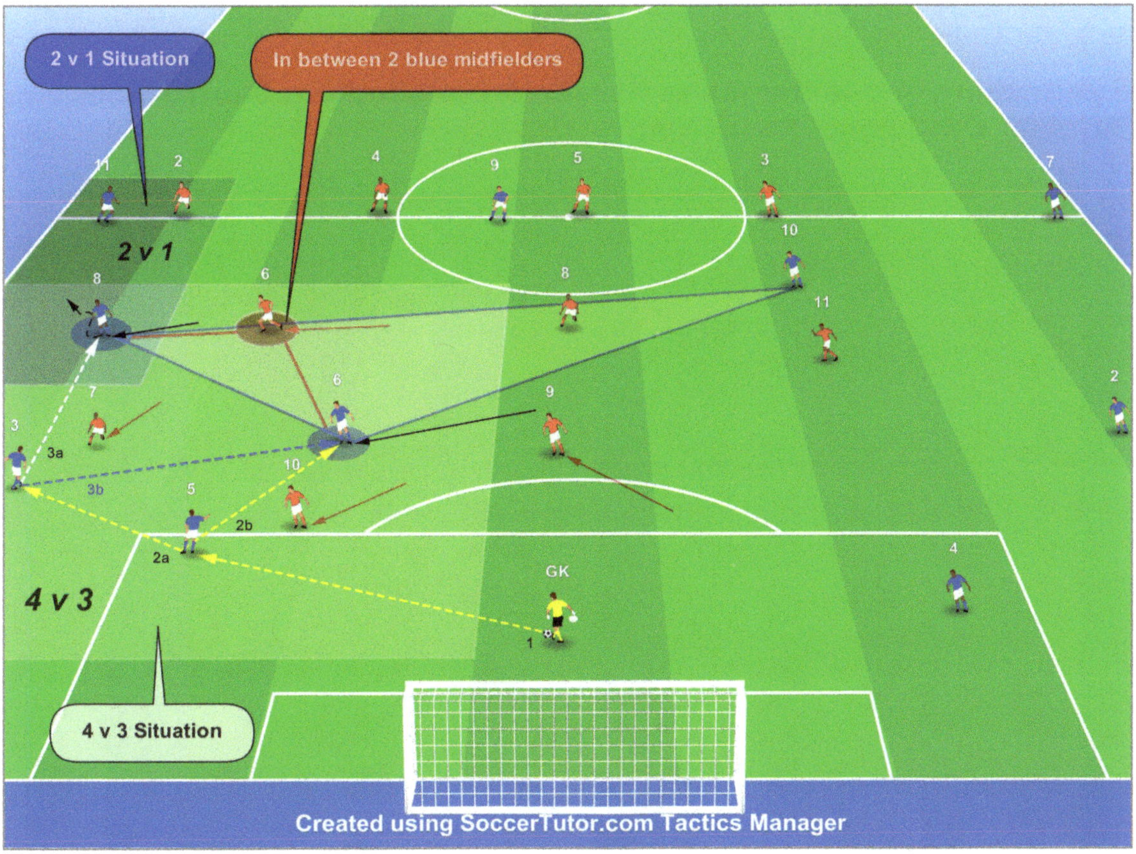

As soon as the **goalkeeper (GK)** passes to the **centre back (N° 5)**, the red N°10 applies pressure.

The possession team (blues) must:

A. Create a numerical superiority near the ball area.

B. Move the ball to the free player.

In the diagram example, when red N°10 presses, the blue **defensive midfielder (N°6)** shifts across quickly and creates a **4v3 numerical advantage** on the left side.

The players must **read the situation and find the free player (N°6 or N°8)**.

The ball can be passed directly to them or via a **link player (full back N°3 in diagram)**.

To be effective, **N°6** and **N°8** maintain a good distance away from each other but also away from nearby opponents. If they are too close, red N°6 can mark both of them easily. **By staying apart, they force their opponent into a dilemma of who to mark closely,** ensuring at least one finds space.

Note: Creating uncertainty for the central midfielder (red N°6) is key to gaining an advantage in possession.

BEAT THE PRESS WITH SINGLE & DOUBLE PIVOTS

Numerical Situations Against High Pressing with Zonal Defending (Double Pivot)

1. Attacking Midfielder is the Key Player to Create a Strong Side Against 4-4-2 Zonal Defending (4-2-3-1)

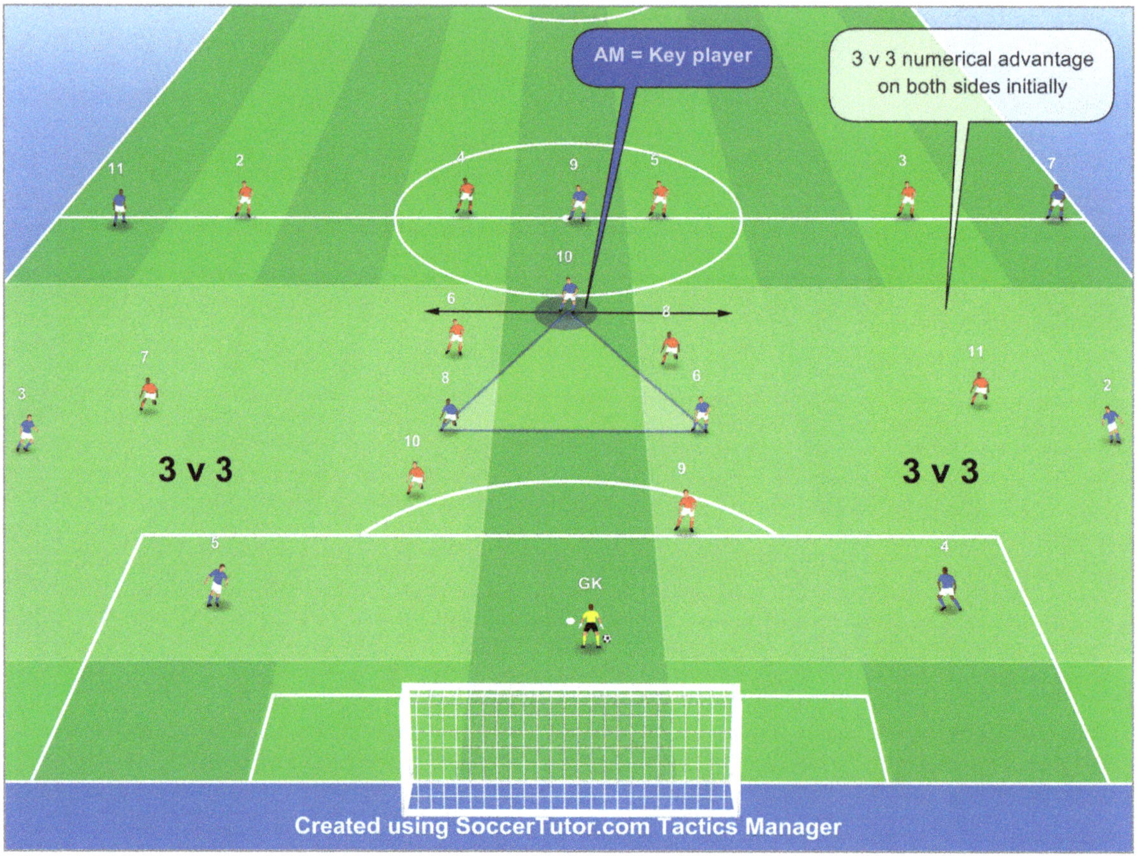

With a double pivot (4-2-3-1), there is a similar dynamic to the 4-3-3 in the early stages. The positioning of players naturally creates a 3v3 situation on both sides of the pitch, with a centre back, full back, and defensive midfielder against the opposing forward, winger, and central midfielder.

In this structure, the **attacking midfielder becomes the key player (N°10)**. After the first pass is made, this **N°10 can shift quickly towards the ball area, arriving in support to create a numerical advantage (4v3) on that side**.

Note: The blue midfielders must create a dilemma for a red central midfielder. Since N°10 starts centrally, he risks being blocked by red N°6 or N°8, who could also mark the blue defensive midfielders. To avoid this, blue N°10 should shift wider before the first pass is played, giving him time to move far enough away from a red midfielder (e.g. N°6) as the ball is played.

Build Up to Beat the Press: Strong Side Advantage vs High Press Zonal Defending

2. Build Up to Bypass Press on the Strong Side by Creating and Exploiting a Numerical Advantage Around the Ball Area (4-2-3-1)

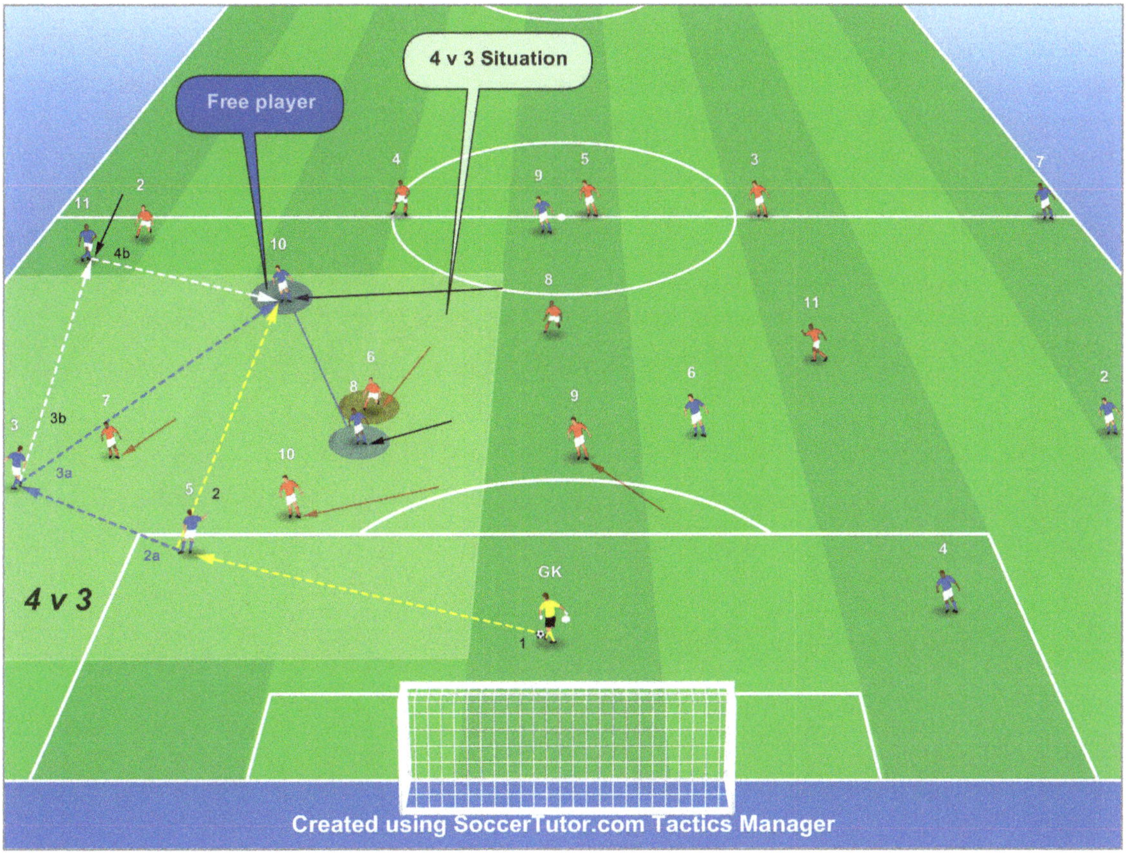

The attacking midfielder (N°10) moves towards the strong side before GK's pass. As soon as **GK** passes to the **centre back (N°5)**, the red N°10 shifts across to press the ball. This movement creates a **4v3 numerical advantage near the ball**.

To make it difficult for red N°6 to control both the defensive midfielder on that side (N°8) and N°10, they must keep a good vertical distance from each other. **N°8 drops deeper while N°10 stays higher**, but still away from the red centre back (N°4).

If red N°6 positions himself between them, both may find time and space. If he marks one (e.g. **N°8**), as in the diagram, the other **(N°10) becomes the free player**. The ball can reach **N°10** directly (yellow arrow) or via link players (blue and white arrows).

If red N°4 steps forward to mark **N°10**, this opens up space behind him for the **forward (N°9)** to run into. In that situation, blue **N°5** should target this space with a long aerial pass.

Note: Good spacing between the blue N°8 and N°10 is essential to cause disruption. By staying apart, they force red N°6 into a decision and one of them will be free.

BEAT THE PRESS WITH SINGLE & DOUBLE PIVOTS

BUILD UP TO BEAT THE PRESS

Training Session 4 (5 Practices)

Strong Side Advantage vs High Press Zonal Defending

Based on Flick, Klopp, and Emery build up patterns

BEAT THE PRESS WITH THE 4-3-3 AND 4-2-3-1

Training Session 4: Build Up with Strong Side Advantage vs High Press Zonal Defending

TRAINING SESSION (5 PRACTICES)
1. Exploiting Numerical Advantage to Find Free Player Continuous Possession Game
1/2: Start to Create and Exploit a Numerical Advantage

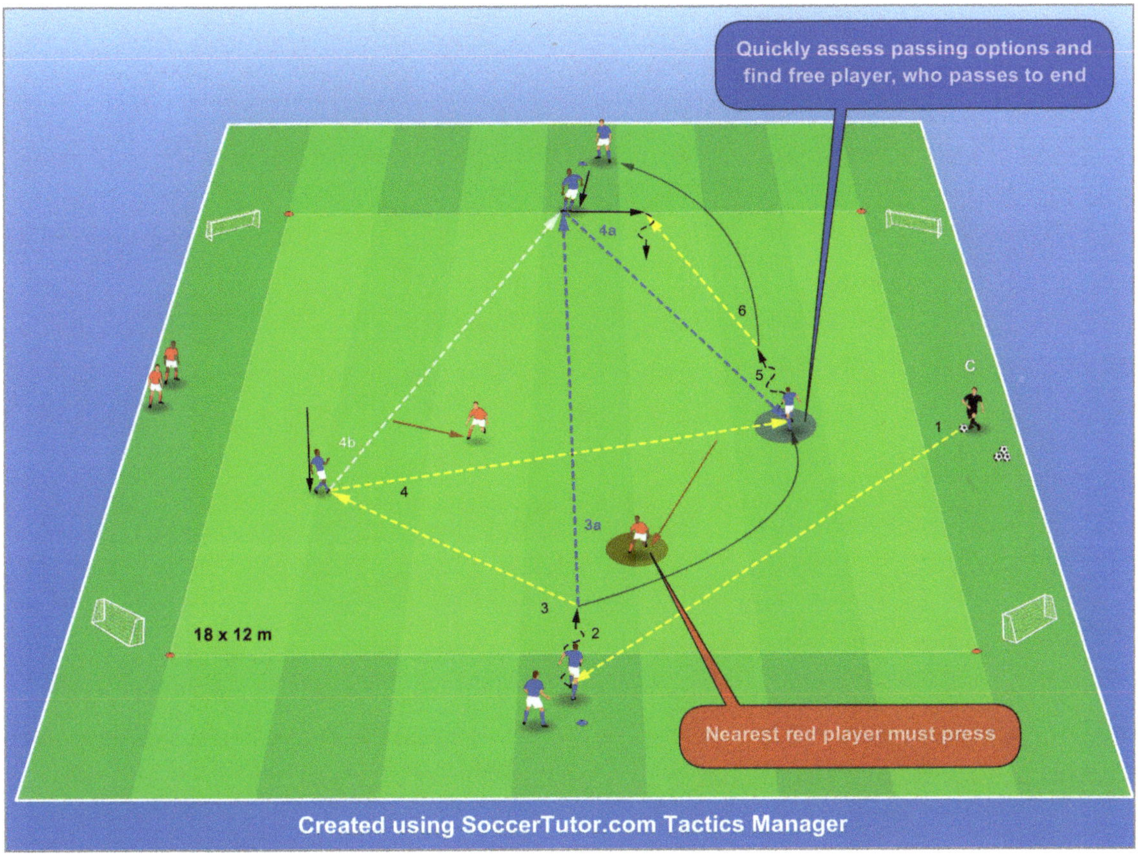

Practice Description (1/2)

NOTE: *This practice also appears in the "Beat the Press with a Box Midfield" book. It is included again here due to its importance to this specific training session.*

- Inside the area, there is a 2v2 situation, with 2 additional blue players on the outside at each end.
- The practice begins with the coach passing to an outside player, who enters the area to create an overload.
- The nearest red defender moves forward to press, forcing the blues to **assess passing options and find the free player**.
- The ball can be moved directly to the free player (yellow arrow) or via the link player at the top (blue and white arrows).
- Once the free player receives the ball, they pass to the player at the opposite end, ensuring **quick ball circulation and continuous positional adjustments**, before rotating to the outside (top).

BEAT THE PRESS WITH SINGLE & DOUBLE PIVOTS

Training Session 4: Build Up with Strong Side Advantage vs High Press Zonal Defending

2/2: Continuous Practice with Opposite End Rotations

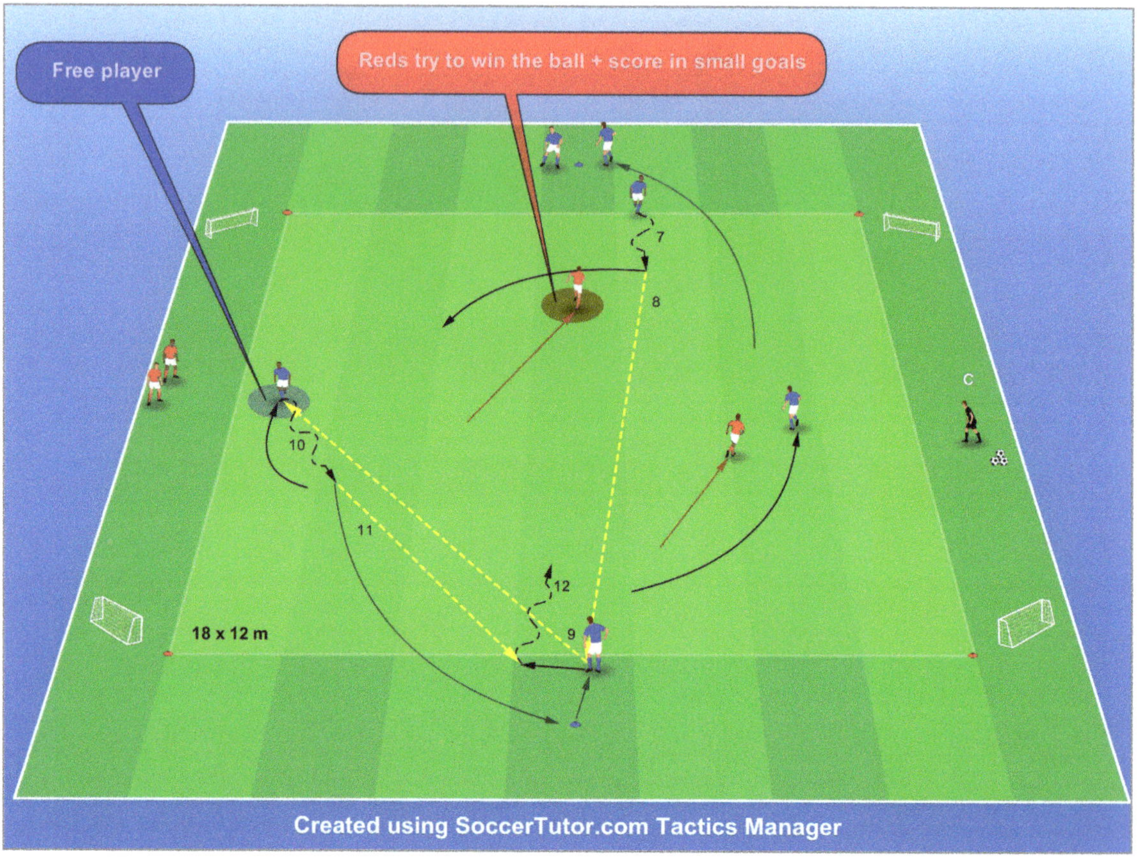

Practice Description (2/2)

NOTE: *This practice also appears in the "Beat the Press with a Box Midfield" book. It is included again here due to its importance to this specific training session.*

- This second diagram shows how the practice continues with the same aims and objectives.
- The outside player (at the top) enters the area to repeat in the opposite direction while the previous starting player remains inside the area.
- Again, the nearest red defender must move forward to press, forcing the blue team to quickly assess passing options and find the free player.

- **The objectives remain the same for the blue team**, trying to find the free player and pass forward.
- **Defending Objective:** Win the ball and score in either of the 2 small goals at the same end you win the ball.

Coaching Points

1. **Assess the situation quickly** and identify passing options.
2. **Adjust positioning** to create passing lanes (diamond shape).
3. **Make intelligent decisions** to move the ball efficiently to the free player.
5. **Keep a high tempo** (continued pressure).

Training Session 4: Build Up with Strong Side Advantage vs High Press Zonal Defending

PROGRESSION

2. Exploiting 4v3 Numerical Advantage 3-Team Small Sided Game

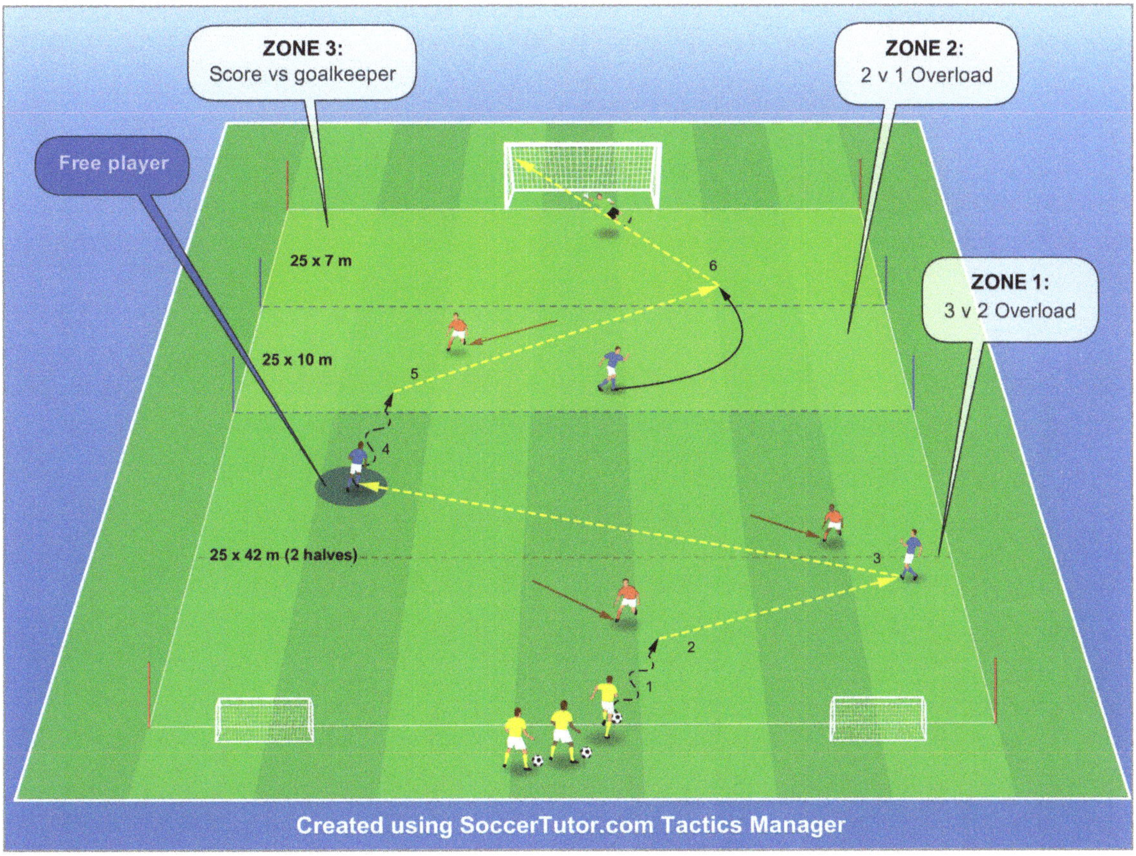

ZONE 3: Score vs goalkeeper

ZONE 2: 2 v 1 Overload

ZONE 1: 3 v 2 Overload

Free player

25 x 7 m
25 x 10 m
25 x 42 m (2 halves)

Practice Description

NOTE: *This practice also appears in the "Beat the Press with a Box Midfield" book. It is included again here due to its importance to this specific training session.*

- There are 2 attacking teams (blue and yellow) and 1 defending team (red).
- The blues and reds start inside the area and the yellows start outside.
- The **initial setup is 1v1 in each half of Zone 1 and 1v1 in Zone 2**. A yellow player enters by dribbling the ball, creating a 2v1 overload in the first half of Zone 1.

- **Attacking Objective:**
  1. **Find the free player in Zone 1.**
  2. **Free player dribbles into Zone 2.**
  3. **Pass into Zone 3 and score.**

- **Defending Objective:** Win the ball and score in either of the 2 small goals.

- **Rules/Restrictions:** After the first pass, all players move freely. Defenders cannot enter Zone 3. After each attack, the player who finishes moves out and the other players move one position forward (new player enters). After a set time, the defending team switch roles.

Training Session 4: Build Up with Strong Side Advantage vs High Press Zonal Defending

PROGRESSION

3. Build Up with Numerical Advantage on Strong Side
Dynamic Split-Pitch Game (Single Pivot)

Practice Description

- The playing area is 3/4 of a full pitch split into 2 halves by a 5-metre vertical zone. In Variation 1, the blue team play with the **4-3-3 formation**. In each half, the red team are in a 2-2-1 defensive shape (combined 4-4-2).

- As soon as the **GK** plays the first pass, a **defensive midfielder (N°6)** enters on both sides to create a **4 v 3** advantage around the ball.

- **On both sides**, the blues build up with **6 v 5** (**+GKs**), so they have an overload.

- **The aim is to find the free player** and then score.

- **Note:** Read the situation quickly to make the best decisions.

- **Defending Objective:** If the reds win the ball (either side), they counter to score within 10-12 seconds.

- After each phase, all players reset to starting positions for the next repetition.

- **Restrictions:** The red players can only press after the first pass from the **goalkeeper** (**GK1** or **GK2**).

BEAT THE PRESS WITH SINGLE & DOUBLE PIVOTS

Training Session 4: Build Up with Strong Side Advantage vs High Press Zonal Defending

VARIATION
4. Build Up with Numerical Advantage on Strong Side
Dynamic Split-Pitch Game (Double Pivot)

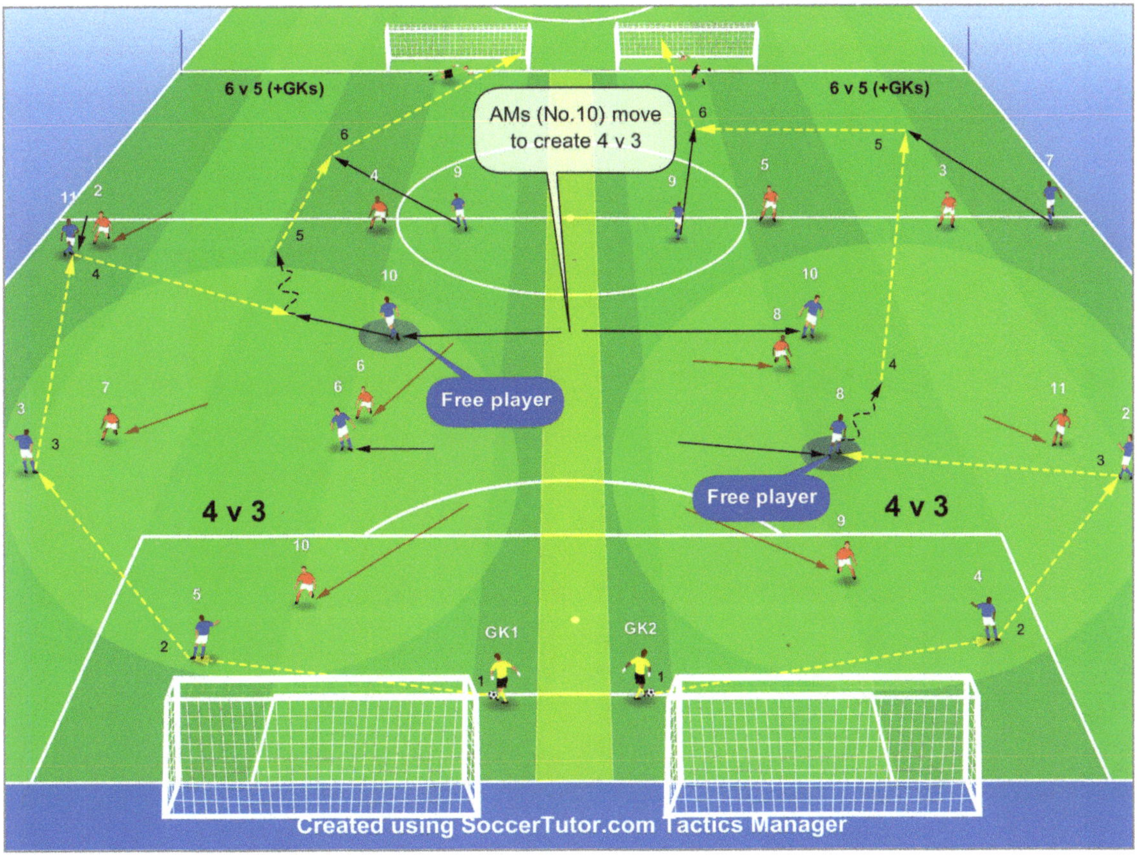

Practice Description

- In Variation 2, the blue team now play with the **4-2-3-1 formation**.
- Instead of 2 defensive midfielders, there are now **2 attacking midfielders (N°10)** instead.
- Just before the **GK** plays the first pass, the **N°10s enter on both sides to create a 4v3 advantage around the ball**.
- On both sides, the blues build up again with **6v5 (+GKs)**, so have an overload.
- **Aim: Find the free player and score.**
- The same rules and restrictions apply.

Coaching Points

1. **Quick reading of the situation + decision making:** Recognise defensive movements and react accordingly.
2. **Support play:** Positioning in passing lanes to provide progressive options.
3. **Create a dilemma for the opposing midfielder and find the free player.**
4. **Fast combination play:** Using quick, sharp passes to break defensive lines.

Training Session 4: Build Up with Strong Side Advantage vs High Press Zonal Defending

PROGRESSION

5. Build Up with Numerical Advantage on Strong Side 11v11 Conditioned Game

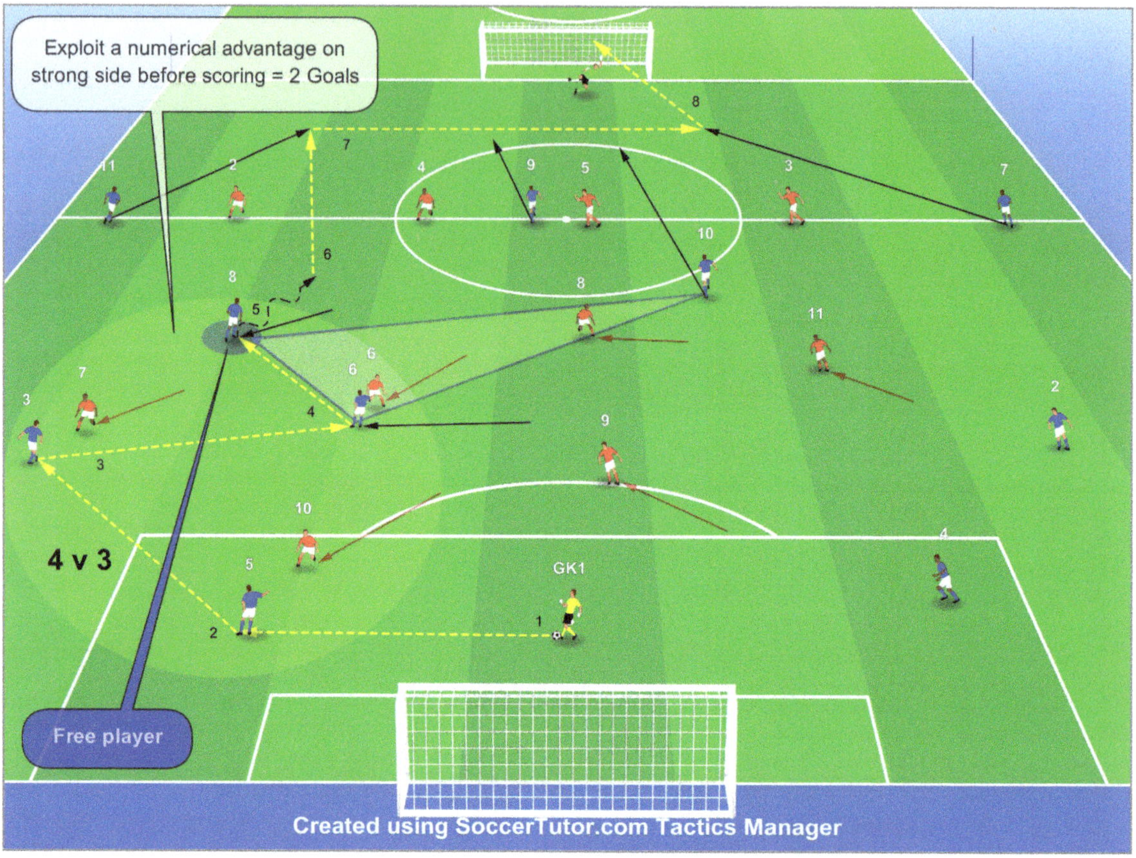

Exploit a numerical advantage on strong side before scoring = 2 Goals

4 v 3

Free player

Practice Description

- 11v11 game in 3/4 of a full pitch.
- **Note:** See previous practices (+ analysis) for different tactics to be applied - this can easily be adapted to 4-2-3-1.
- **Blue Objective 1:** Build up play from GK and score (1 goal).
- **Blue Objective 2:** Build up play and successfully exploit a numerical advantage on the strong side before scoring (2 goals).
- **Red Objective:** Win ball and counter.
- Play always restarts with the blue **GK**. Switch the team roles after a set time.

Coaching Points

1. **Quickly assess the situation** to identify passing options and position effectively to create and maintain passing lanes.
2. **Make intelligent decisions** to exploit numerical superiority.
3. **Execute fast combination play** to break defensive lines.
4. **Maintain a high tempo** to sustain attacking momentum.

BUILD UP TO BEAT THE PRESS

Tactical Analysis

Strong Side Equality vs High Press Zonal Defending

Build up play patterns from Flick, Klopp, and Emery's teams

Build Up to Beat the Press: Strong Side Equality vs High Press Zonal Defending

Switching Play from Strong to Weak Side with Single Pivot Midfield (4-3-3)

1. Equality in Numbers on the Strong Side Creates a Numerical Advantage and Available Space on the Weak Side

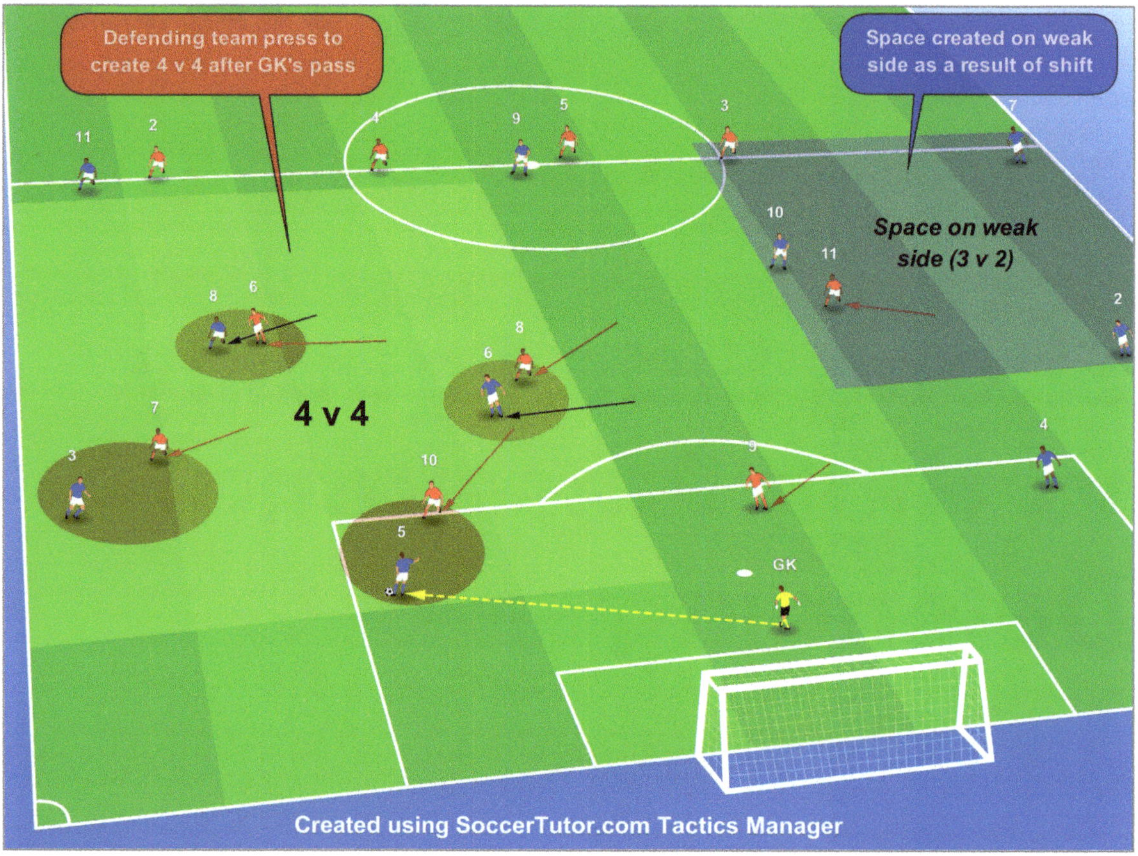

When building up play from the back using the 4-3-3 and the opposing players shift quickly towards the strong side after the **goalkeeper's** (**GK**) first pass, equality in numbers may be created (4v4 highlighted area in diagram). This indicates there is likely to be a numerical advantage and available space elsewhere on the pitch.

In the diagram example, once the pass is played to the **centre back** (**N°5**), the red forward (N°10) closes the ball and the red central midfielder (N°8) quickly shifts across to mark the **defensive midfielder** (**N°6**), preventing any advantage for the blues on that side.

This **4v4 situation on the strong side creates a 3v2 situation on the weak side**, with available space for the **right back** (**N°2**) and **winger** (**N°7**) to exploit.

©SOCCERTUTOR.COM BEAT THE PRESS WITH SINGLE & DOUBLE PIVOTS

Build Up to Beat the Press: Strong Side Equality vs High Press Zonal Defending

2. Reset through the Goalkeeper or Centre Back to Switch Play to the Weak Side

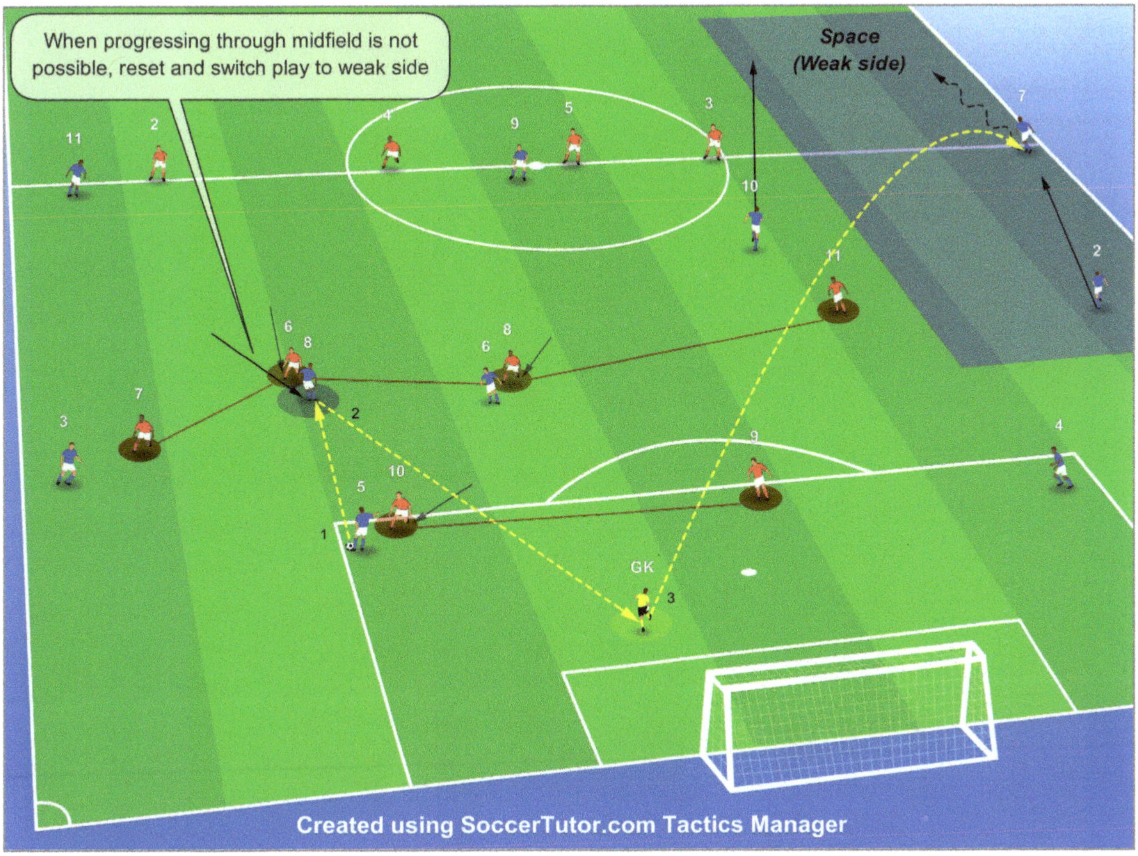

Although the numerical situation does not favour building up play on the strong side with an advantage (see previous page), that does not mean it cannot be carried out effectively.

As the situation evolves, the **attacking team must identify where the advantage lies** and in this case, it's on the weak side.

The possession team (blues) must take the following steps:

A. The players on the strong side should overcome the pressing by **finding a teammate with time and space who can play a pass to the opposite side**.

B. **If no such option exists near the ball, possession should be retained** and the ball directed to the closest free player (e.g. the goalkeeper), who has both space and time to switch play.

In the diagram example, the ball is directed back to the **goalkeeper (GK)**, who is free to switch play to the opposite side, where there is space available (blue highlighted area) for the **full back (Nº2)** and **winger (Nº7)** to exploit.

Note: GK's switch of play pass neutralises 6 red players and sets up a 4v4 attack in an advanced area.

BEAT THE PRESS WITH SINGLE & DOUBLE PIVOTS

Build Up to Beat the Press: Strong Side Equality vs High Press Zonal Defending

3. Centre Back's Aerial Pass to Forward or Winger with Immediate Support Play

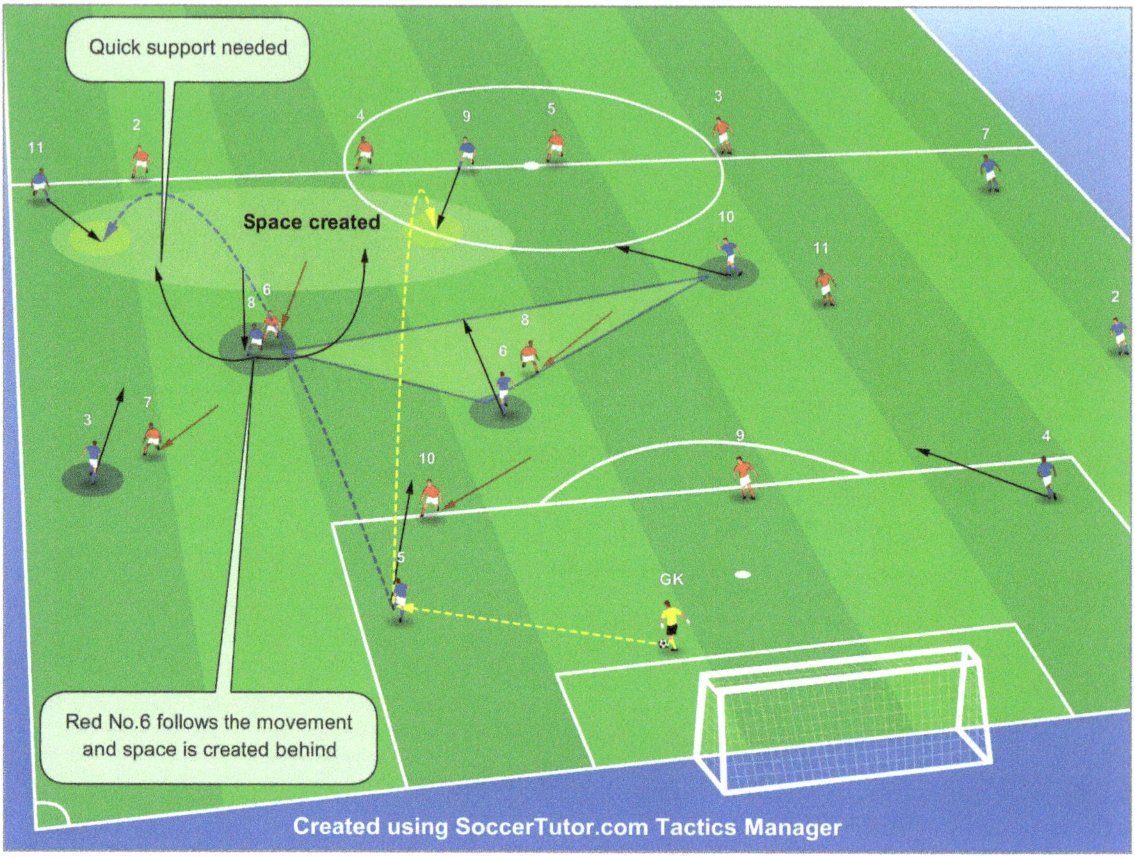

Generally, the creation of equality in numbers on the strong side does not favour building up play there unless the individual and collective quality of the attacking players allows them to play under pressure.

A forward with strong hold-up play can be effective if the supporting players' movements are organised and well-timed.

In the diagram example, as the **centre back (N°5) receives under pressure, the attacking midfielder (N°8) drops back to escape his marker and create space for advancing teammates**. Red N°6 is likely to follow, creating space behind.

This opens a gap for the winger N°11 (blue arrow) or forward N°9 (yellow arrow) to challenge for the first ball without being double-marked.

N°8 can also change direction after **N°5's** pass to run into the vacated space.

If N°11 or N°9 can receive the long pass and hold possession, immediate support will be available. As nearby players move in, the blue team **increases its chances of winning the second ball**.

Note: The synchronised movement of the centre backs (N°5 and N°4) pushes the 2 red forwards into an offside position.

BEAT THE PRESS WITH SINGLE & DOUBLE PIVOTS

Build Up to Beat the Press: Strong Side Equality vs High Press Zonal Defending

4. Full Back's Aerial Pass to Exploit Space Behind the Pressing Full Back who Follows the Winger's Movement

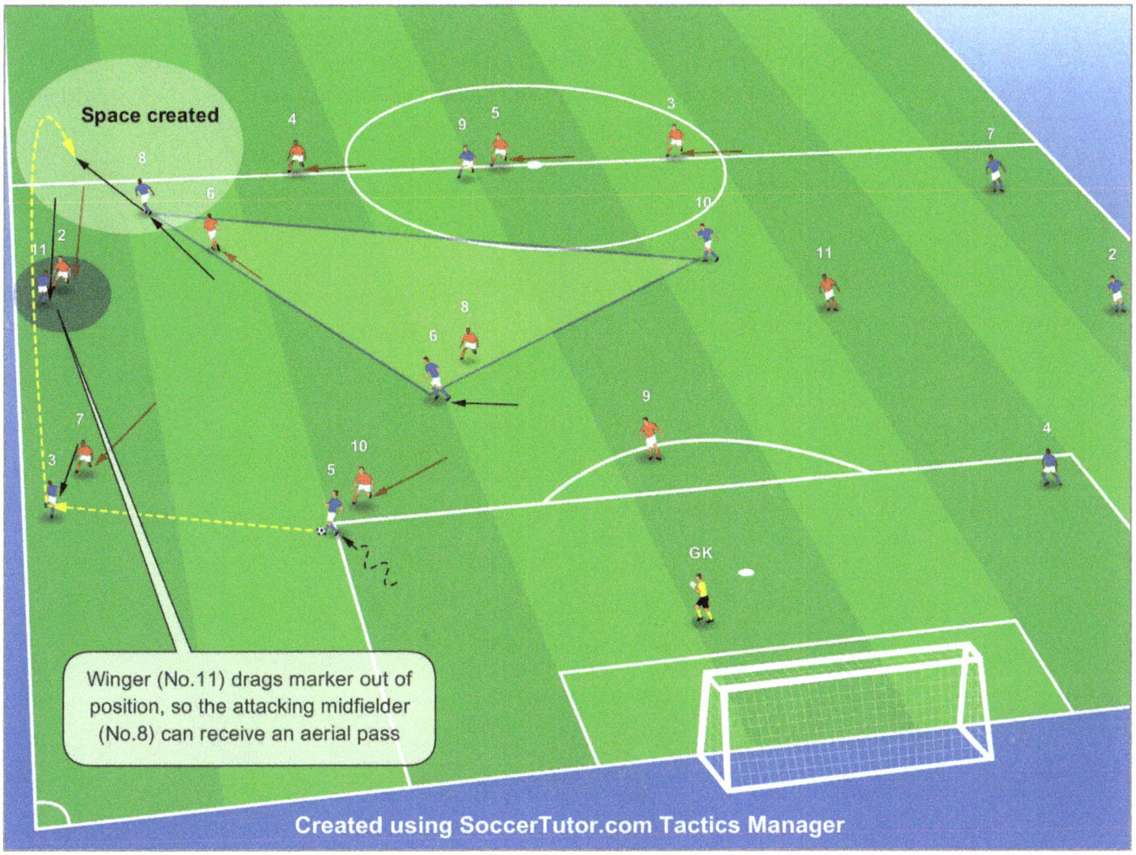

Winger (No.11) drags marker out of position, so the attacking midfielder (No.8) can receive an aerial pass

When numbers are equal, off-the-ball movement becomes essential. Attacking players must move intelligently and dynamically to open up space and create passing options.

The attacking players should use off-the-ball movements and high quality combination play to create and exploit potential available spaces. The high collective quality of the attacking team players can be crucial in this occasion.

In this example, the **left back (N°3)** drops back to receive from the **centre back (N°5)** and turns forward.

At the same time, the **left winger (N°11) drops back and drags the opposing right back (red N°2) out of position.**

This opens up space behind red N°2, so the **attacking midfielder (N°8) makes a well-timed forward run into the created space.**

If the red central midfielder (N°6) does not track **blue N°8's** run quickly enough, **N°3** can exploit this by playing an aerial pass, as shown.

Note: This sequence has the potential to eliminate 7 opposing players and move the ball into a dangerous attacking area.

BEAT THE PRESS WITH SINGLE & DOUBLE PIVOTS

5. Combination Play and Movements to Create Space for Switch to Weak Side Winger

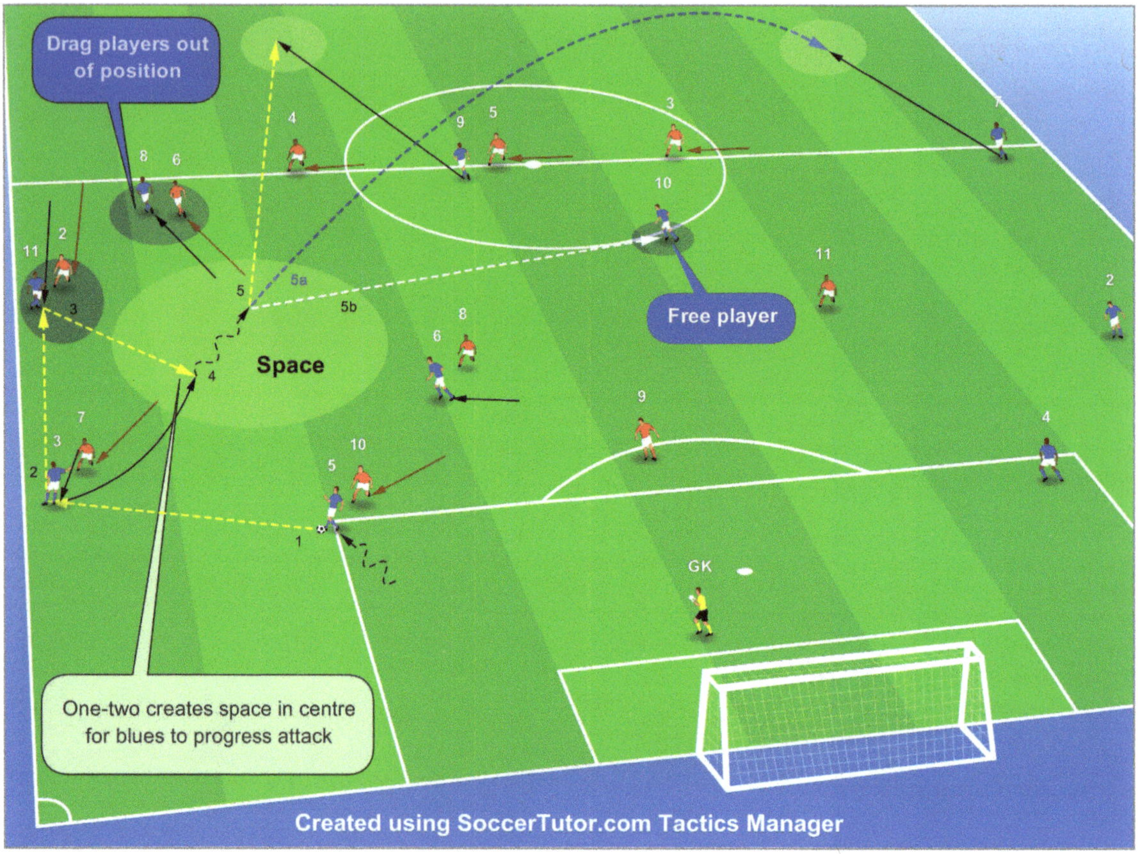

In a variation of the previous example, we show what happens if the **red central midfielder (N°6) follows the blue attacking midfielder (N°8) tightly** and prevents the opening for the **left back (N°3)** to play an effective aerial pass to **N°8**.

In this situation, **space is instead created in the central area (highlighted), which can be exploited by playing a one-two combination with the left winger (N°11)**.

As soon as **N°3** receives in the centre, **passes towards the forward (N°9 - yellow arrow) or the weak side winger (N°7 - blue arrow)** open up. Both options get the team in behind the opposition's defensive line.

There is also an **option to pass inside to the other attacking midfielder (N°10 - white arrow)**, who is available in lots of space.

Note 1: This combination allows the blue team to bypass at least 4 opponents, but its success relies on good decision making, communication, awareness, and technical quality under pressure to move the ball accurately and at speed.

Note 2: Everything depends on reading the situation well, appropriate decision making, and good technique to pass the ball accurately and exploit the situation effectively.

Build Up to Beat the Press: Strong Side Equality vs High Press Zonal Defending

6. Using the Forward to Link Play to Create and Exploit a Wide Overload

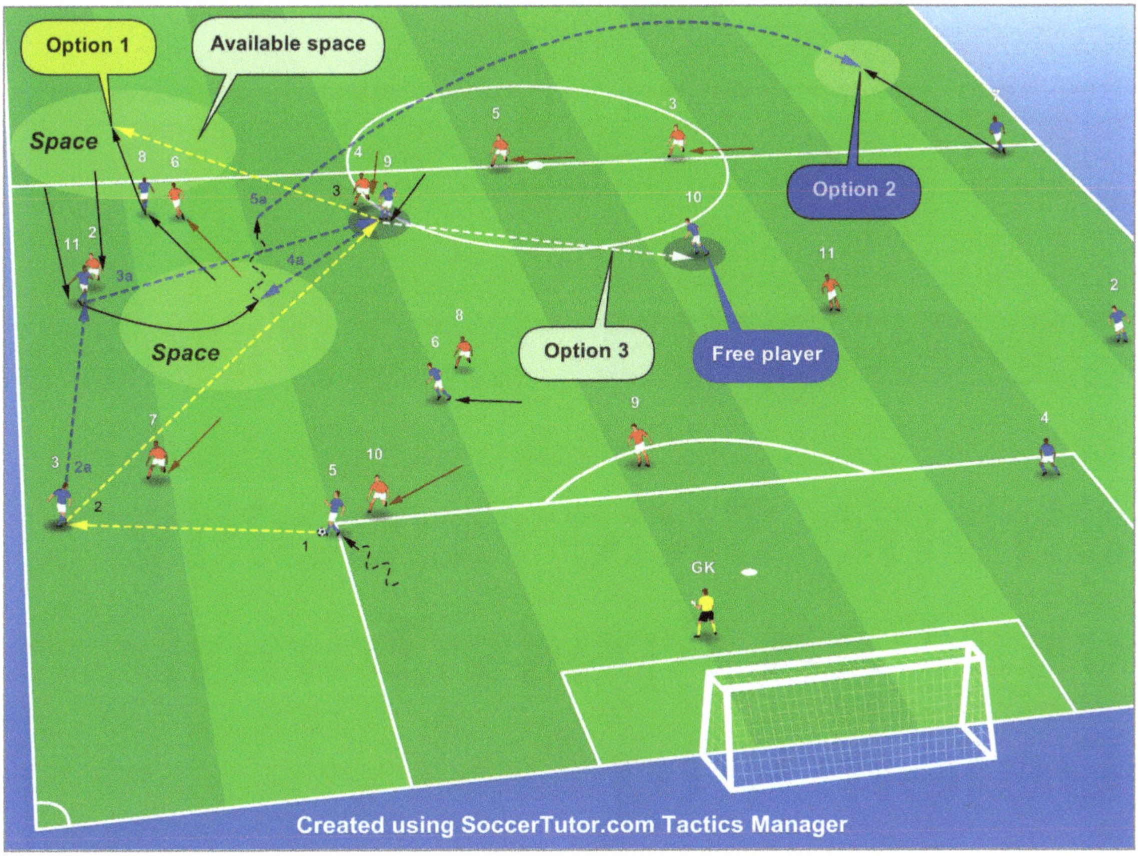

Here we show another way to beat the press with combination play using the same coordinated movements of the winger and attacking midfielder, but now with the forward dropping back to link up.

This time there is either an available passing lane for the **full back** (**N°3**) to pass to the **forward** (**N°9**), who drops back (yellow arrow) or the **winger** (**N°11**) can be used as a link player (blue arrow).

In this example, as **N°3** receives, **N°11** and the **attacking midfielder on that side** (**N°8**) move together, as **N°9** drops back to offer support (all in sync).

Option 1: **N°9** can play forward and in behind for the run of **N°8** (yellow arrow).

Option 2: Lay the ball back into space for **N°11** to receive and switch play to the opposite **winger N°7** (blue arrows).

Option 3: Pass to **AM** (**N°10**), who is available in lots of space (white arrow).

Note: If opponents nullify the numerical advantage near the ball, switching play to the weak side is the most effective way to find space. On the strong side, use quick combinations (if players are technical). Also, a long ball to a target forward with well-timed support runs can be effective.

BUILD UP TO BEAT THE PRESS

Training Session 5 (4 Practices)

Strong Side Equality vs High Press Zonal Defending

Based on Flick, Klopp, and Emery build up patterns

Training Session 5: Build Up with Strong Side Equality vs High Press Zonal Defending

TRAINING SESSION (4 PRACTICES)
1. Build Up Combinations and Switching Play with Target Areas
Variation 1: Wide Support with Deep Switch

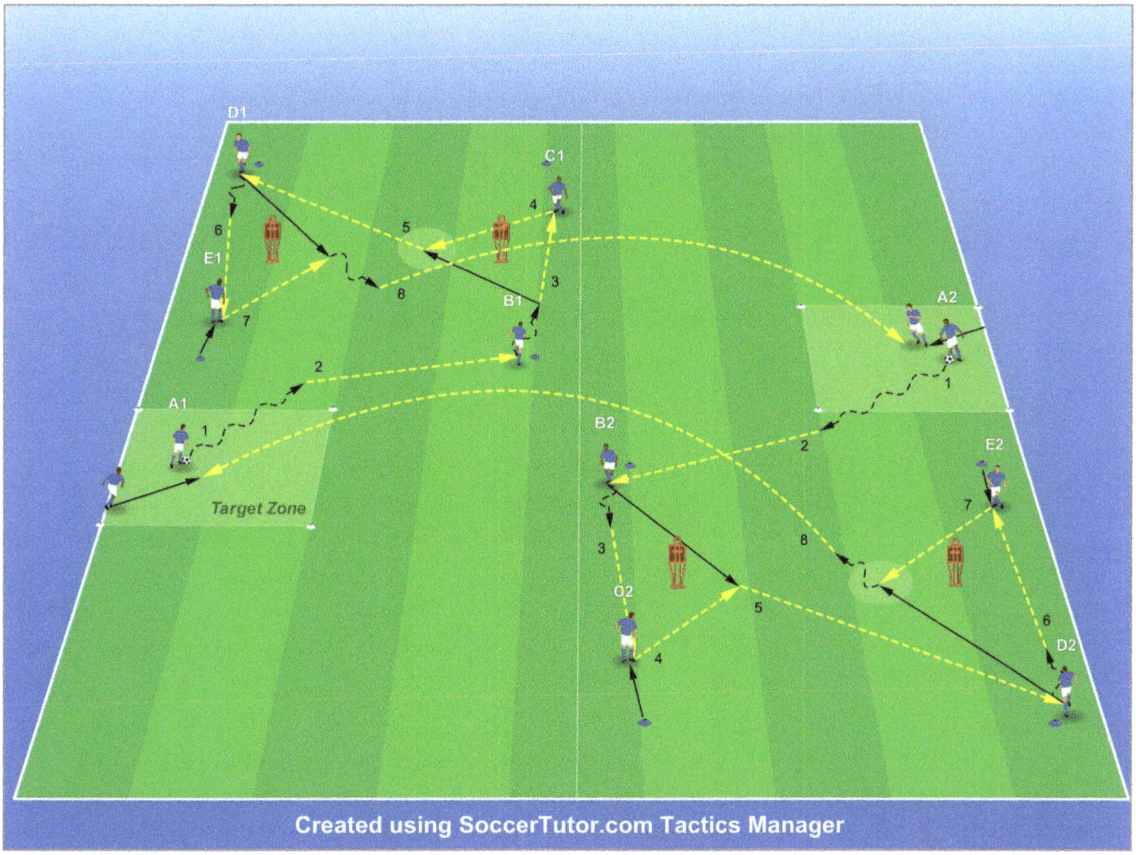

Practice Description (Variation 1)

NOTE: *This practice also appears in the "Beat the Press with a Box Midfield" book. It is included again here due to its importance to this specific training session.*

The practice is set up in a 40x60m area divided vertically into 2 zones, with 8x5m target areas on each side. The combination runs simultaneously on both sides

1-2. **A** starts by dribbling out of the target zone and passing to **B**.

3-6. **B** combines with **C** and receives the return pass. **B** then finds **D**, who takes a forward touch and passes to **E**.

7-8. **D** receives a return pass from **E** and switches play to the opposite target zone for the next player waiting.

→ The practice continues.

→ **Player Rotations: A1 → B1 → C1 → D1 → E1 → A2 → B2 → C2 → D2 → E2 → A1.**

BEAT THE PRESS WITH SINGLE & DOUBLE PIVOTS

Training Session 5: Build Up with Strong Side Equality vs High Press Zonal Defending

Variation 2: Forward Combination with 2 Switch Options

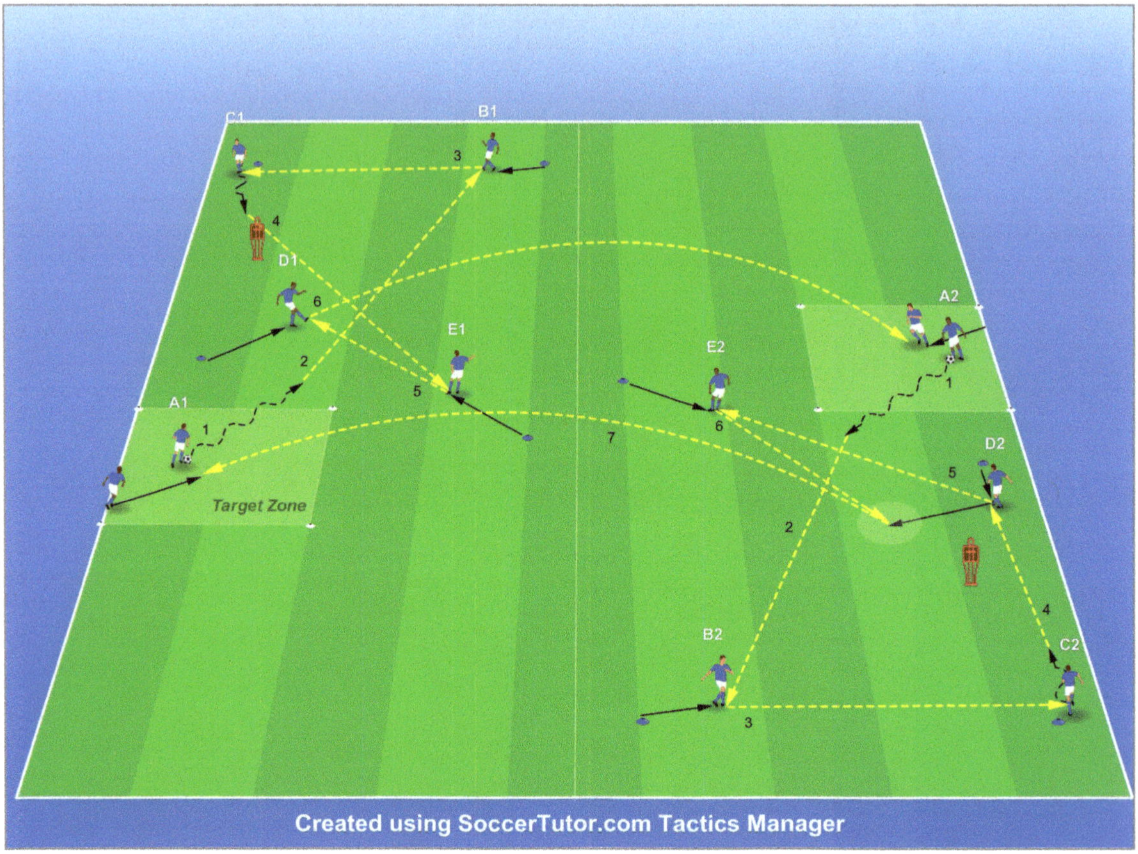

Practice Description (Variation 2)

NOTE: *This practice also appears in the "Beat the Press with a Box Midfield" book. It is included again here due to its importance to this specific training session.*

- In this variation, the sequence changes.

- **A** starts by dribbling out of the target zone and passing to **B**, who passes to **C**.

- **C** moves forward and has 2 options: Pass to **E** (left side of diagram) or pass to **D** (right side).

- If **E** receives, they lay it off for **D**.

- **D** switches play to the opposite target zone for the next player waiting and the practice continues.

→ **Player Rotations:** A1 → B1 → C1 → D1 → E1 → A2 → B2 → C2 → D2 → E2 → A1.

Coaching Points

1. **Quick, purposeful combination play** to break lines and maintain control.
2. **Precision passing** (short and long) to support fluid ball movement.
3. **Consistent high tempo** with sharp movement and fast decision making.

Training Session 5: Build Up with Strong Side Equality vs High Press Zonal Defending

PROGRESSION
2. Build Up Play with Equal Numbers and Switch Play in a Dynamic 3-Team Game
1/2: 4v4 with Outside Support and Switching Objective

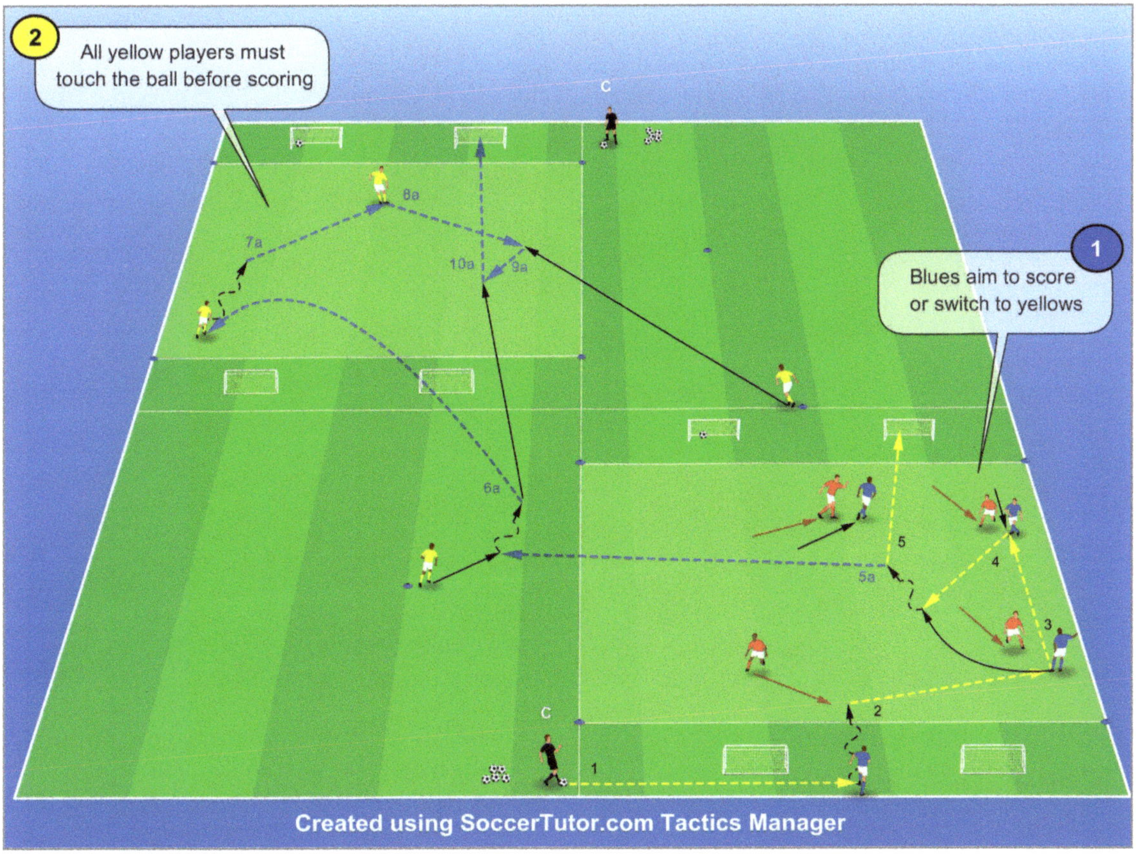

Practice Description (1/2)

NOTE: *This practice also appears in the "Beat the Press with a Box Midfield" book. It is included again here due to its importance to this specific training session.*

- We use two 25x15m areas with 3 teams of 4 (blue, red, and yellow).
- **The blues play 4v4 against the reds (+ outside yellow player at top) and aim to score in the 2 small goals or pass to the wide yellow outside support player.**
- The positioning replicates the centre back, full back, winger and attacking midfielder for build up play out wide.
- **Defending Objective:** Win the ball and counter to score in other 2 small goals.
- If the outside yellow player receives (as in the diagram), they then **switch play to a teammate** in the other area. From there, the 2 outside players must sprint into the new area.
- **All yellow players must touch the ball before scoring a goal.**

BEAT THE PRESS WITH SINGLE & DOUBLE PIVOTS

Training Session 5: Build Up with Strong Side Equality vs High Press Zonal Defending

2/2: Transition and Rotation After Switch or Goal

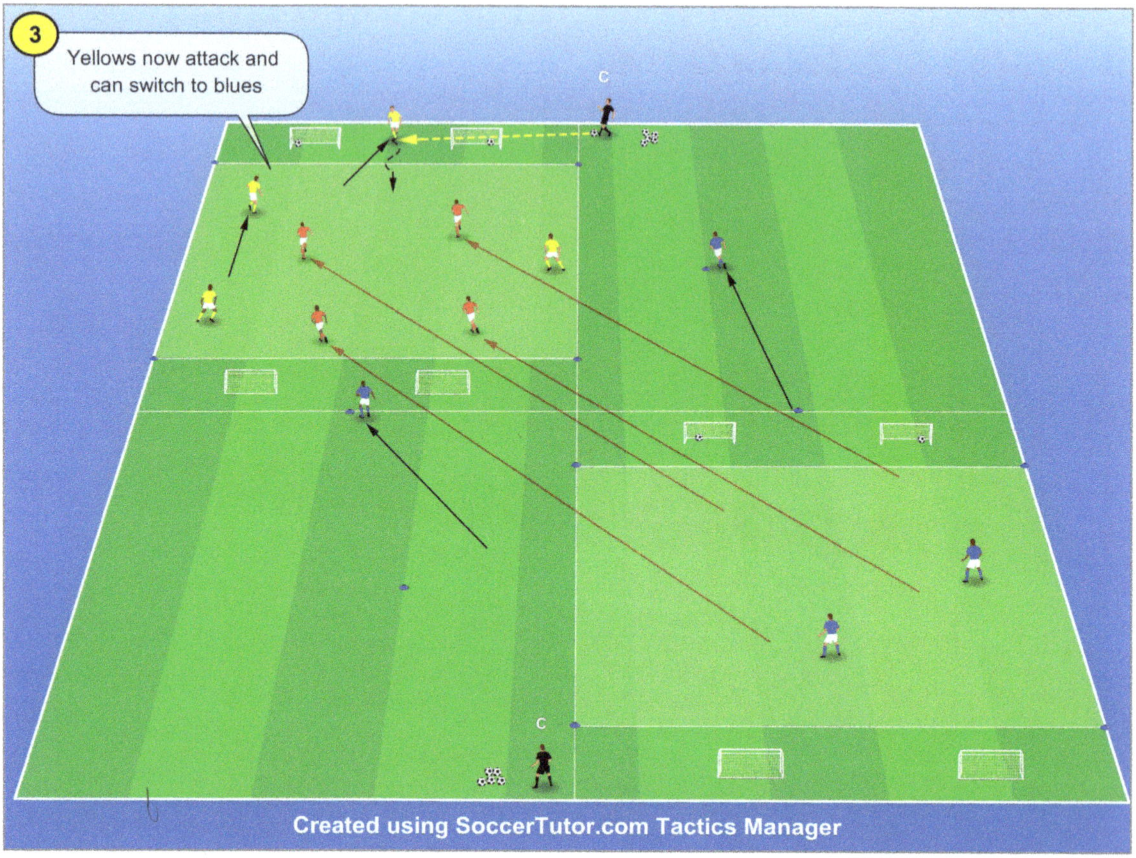

3 Yellows now attack and can switch to blues

Practice Description (2/2)

NOTE: *This practice also appears in the "Beat the Press with a Box Midfield" book. It is included again here due to its importance to this specific training session.*

- After a goal or a completed switch, **all 4 red players quickly transition to defend in the second area**. 2 blue players move outside and 2 stay in the first area.
- The **coach passes a new ball in with the yellow team now aiming to score or switch play** to the blues back in the opposite direction.
- If the ball goes out at anytime, the practice restarts from the coach.

- **Rule:** The attacking team must complete their objective within a set time. If they fail, the coach blows the whistle and they become the defending team.
- Area dimensions can be adjusted based on the player level and/or age group.

Coaching Points

1. **Intelligent off-the-ball movement** to offer clear passing options.
2. **Supporting players adjust positions** to open new passing lanes.
3. **Fast, coordinated combination play**.
4. **Quality long passes** with immediate forward support.

Training Session 5: Build Up with Strong Side Equality vs High Press Zonal Defending

PROGRESSION

3. Split-Pitch Build Up Tactical Game to Beat the Press with Equal Numbers (4-3-3)

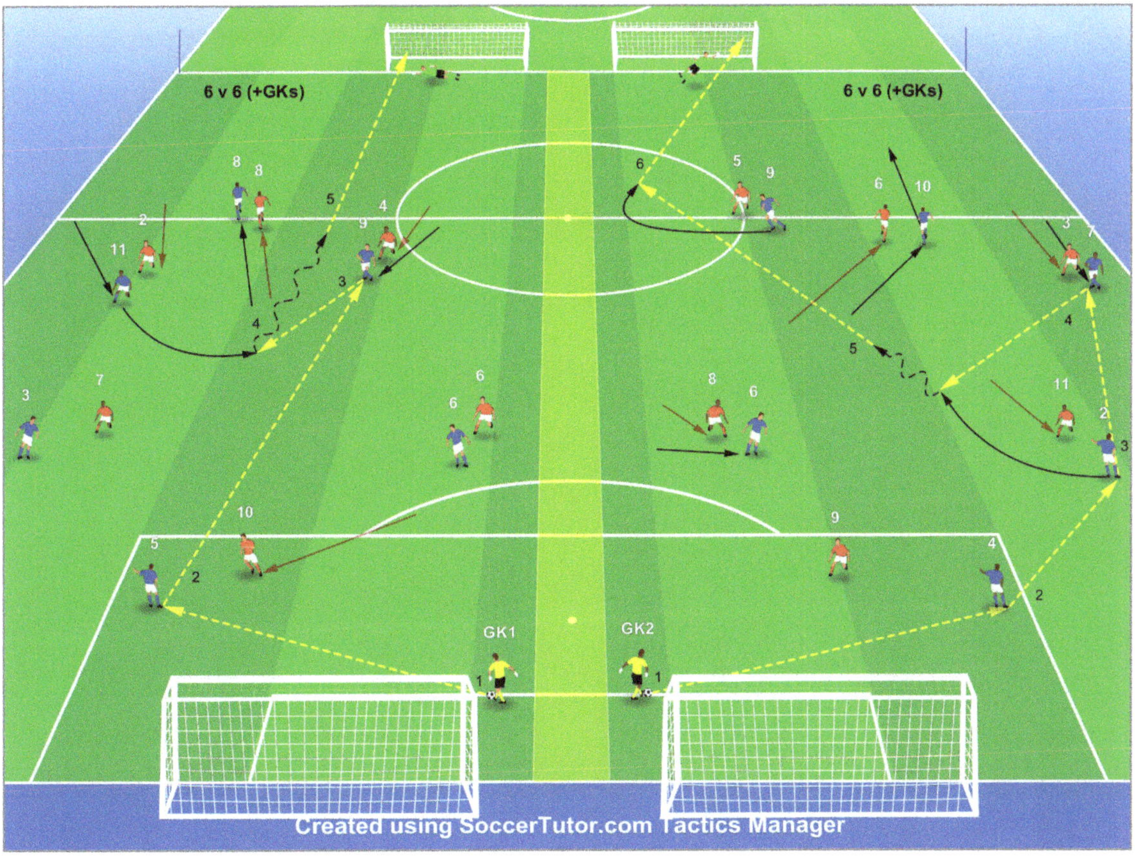

Practice Description

- The pitch is split into 2 halves, with both 6v6 (+GKs) games active at the same time. This is so the players do more repetitions than normal.

- The blues have a **defensive midfielder (Nº6) and forward (Nº9) on both sides**. The reds have 2 forwards (Nº6 and Nº8) on both sides.

- **Defending Objective:** Press first receiver (after first pass), win the ball and counter to score within 10-12 seconds.

- **Attacking Objective:** Use dynamic and synchronised movements of 2 or 3 players to create and/or exploit available spaces with a numerical equality on the strong side - *see analysis pages in this section for all options and full details*.

- The blues **build up play through short combinations or play long**, then support the second ball.

- The aim is to beat the press, play in behind, and score.

BEAT THE PRESS WITH SINGLE & DOUBLE PIVOTS

Training Session 5: Build Up with Strong Side Equality vs High Press Zonal Defending

PROGRESSION
4. Reading the Game Situation (Advantage or Equal Numbers) 11v11 Conditioned 3 Zone Game

Variation 1: Exploiting Strong Side Overloads

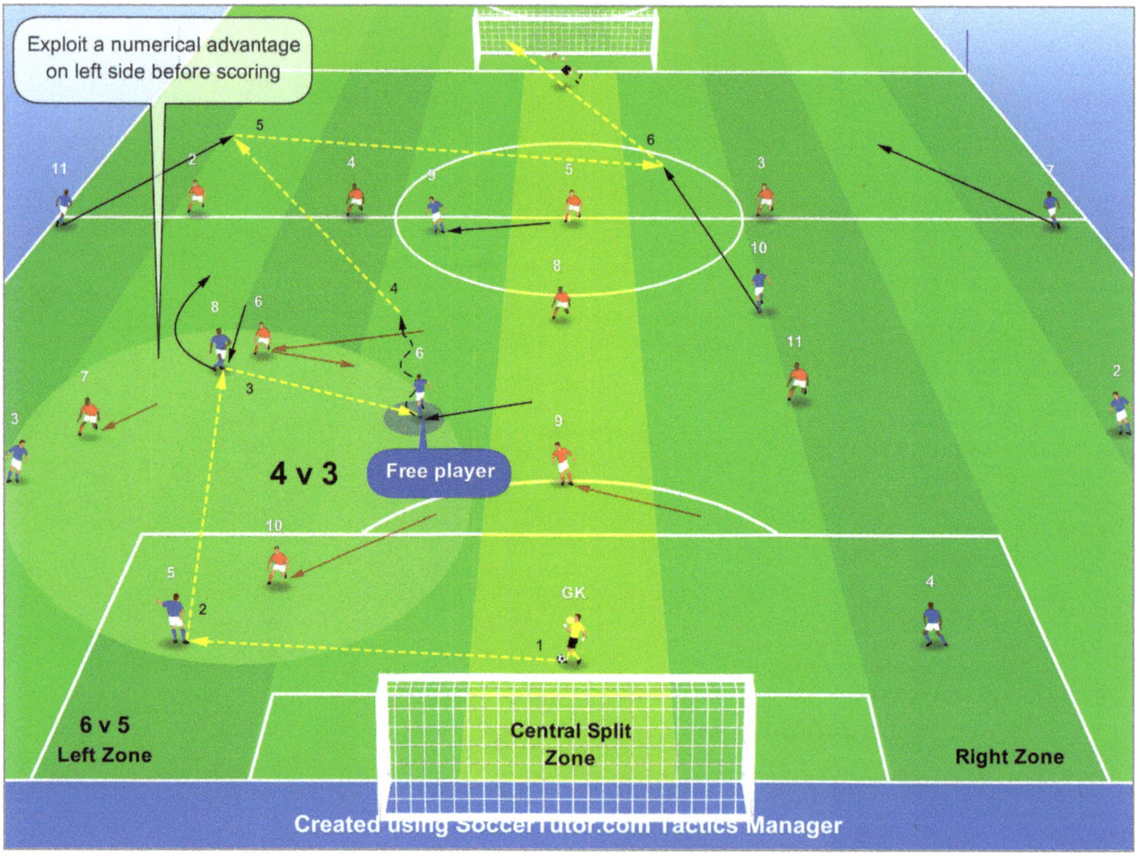

Practice Description (Variation 1)

- Using 3/4 of a full pitch, the yellow 7 metre middle zone splits the pitch to help the players read the situation.
- The **goalkeeper (GK)** starts by passing into either wide zone.
- When there is a **numerical advantage on that side (Variation 1 diagram)**, the blues aim to exploit it by using quick combination play before scoring.

- There is a **4v3 advantage for the build up (highlighted)** and the blues move the ball to the free player **(defensive midfielder N°6)**. Overall there is a 6v5 advantage on the left side.
- **Defending Objective:** If the reds win the ball, they counter attack and try to score within 10-12 seconds.
- **Restriction:** The reds can only press after the first pass from the **GK** is played.

BEAT THE PRESS WITH SINGLE & DOUBLE PIVOTS

Training Session 5: Build Up with Strong Side Equality vs High Press Zonal Defending

Variation 2: Switching from Equal Numbers to the Weak Side

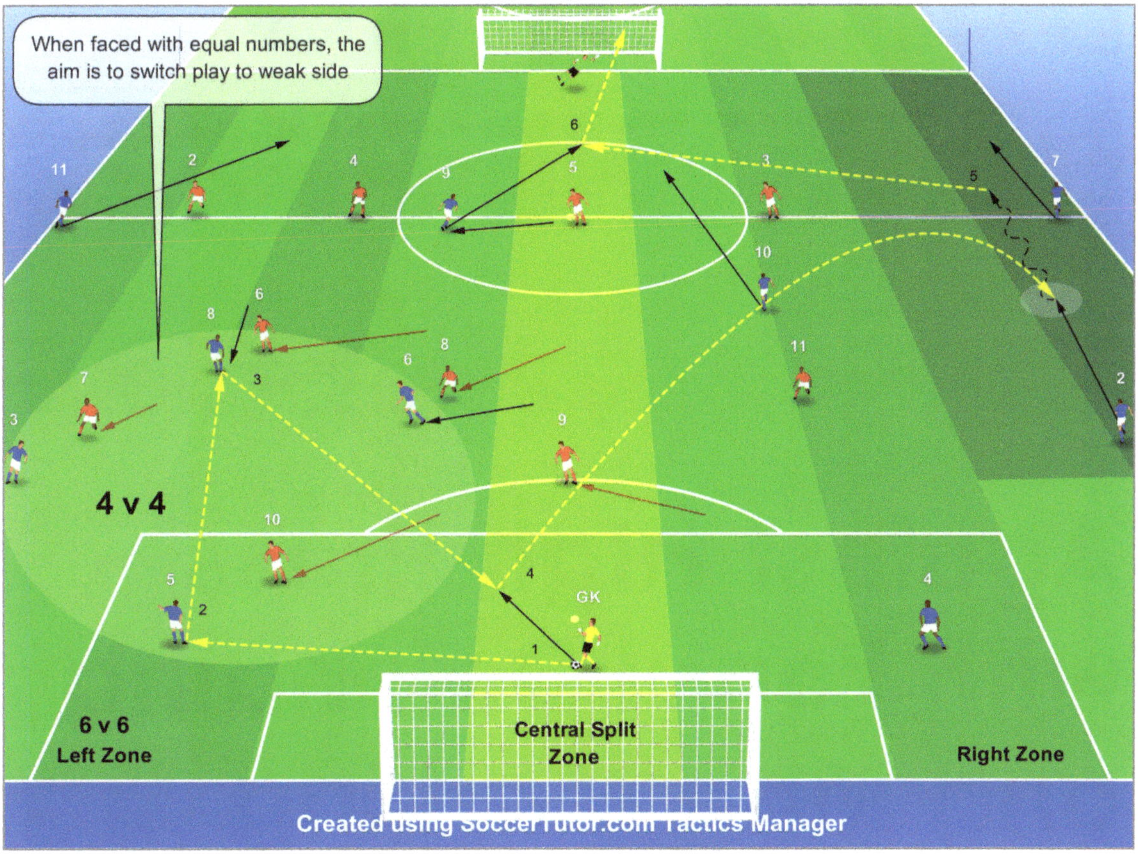

When faced with equal numbers, the aim is to switch play to weak side

4 v 4

6 v 6 Left Zone | **Central Split Zone** | **Right Zone**

Practice Description (Variation 2)

- In **Variation 2**, the red players shift across early to create a **numerical equality** on the relevant side of the pitch.
- **The blues must decide the best option**:
  1. Continue using combination play.
  2. Pass long and provide support for the second ball.
  3. Switch to the weak side where space may be available (**diagram example**).
- Clear communication is essential to identify whether an overload, equality, or a switching opportunity exists
- **Progression:** Remove the zones for players to play naturally.

Coaching Points

1. **Read and react quickly** to changing situations.
2. **Use verbal cues** to support team decision making.
3. **Offer passing options** through intelligent positioning.
4. **Switch play with accuracy and awareness**.
5. **Maintain a high tempo** throughout the practice.

BUILD UP TO BEAT THE PRESS

Tactical Analysis

Against High Press with Zonal Defending and Man Marking

Build up play patterns from Flick, Klopp, and Emery's teams

Build Up Against High Press with Zonal Defending and Man Marking (Single Pivot)

1. Opposition Positioning Adjustments to Apply Marking Against a 4-3-3 Build Up Shape

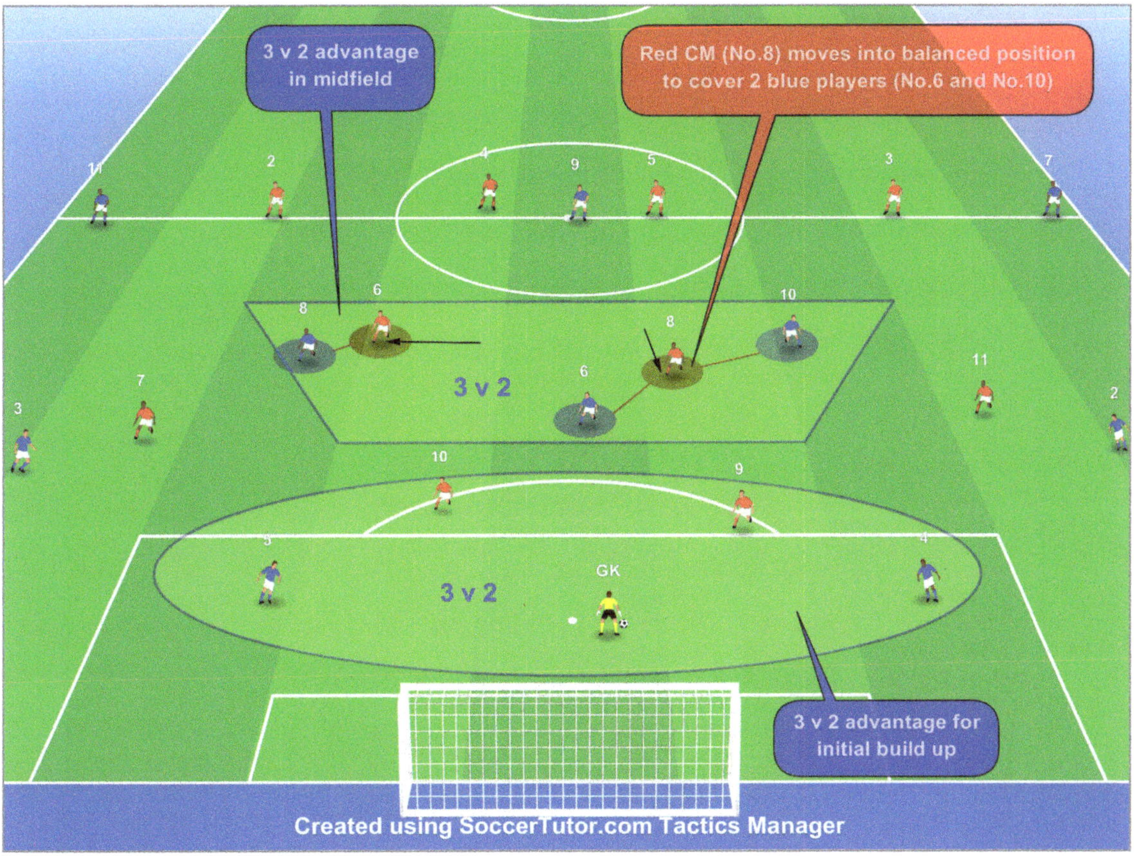

Another type of defending that can be used when applying a high press is a hybrid of zonal defending and man marking. Defenders mark opponents in their zone more aggressively. However, due to a **numerical disadvantage (2 v 3)** for the red team, one of the central midfielders must position himself between 2 opponents. As shown in the diagram, **red N°6 moves close to blue N°8, while red N°8 positions himself between blue N°6 and N°10**.

Principles needed:

A. **Make it difficult for the opposing midfielder** to control 2 players.

B. **Move the ball to the midfielder who has the most available space**.

Note: The following pages outline tactical solutions against a high press with zonal defending and man marking (hybrid), exploiting the red player that has to cover 2 players in midfield to progress the play.

Build Up to Beat the Press: Against High Press with Zonal Defending and Man Marking

2. Reactions and Movements of Midfielders to Create Space to Receive from Goalkeeper (4-3-3)

No.6 and No.10 increase the distance between each other to stretch the press and create space

Red CM (No.8) forced to cover 2 players

Passing lane

Passing lane

The first action needed to be effective in is for the **defensive midfielder (Nº6)** and an **attacking midfielder (Nº10)**, who are being covered by red Nº8, to increase their distance between each other while also staying away from nearby red players.

In the diagram example, **Nº6 moves away from Nº10 and red Nº8**, while maintaining equal distance from red Nº6 and Nº10. At the same time, **Nº10 also moves away from Nº6 and red Nº8**, keeping an equal distance from red Nº3 and Nº11.

The positioning of Nº6 and Nº10 is ideal when both are aligned with available passing lanes to receive directly from GK.

The next step is to move the ball to the player with the most available space.

Since red Nº8 is positioned between them, **both Nº6 and Nº10 have enough space to receive**.

Nº6 is well-positioned in a passing lane and can receive directly from the **goalkeeper (GK)**.

Nº10 is behind the second pressing line and, so the direct passing lane would be more risky. However, he can **receive a lofted medium-range pass that skips over 2 pressing lines**.

©SOCCERTUTOR.COM

BEAT THE PRESS WITH SINGLE & DOUBLE PIVOTS

Build Up to Beat the Press: Against High Press with Zonal Defending and Man Marking

3. Options to Exploit the Numerical Superiority in Midfield when the Defensive Midfielder Receives (4-3-3)

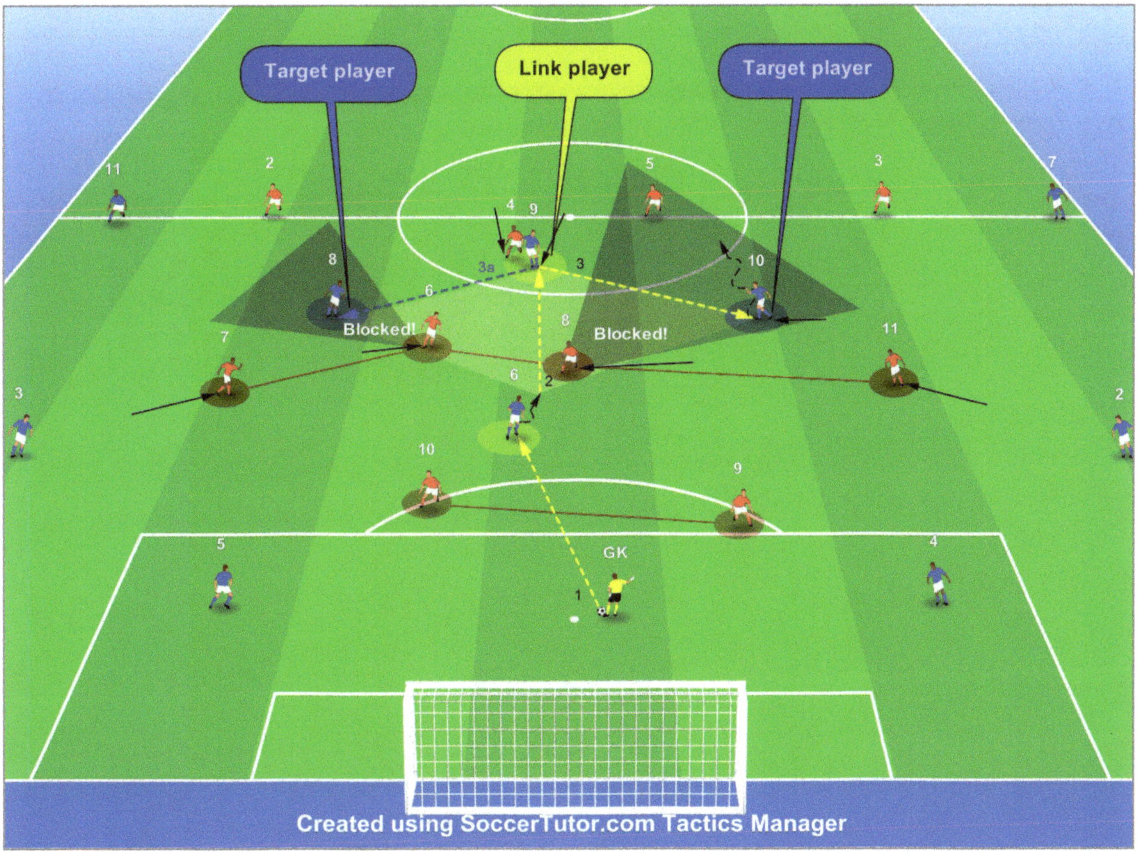

If the ball is moved to the **defensive midfielder** (**Nº6**), the first line of pressure is broken. The advanced players must then increase options for the player in possession to help break the second line.

The 2 attacking midfielders (Nº8 and Nº10) and the forward (Nº9) should each move into different available passing lanes, creating 2 triangles or a diamond shape. This makes it impossible for the red team to block all of Nº6's passing options.

As shown in the diagram, once **Nº6** receives and red Nº8 presses, **Nº8** and **Nº10** offer support. However, since direct passes to both of them are blocked by opponents (highlighted), **Nº9 becomes the key player forming the diamond shape and acting as the link player** to move the ball to either of the free **target players** (**Nº8 or Nº10**) behind the second pressing line.

©SOCCERTUTOR.COM

BEAT THE PRESS WITH SINGLE & DOUBLE PIVOTS

Build Up Against High Press with Zonal Defending and Man Marking (Double Pivot)

1. Opposition Positioning Adjustments to Apply Marking Against a 4-2-3-1 Build Up Shape

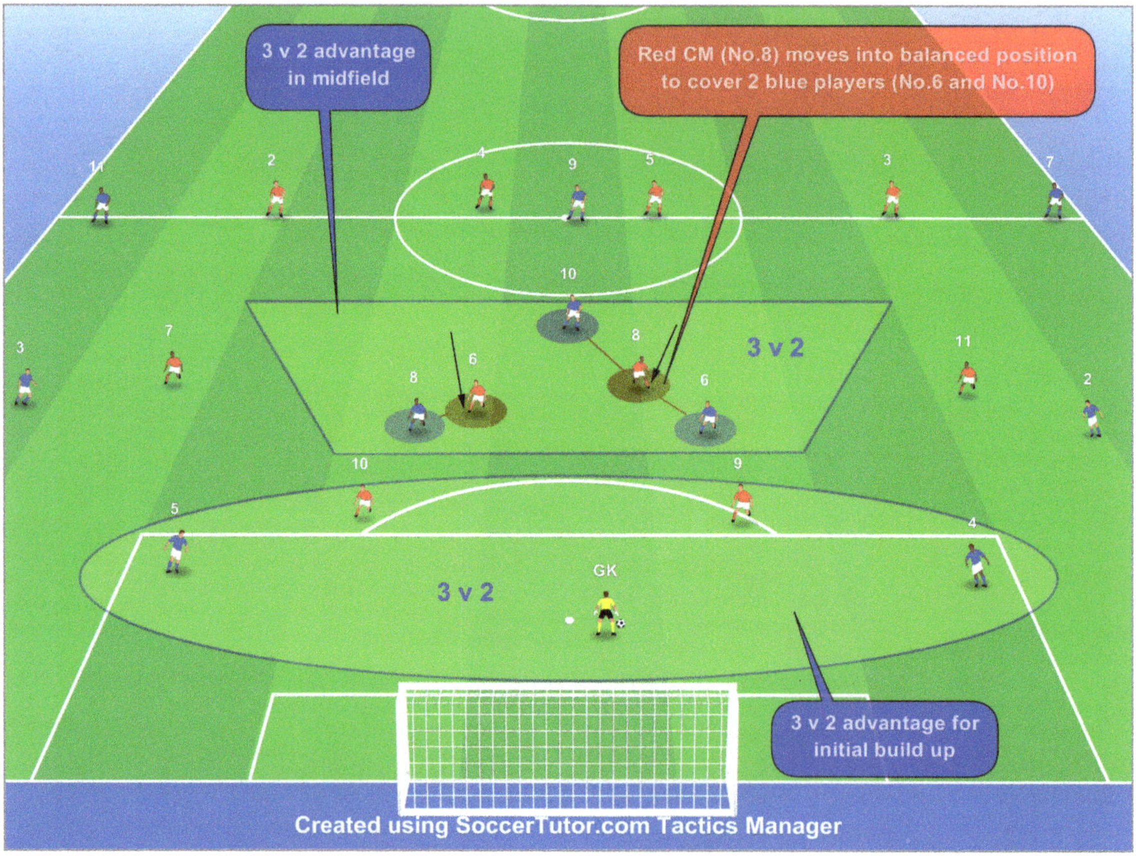

We now focus on building up play with the 4-2-3-1 formation against a hybrid of zonal defending and man marking. Defenders mark opponents in their zone more aggressively. However, due to a **numerical disadvantage (2 v 3)** for the red team, one of the central midfielders must be positioned between 2 opponents. As shown in the diagram, **red Nº6 moves close to blue Nº8**, while red Nº8 positions himself between blue Nº6 and Nº10.

The principles and actions the possession team (blues) apply to be effective building up against this type of defending are:

A. **Make it difficult for the opposing midfielder** to control 2 players at the same time.

B. **Move the ball to the midfielder who has the most available space**.

Build Up to Beat the Press: Against High Press with Zonal Defending and Man Marking

2a (Option 1). Playing to the Attacking Midfielder (Target Player) in Space Between the Lines (4-2-3-1)

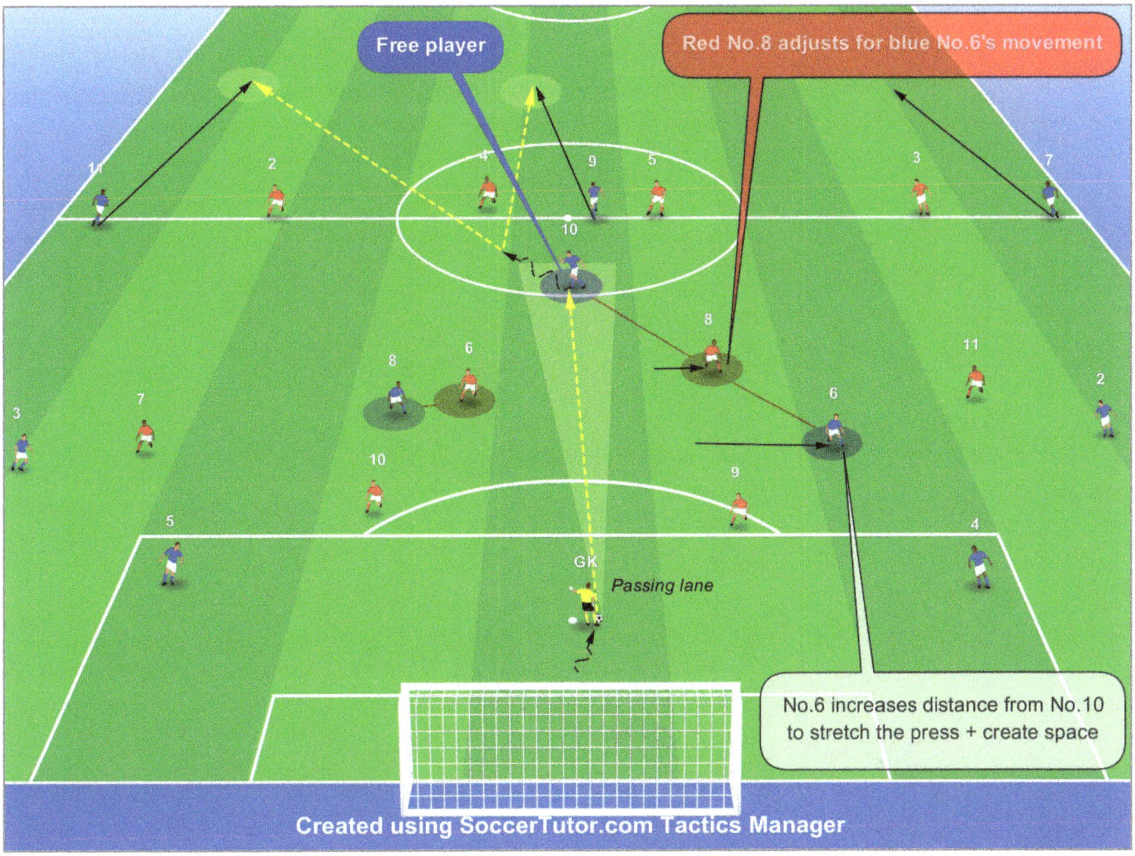

The team building up play from the back with a 4-2-3-1 structure can be effective against this type of defending if they **make it more difficult for red Nº8 to control 2 players (Principle A) on previous page**.

The defensive midfielder (Nº6) and attacking midfielder (Nº10) increase their distance from each other and, at the same time, try to stay equal distances away from nearby opponents while positioning themselves in available passing lanes. As shown in the diagram, this positioning is possible for **Nº10** but not for **Nº6**.

Based on red Nº8's reaction, the **goalkeeper (GK) decides the best option to move the ball to the free player with the most available space (Principle B on previous page)**.

If red Nº8 remains between the 2 blue players (as shown in this diagram example), the through passing lane to Nº10 will likely be available.

A pass to **Nº10** breaks the 2 pressing lines and neutralises 6 red players. The next step is a forward pass in behind the red team's defensive line.

BEAT THE PRESS WITH SINGLE & DOUBLE PIVOTS

Build Up to Beat the Press: Against High Press with Zonal Defending and Man Marking

2b (Option 2). Playing to the Defensive Midfielder when the Passing Lane to the Attacking Midfielder is Blocked (4-2-3-1)

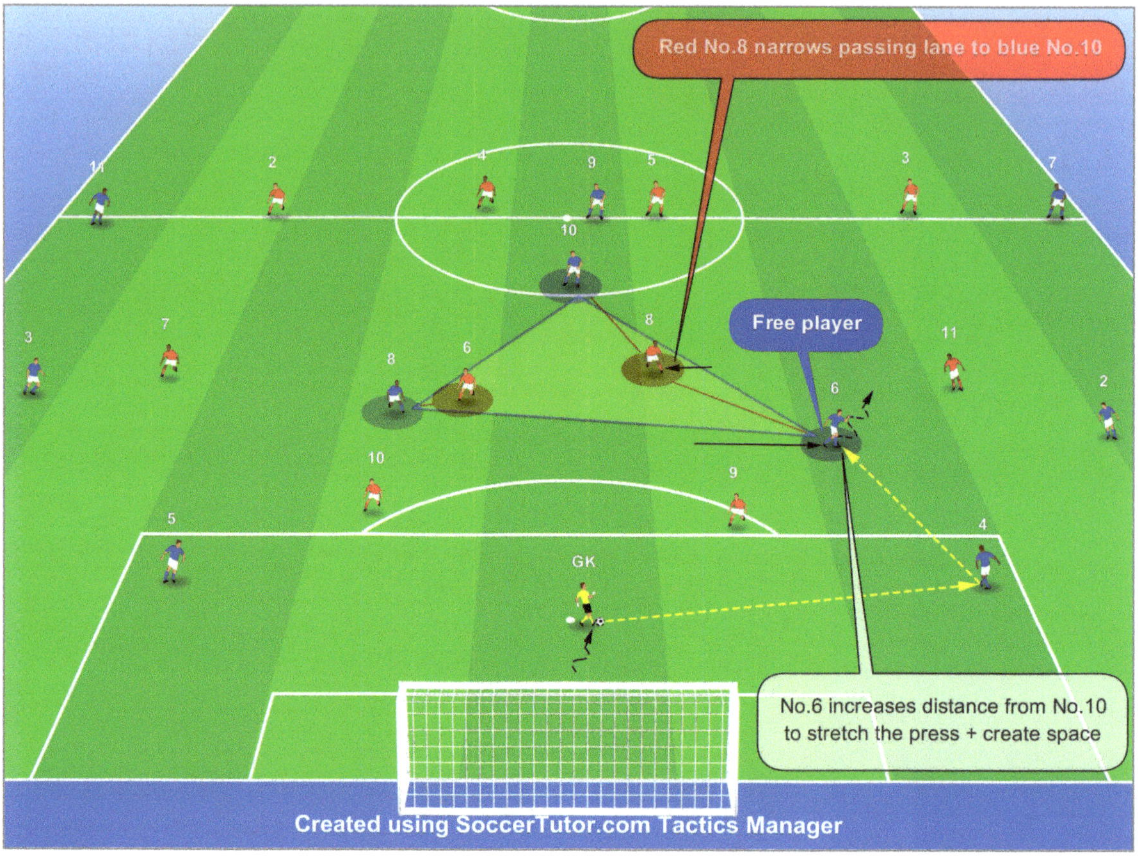

If **red N°8 decides to shift inside** and narrow the through passing lane to the **attacking midfielder (N°10)**, his distance from the **defensive midfielder (N°6)** increases.

As a result, **N°6 is no longer in a direct passing lane from the goalkeeper (GK)**, but this does not exclude him from the play.

The ball can be directed to N°6 via the centre back (N°4), who, after receiving from the **GK**, can act as the link player to play a forward pass into **N°6**'s feet.

This indirect route keeps **N°6** actively involved in the build up phase, maintaining central presence and passing continuity. It also enables the team to exploit the space left behind by red N°8's movement, ensuring they **retain midfield control and increase the chances of progressing past the pressing lines**.

3. Options to Exploit the Numerical Superiority on the Strong Side when the Defensive Midfielder Receives (4-2-3-1)

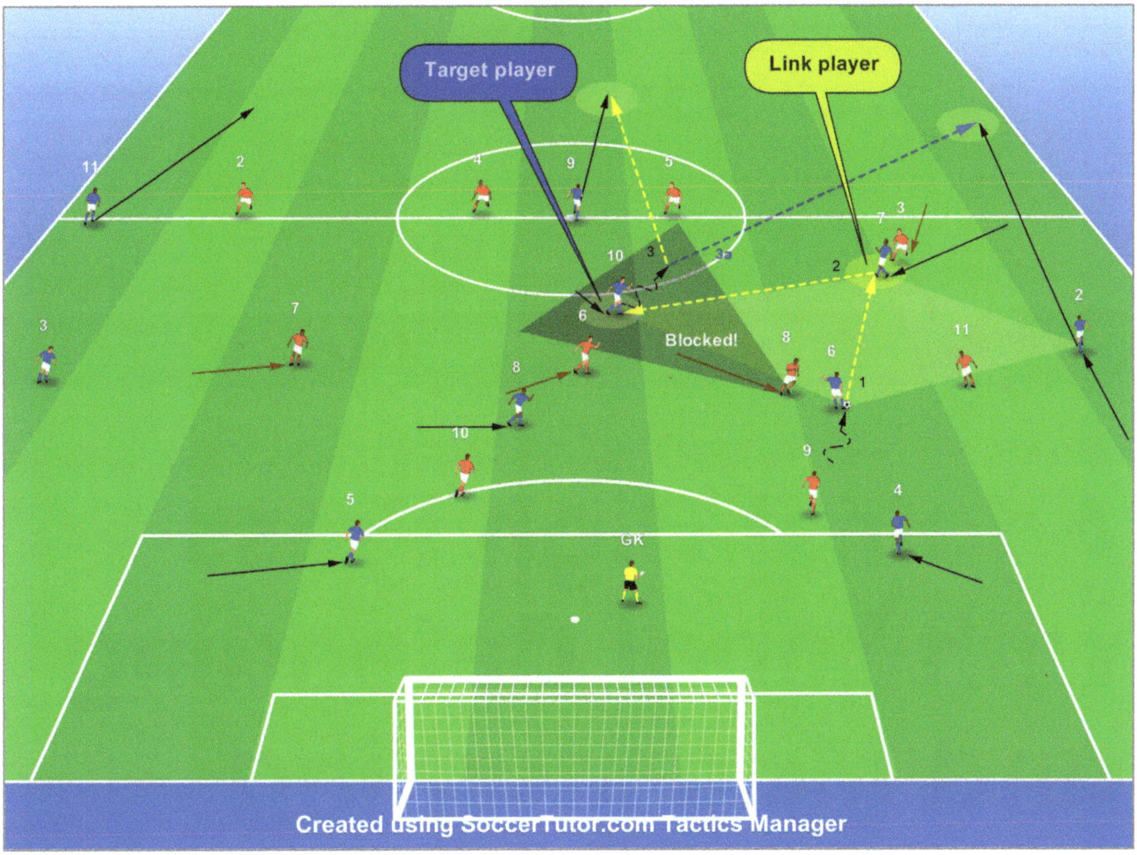

Following on from the previous page, as soon as this action is completed, the receiver will have time and space to turn and move the ball beyond the second line. A free target player - the **attacking midfielder (N°10)** - is already positioned between the lines, but for the ball to reach him, the **defensive midfielder (N°6)** needs more passing options.

To support the progression of the play, the **winger (N°7) moves inside while the full back (N°2) pushes forward**. This coordinated movement **creates a dilemma for the red full back N°3**, potentially leaving a second player free between the lines if red N°3 chooses not to follow **N°7**.

These synchronised movements increase the passing options for N°6, forming 2 triangles or a diamond.

The pass to N°10 is blocked, but the ball can be played to him via N°7, who acts as a link player.

Once **N°10** receives, the next step is to move the ball in behind the red team's defensive line into space for the runs of the **forward (N°9** -yellow arrow) or the **full back (N°2** -blue arrow).

BUILD UP TO BEAT THE PRESS

Training Session 6 (3 Practices)

Against High Press with Zonal Defending and Man Marking

Based on Flick, Klopp, and Emery build up patterns

BEAT THE PRESS WITH THE 4-3-3 AND 4-2-3-1

Training Session 6: Build Up Against High Press with Zonal Defending and Man Marking

TRAINING SESSION (3 PRACTICES)
1. Exploit 3v2 Numerical Advantage with Single Pivot Midfield Positional Small Sided Game

Variation 1: GK's Direct Pass to Defensive Midfielder Available

Red CM (8) has to cover 2 blue players

Blues find midfielder with most space to progress forward and score

Practice Description (Variation 1)

- The blues build up in a 2-3-1 shape (from 4-3-3) with 1 defensive midfielder - single pivot. The reds defend in a 2-2 shape.
- The defensive midfielder (N°6) and N°10 increase the distance between each other to maximise space.
- **Blue Objective:** Exploit 3v2 numerical advantage in midfield and red midfielder (N°8 in diagram), who has to control 2 blue players.
- The next step is to move the ball to the **free attacking midfielder (N°10 in diagram)** and score in the small goals.
- To start, **GK** reads the situation to play the correct pass. **In Variation 1 example, the through pass to N°6 is possible**, who receives with space to turn. **The forward (N°9) is used as a link player to move the ball to N°10 in the end zone.**
- **Red Objective:** Press to win the ball and counter to score within 8–10 seconds.

BEAT THE PRESS WITH SINGLE & DOUBLE PIVOTS

Training Session 6: Build Up Against High Press with Zonal Defending and Man Marking

Variation 2: GK's Direct Pass to Defensive Midfielder Unavailable

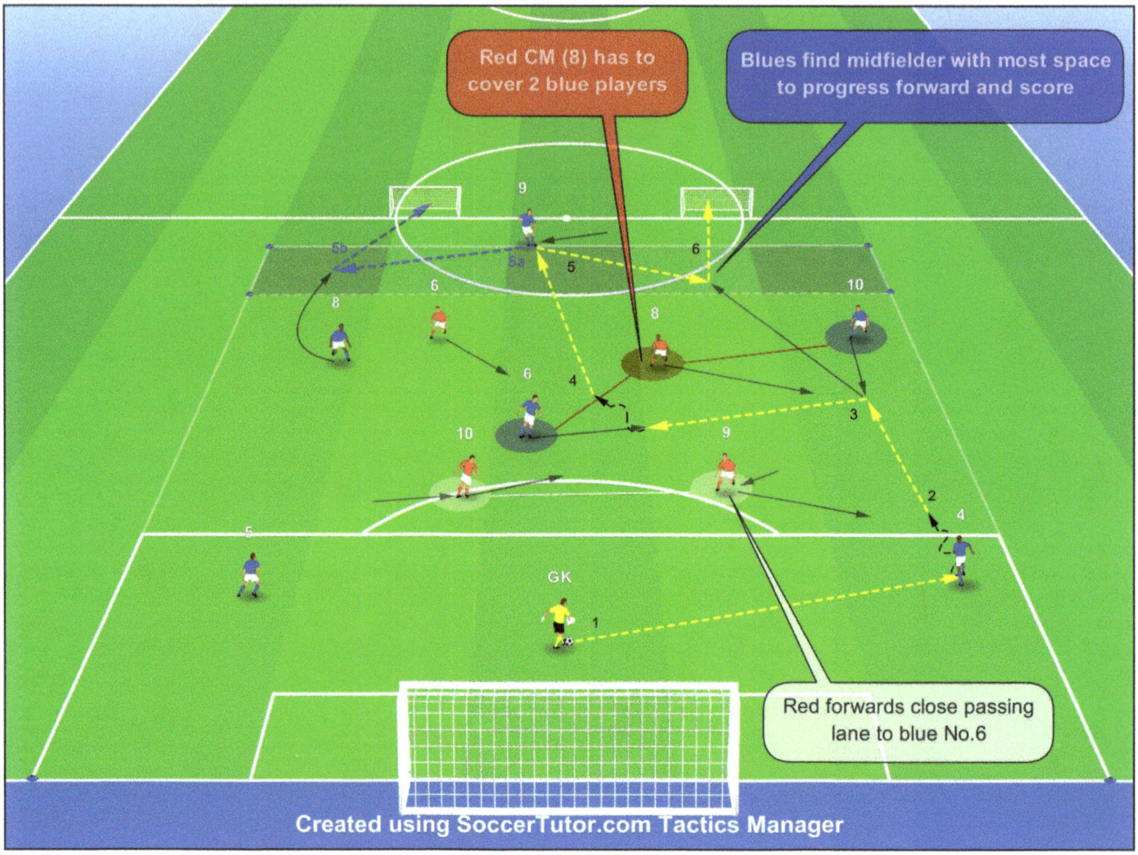

Practice Description (Variation 2)

- In **Variation 2**, the through pass from the GK to the defensive midfielder (**N°6**) is blocked by the 2 red forwards (N°9 and N°10), who have both shifted inside.

- **GK instead passes to the centre back (N°4)**, who uses the attacking midfielder (N°10) as a link to move the ball to N°6.

- From there, the **forward (N°9)** is again used as a link player to move the ball to either **attacking midfielder (N°8 or N°10)** in the end zone, as shown.

- **Restrictions:** Red midfielders are not allowed in the end zone to prevent them standing in front of the small goals.

Coaching Points

1. **Apply the appropriate principles** to exploit the opponent who must control 2 players.

2. **Timing and synchronisation** of supporting runs.

3. **Read the pressing cues** to identify the free player.

BEAT THE PRESS WITH SINGLE & DOUBLE PIVOTS

Training Session 6: Build Up Against High Press with Zonal Defending and Man Marking

VARIATION

2. Exploit 3v2 Numerical Advantage with Double Pivot Midfield Positional Small Sided Game

Variation 1: GK's Direct Pass to Attacking Midfielder Available

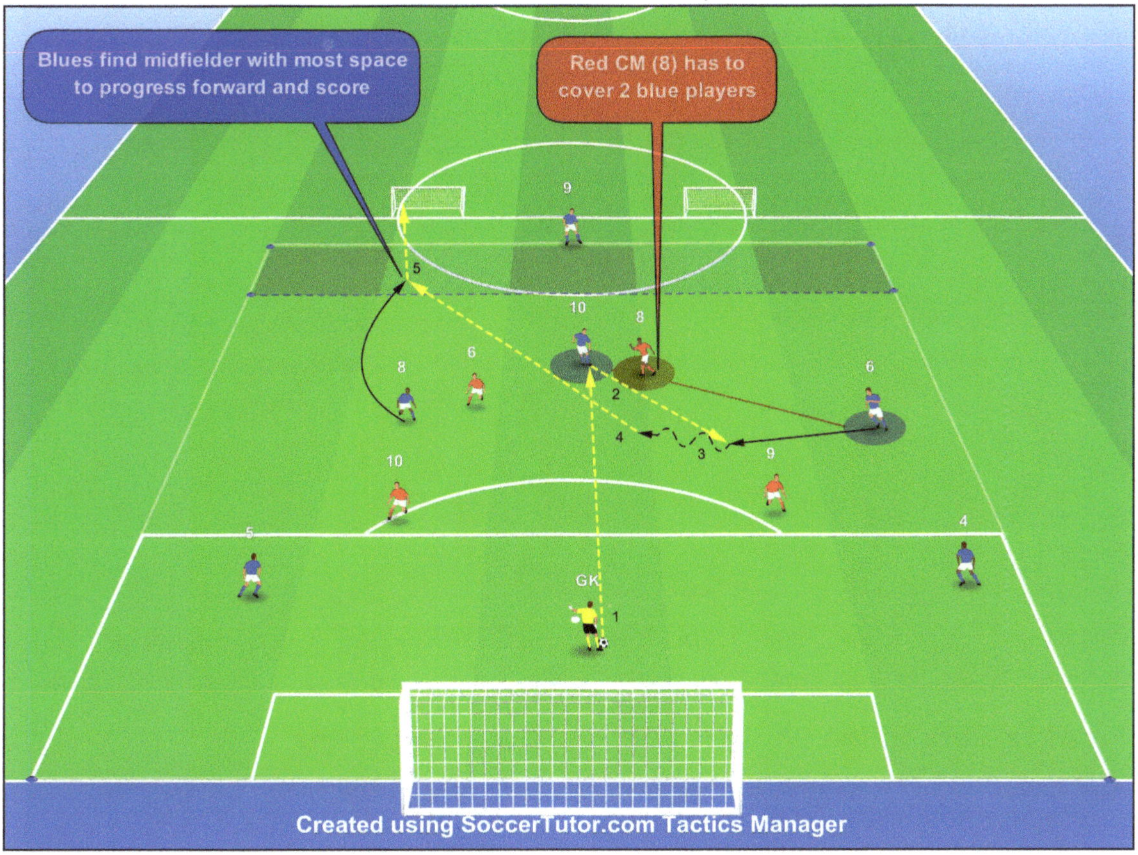

[Diagram: Blues find midfielder with most space to progress forward and score. Red CM (8) has to cover 2 blue players.]

Practice Description (Variation 1)

- The blues build up in a 2-2-1-1 shape (from 4-2-3-1) with 2 defensive midfielders - double pivot. The reds defend in a 2-2 shape.
- **Blue Objective:** Exploit 3v2 numerical advantage in midfield and red midfielder (**N°8 in diagram**), **who has to control 2 blue players**. The next step is to move the ball to the **free midfielder (N°8 in diagram)**, who scores in a small goal.

- To start, **GK** reads the situation to play the correct pass.
- **In Variation 1, the through pass to the attacking midfielder (N°10) is possible**, who receives with space to turn.
- **The defensive midfielder (N°6) is used as a link player to move the ball to N°8 in the end zone**, as shown.
- **Red Objective:** Press to win the ball and counter to score within 8–10 seconds.

BEAT THE PRESS WITH SINGLE & DOUBLE PIVOTS

Training Session 6: Build Up Against High Press with Zonal Defending and Man Marking

Variation 2: GK's Direct Pass to Attacking Midfielder Unavailable

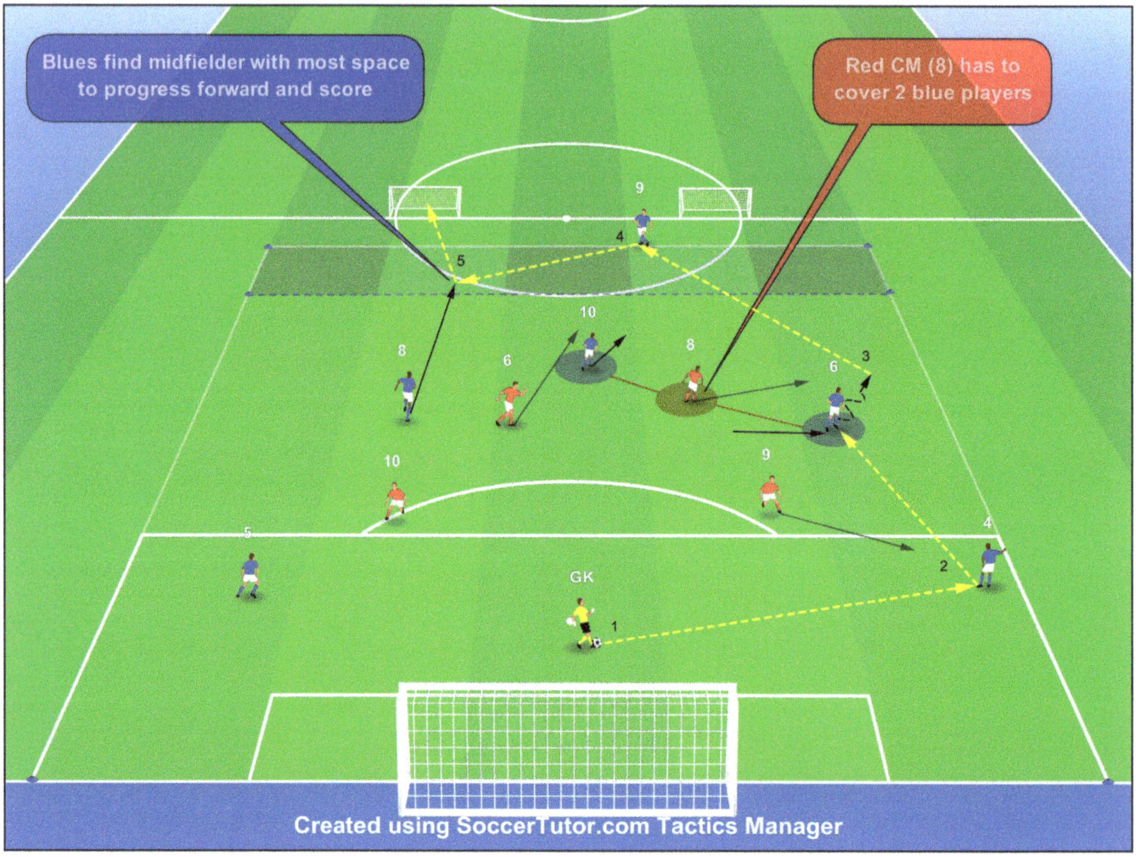

Blues find midfielder with most space to progress forward and score

Red CM (8) has to cover 2 blue players

Practice Description (Variation 2)

- In **Variation 2**, the **through pass to the attacking midfielder (N°10) is too risky** due to the positioning of the 2 red central midfielders (N°6 and N°8).
- **The GK instead passes to the centre back (N°4)**, who moves the ball to the **defensive midfielder (N°6)**.
- From there, the **forward (N°9) is used as a link player to move the ball to the free midfielder (N°8 in diagram example)** in the end zone.
- **Restrictions:** Red midfielders are not allowed in the end zone to prevent them standing in front of the small goals.

Coaching Points

1. **Apply the appropriate principles** to exploit the opponent (red N°6 in diagram) who must control 2 players.
2. **Timing and synchronisation** of supporting runs.
3. **Read the pressing cues** to identify the free player.

Training Session 6: Build Up Against High Press with Zonal Defending and Man Marking

PROGRESSION

3. Exploit 3v2 Midfield Advantage Against High Press with Zonal and Man Marking Conditioned Game

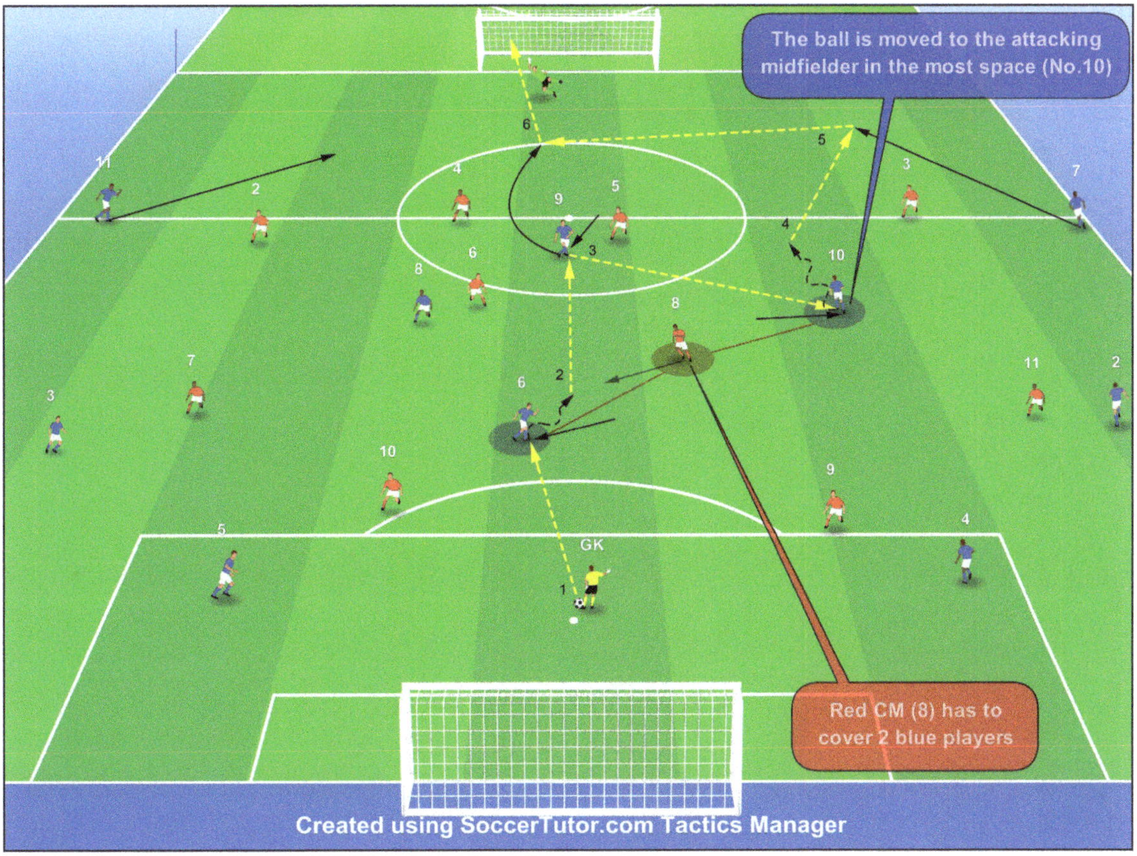

The ball is moved to the attacking midfielder in the most space (No.10)

Red CM (8) has to cover 2 blue players

Practice Description

- This final practice is an 11v11 game. The attacking team either build up play using the 4-3-3 formation (diagram example) or the 4-2-3-1. The red defending team press high after the first pass with zonal defending and man marking in midfield.

- **Blue Objective:** Exploit 3v2 numerical advantage in midfield and red midfielder (**N°8 in diagram**), who has to control 2 blue players.

- The **defensive midfielder (N°6)** and **attacking midfielder (N°10)** increase the distance between each other to maximise space.

- The next step is to **move the ball to the free attacking midfielder (N°10 in diagram example)**, who then looks to finish the attack quickly with support from teammates.

- **Coaching Points:** Create distance from the opposing midfielder marking 2 players using coordinated movements to open passing lanes and create space. Recognise pressing triggers early and make quick, effective decisions.

BEAT THE PRESS WITH SINGLE & DOUBLE PIVOTS

BUILD UP TO BEAT THE PRESS

Tactical Analysis

Against Ultra-Aggressive Pressing with Zonal Defending and Man Marking

Build up play patterns from Flick, Klopp, and Emery's teams

Build Up Against Ultra-Aggressive Pressing with Zonal Defending and Man Marking

We have already mentioned that when high pressing is applied (see page 83), there is a 7v6 situation in favour of the possession team.

When this pressing extends up to the goalkeeper (ultra-aggressive pressing), the defending team must also account for the goalkeeper, who becomes actively involved in the build up play.

The possession team, therefore, has a **+2 numerical advantage (7 outfield players + GK vs 6 defenders)** in this specific part of the pitch.

When the objective of the defending team is to apply ultra-aggressive pressing, some principles must be applied.

1. **First Principle:** When pressing is applied to the goalkeeper, it is to **block the passing lane towards one of the centre backs, who stays free**.

   This eliminates the first numerical advantage problem for the pressing team.

   If the first principle is not applied properly, a pass to the centre back would at least neutralise the player who presses the goalkeeper.

2. **Second Principle:** Set up to **control all the receivers of a potential short pass** from the goalkeeper.

   If the second principle is not applied properly, an easy short pass can be played to a free player.

   This pass will again at least neutralise the player who presses the goalkeeper, and potentially more players.

To achieve the second principle, the defending team must apply close marking to all opponents near the ball. One way to carry this out is by using a **hybrid of zonal defending and man marking in midfield**, which we will fully analyse in this section.

This means that the **midfielders should mark the opponents within their zone of responsibility** and especially the defensive midfielders, who are potential receivers of a short first pass. If they do receive, the aim is to use close marking to prevent them from turning.

Note: Although we set out the opposition's pressing structure and aims, the focus of this section is on how to build up play with a single pivot (4-3-3) and double pivot (4-2-3-1) against this type of defending/pressing, with tactical solutions provided.

Build Up: Against Ultra-Aggressive Pressing with Zonal Defending and Man Marking

Build Up Against Ultra-Aggressive Pressing with Zonal Defending and Man Marking (Single Pivot)

1. Opposition Positioning Adjustments to Apply Marking Against a 4-3-3 Build Up Shape

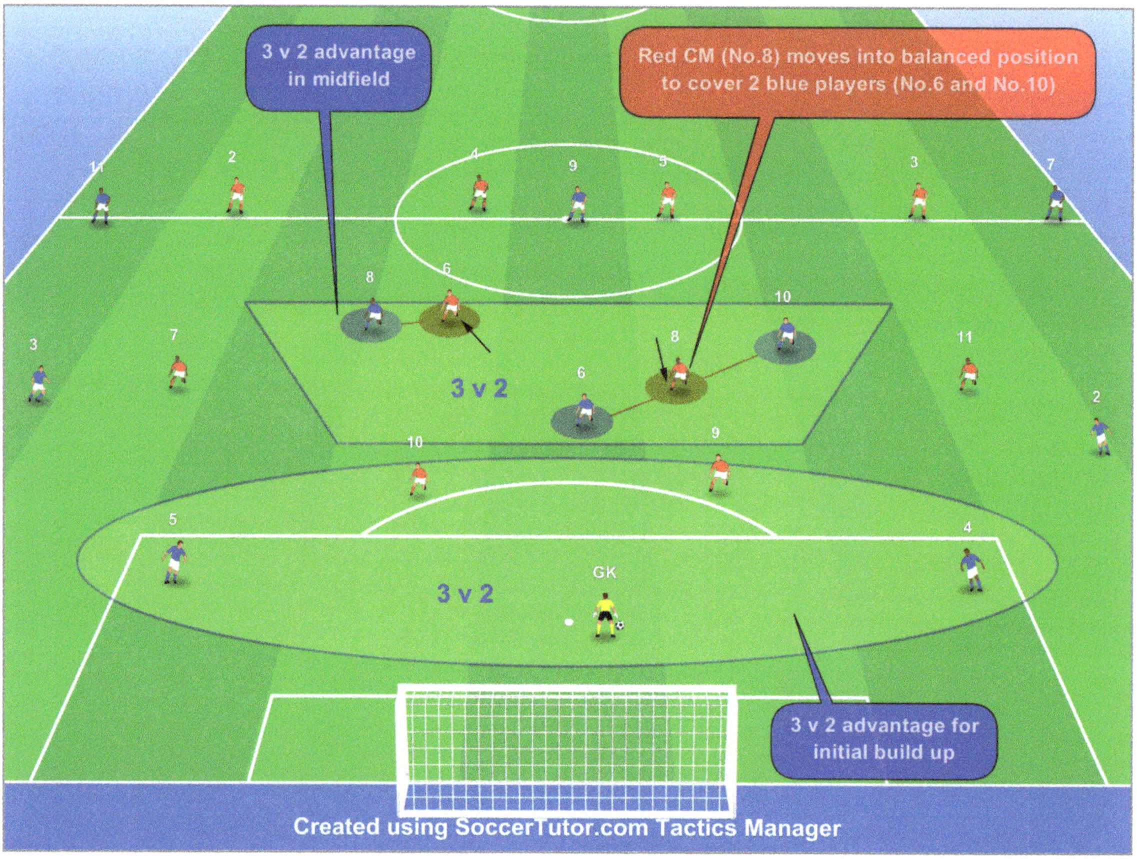

This first diagram reflects the second principle outlined on the previous page: **The opposition set up to control all the receivers of a potential short pass from the goalkeeper (GK)**.

The red central midfielder Nº6 marks the **left attacking midfielder (Nº8)**, while red Nº8 is positioned between the **defensive midfielder (Nº6)** and the **right attacking midfielder (Nº10)** to control both players.

This is because a **3 v 2 disadvantage exists for the reds in the key central midfield area** for the reds, so a midfielder must cover 2 opponents.

Note: Red Nº8 must be close enough to press Nº6 if he receives, while limiting potential passing lanes towards Nº10.

Build Up: Against Ultra-Aggressive Pressing with Zonal Defending and Man Marking

2. Opposition Press the Goalkeeper and Ensure All Nearby Passing Options are Marked (4-3-3)

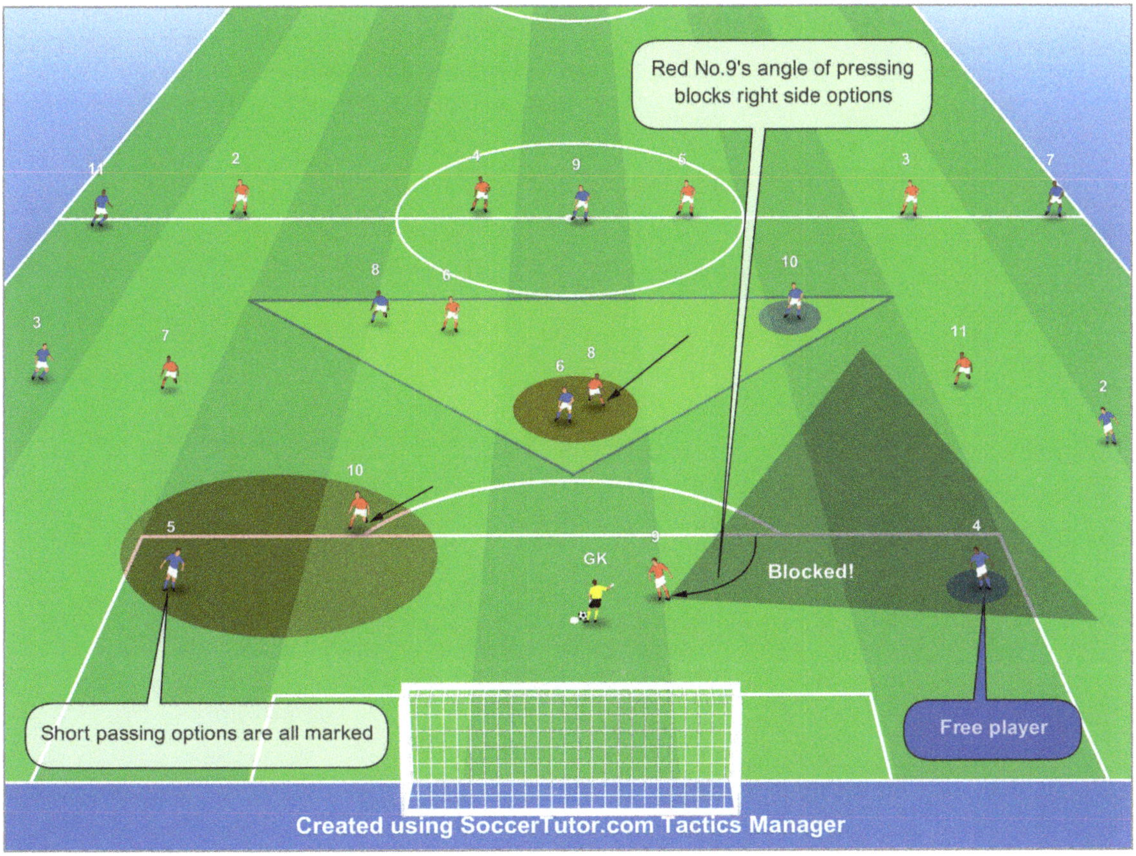

When playing against ultra-aggressive pressing with zonal defending and man marking, **as soon as the opposing forward (N°9 in diagram) decides to press the goalkeeper (GK), a red central midfielder (N°8) must move forward to mark the defensive midfielder (N°6).**

The other red forward (N°10) reduces his distance to the blue centre back (N°5), so that he is able to put him under pressure immediately if he receives.

Red N°9 presses in a way that blocks a direct pass to his direct opponent (blue centre back N°4).

All potential receivers of a short pass are either marked or passing lanes towards them are blocked.

However, in this situation there are **2 free players**:

1. **Centre back (N°5)** who is in the shadow of red N°9's pressing.
2. **Attacking midfielder (N°10)**, who stays completely free of marking after the forward movement of red N°8.

BEAT THE PRESS WITH SINGLE & DOUBLE PIVOTS

Build Up: Against Ultra-Aggressive Pressing with Zonal Defending and Man Marking

3. Using the Link Player Closest to the Ball to Move the Ball to the Free Player (4-3-3)

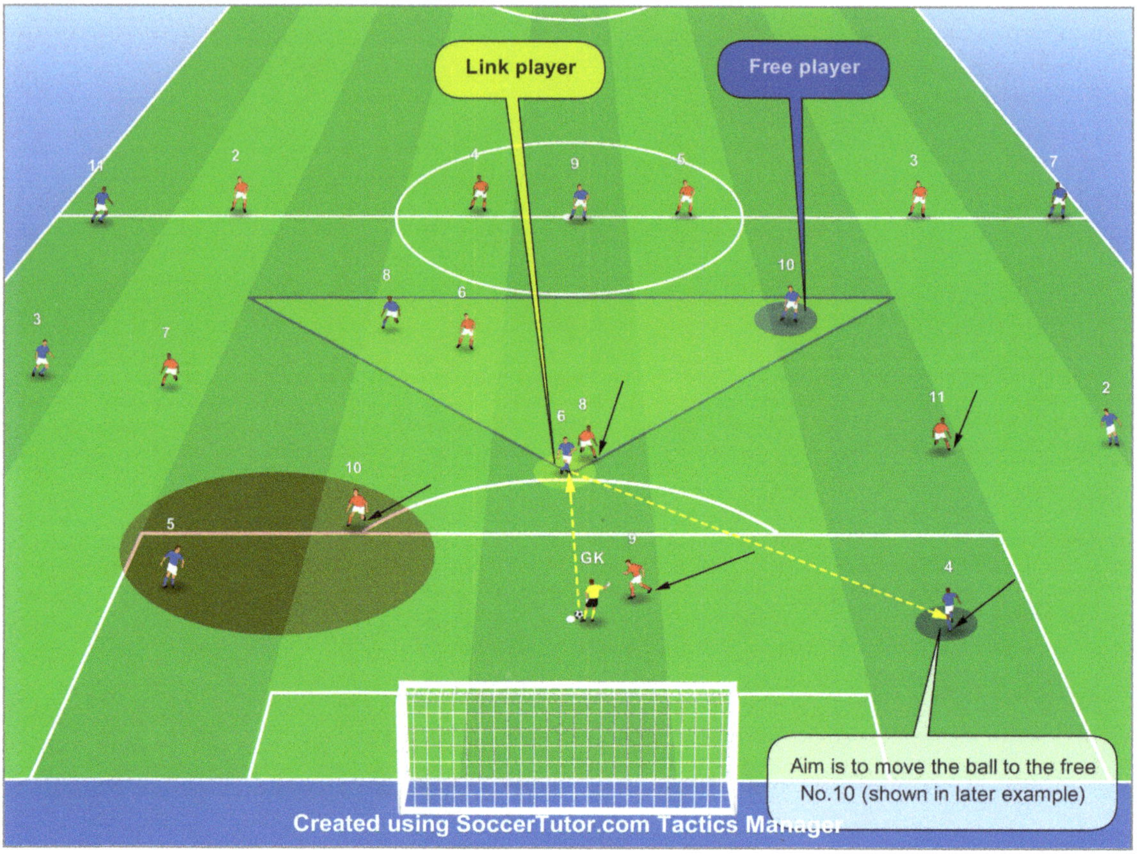

Principles to apply or actions to take in order to build up effectively are:

1. Use the link players near the ball carrier to move the ball to the free defender.
2. Move the ball to the free midfielder (directly or indirectly via a link player).

In the diagram example, the blue team manage to apply the first principle successfully.

The goalkeeper (GK) passes to the closest available link player - the defensive midfielder (N°6) who is in a good position to direct the ball to the closest free player - the **centre back (N°4)**.

From there, the aim is to move the ball to the **advanced free player in between the lines - the attacking midfielder (N°10)**.

If **N°4** carries the ball forward, a numerical advantage on that side can be quickly exploited to make this a fairly easy option.

Build Up: Against Ultra-Aggressive Pressing with Zonal Defending and Man Marking

4. Potential Link Player Positioning and Scanning to Support the Free Defender Before Pressure is Applied (4-3-3)

Key principles link players follow to be effective:

1. Stay high enough to form an effective passing angle.
2. Constantly scan for teammates and opposing players' positions, especially in the area likely to be used after the goalkeeper (GK) is pressed.

Before pressure is applied to the goalkeeper (GK), the defensive midfielder (N°6) must scan the space around him and the positioning of players in the highlighted yellow area.

Once a red player presses **GK**, it becomes clear which defender is free and will act as the target player (**N°4** in diagram example).

N°6's focus then shifts to the red winger N°11, who is the opponent most likely to intervene and intercept a pass, making it essential for **N°6** to be aware of this while being ready to offer support to **GK**.

BEAT THE PRESS WITH SINGLE & DOUBLE PIVOTS

Build Up: Against Ultra-Aggressive Pressing with Zonal Defending and Man Marking

5a. Timing of Link Player's Movement Creates a Narrow Passing Angle to Prevent Interceptions (4-3-3)

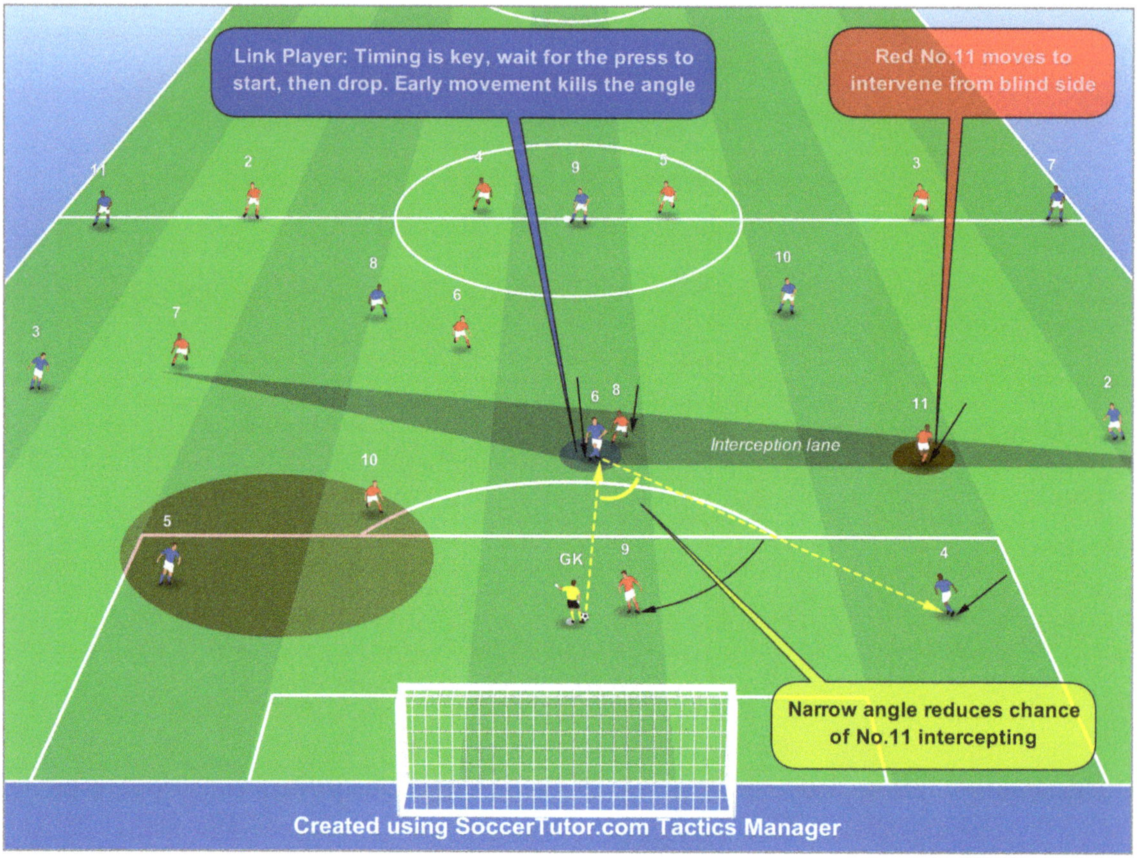

Following on from the 2 principles outlined on the previous page, the link player must also apply a third principle:

3. **Offer support at the right moment (not too early)**, otherwise the passing angle becomes ineffective.

To do this, the **potential link player should start from a relatively high position**. As the red N°9 moves to press the goalkeeper, the **defensive midfielder (N°6) should drop back to support**.

Both of these actions must be perfectly synchronised. The correct timing is key to creating an effective passing angle.

In the diagram example, **N°6 moves in sync with the red forward N°9 pressing the goalkeeper (GK)**. This allows **N°6** to stay high and then drop to receive with enough space, resulting in a **narrow diagonal passing angle**.

Importance of Narrow Passing Angle: The nearest opponent (red N°11), arriving from the blind side, is kept far enough from the passing line to the target player (centre back - N°4), lowering the risk of interception. Red N°11 may be seen during N°6's scanning, but by the time the pass is made, he is usually out of the link player's view.

©SOCCERTUTOR.COM

BEAT THE PRESS WITH SINGLE & DOUBLE PIVOTS

Build Up: Against Ultra-Aggressive Pressing with Zonal Defending and Man Marking

5b (Variation). Early or Deep Movement by the Link Player Creates a Wide Passing Angle that Increases Risk (4-3-3)

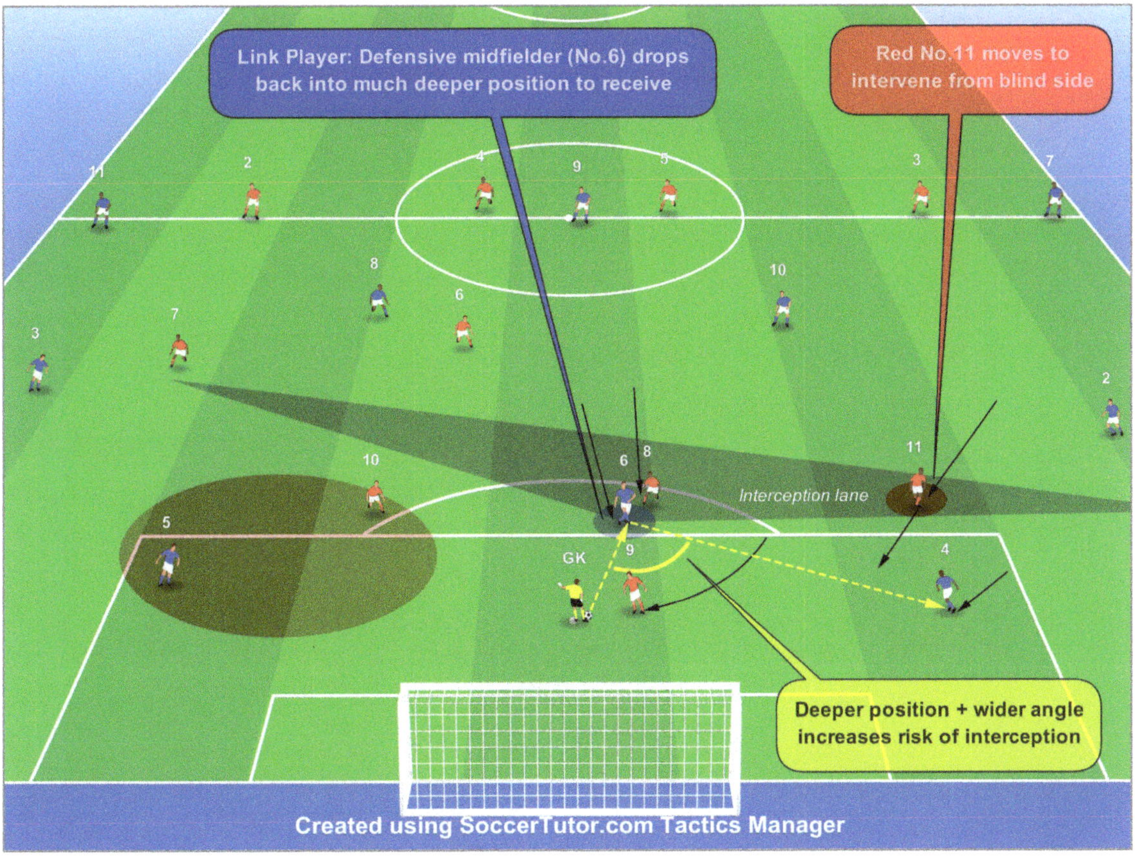

If the link player starts too deep or drops too early, he receives the pass from the goalkeeper (GK) in a deep position, which flattens the angle of the pass and makes it easier to predict and intercept. A deep link player position leads to a more horizontal or wide passing line.

In the example shown in the diagram, **the red winger (N°11), who arrives from the blind side, is positioned much closer to the passing line**. This positioning significantly increases the chances of intercepting the ball when the **defensive midfielder (N°6)** attempts to play a pass to the free **centre back (N°4)**.

Note: To create a sharper, more effective passing angle, the link player must start higher and move at the correct time.

BEAT THE PRESS WITH SINGLE & DOUBLE PIVOTS

6. Free Defender Must Act Quickly to Exploit Available Space or 3v1 Situation Near the Ball (4-3-3)

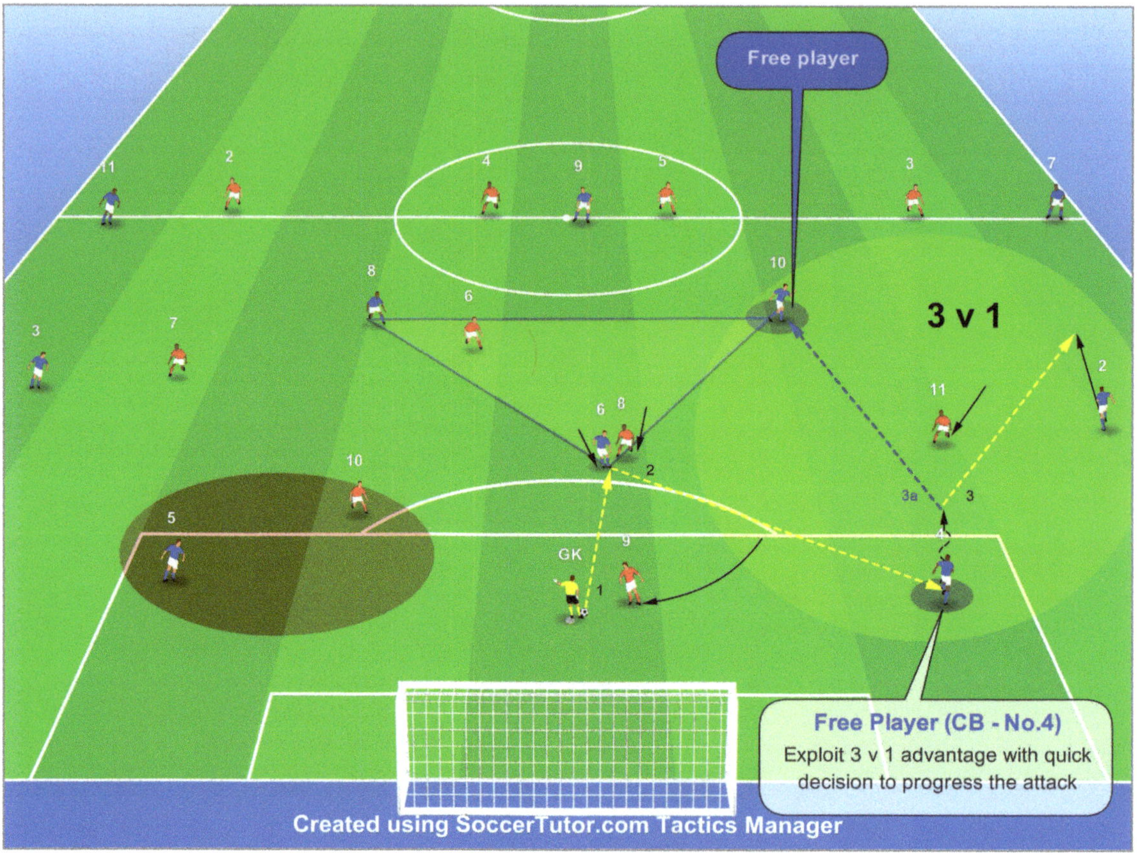

Note: As soon as the pass is directed to the free player via the link player, the receiver will find available space, a numerical advantage, or both - if he acts quickly.

In the diagram example, the blue **centre back (N°4)** receives from the **defensive midfielder (N°6)** and has space in front of him, while a **3v1 situation forms near the ball area**.

The next action depends on how red N°11 reacts. For example, if red N°10 presses **N°4** in a way that blocks the passing lane to the **attacking midfielder (N°10)**, then the pass to the **full back (N°2** - yellow arrow) becomes available.

If red N°11 blocks the pass to blue **N°2**, then **N°10** becomes the clear passing option (blue arrow).

If red N°11 drops deeper to try and avoid being bypassed, **N°4** will have more room to drive forward with the ball.

The key to exploiting this situation is the speed of action by N°4. If there is a delay, the red central midfielder N°8 will have time to shift across and narrow the passing lane to blue **N°10**, allowing red N°11 to focus solely on controlling blue **N°2**, and reducing the original numerical advantage.

Build Up: Against Ultra-Aggressive Pressing with Zonal Defending and Man Marking

7. Potential Options to Move the Ball Directly to the Free Attacking Midfielder when the Goalkeeper is Pressed (4-3-3)

Here we show an alternative and more direct option of moving the ball to the free attacking midfielder.

As the red central midfielder (Nº8) shifts closer to the defensive midfielder (Nº6), more space opens up for the attacking midfielder (Nº10) in between the lines and he is left completely unmarked.

If the **goalkeeper (GK)** recognises this and has the time and space to pass directly to **Nº10** (blue arrow), it is the best option, as it neutralises 6 red players immediately.

However, if **GK** is under heavy pressure from the red forward (Nº9) and is unable to see the free teammate or find a passing lane, he can instead play a long straight pass towards the **forward (Nº9)**, who acts as a link player to set the ball back for **Nº10** (yellow arrows).

Build Up Against Ultra-Aggressive Pressing with Zonal Defending and Man Marking (Double Pivot)

1. Opposition Positioning Adjustments to Apply Marking Against a 4-2-3-1 Build Up Shape

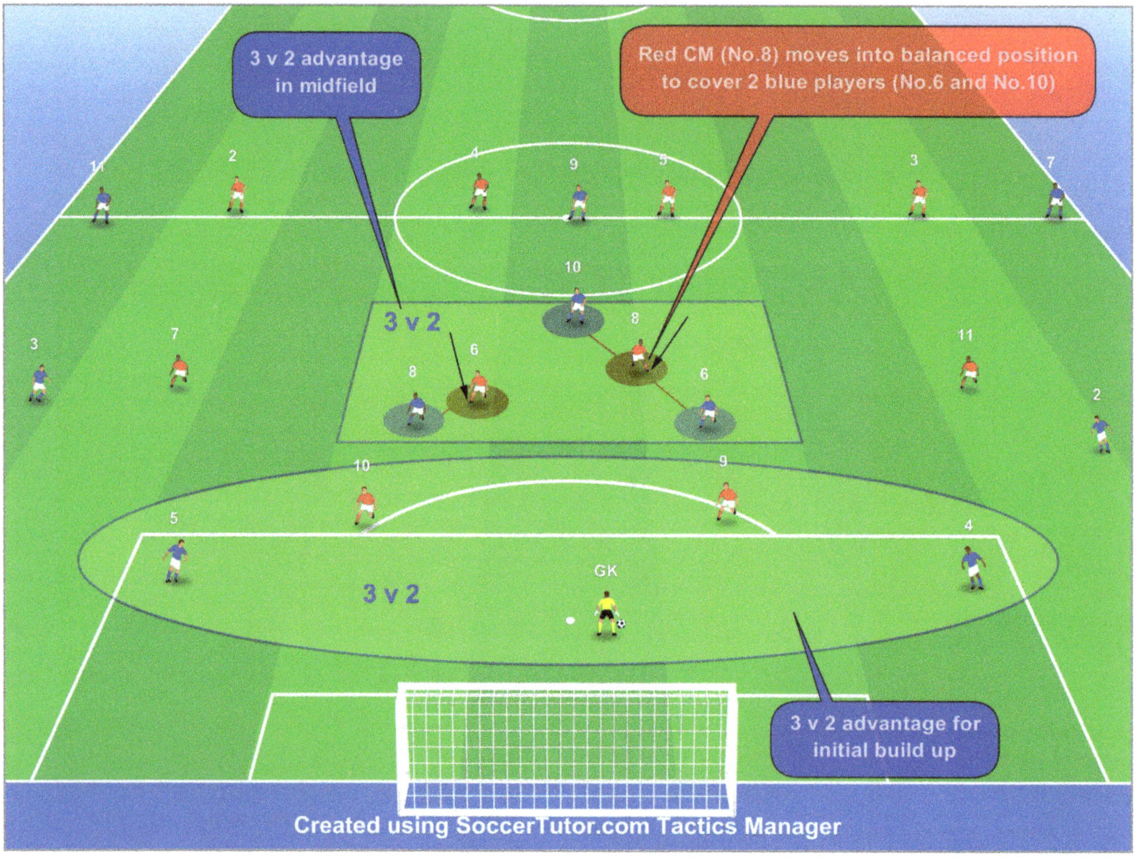

This diagram reflects the second principle outlined on page 125: **The opposition set up to control all the receivers of a potential short pass from the goalkeeper**.

Red central midfielder N°6 marks the **left defensive midfielder (N°8)**.

Red N°8 is positioned between **right defensive midfielder (N°6)** and **attacking midfielder (N°10)** to control both players.

This is because a 3v2 disadvantage exists in the key central midfield area for the reds, so a midfielder must cover 2 opponents.

Note: Red N°8 must be close enough to press N°6 if he receives, while limiting potential passing lanes towards N°10.

Build Up: Against Ultra-Aggressive Pressing with Zonal Defending and Man Marking

2. Opposition Press the Goalkeeper and Ensure All Nearby Passing Options are Marked (4-2-3-1)

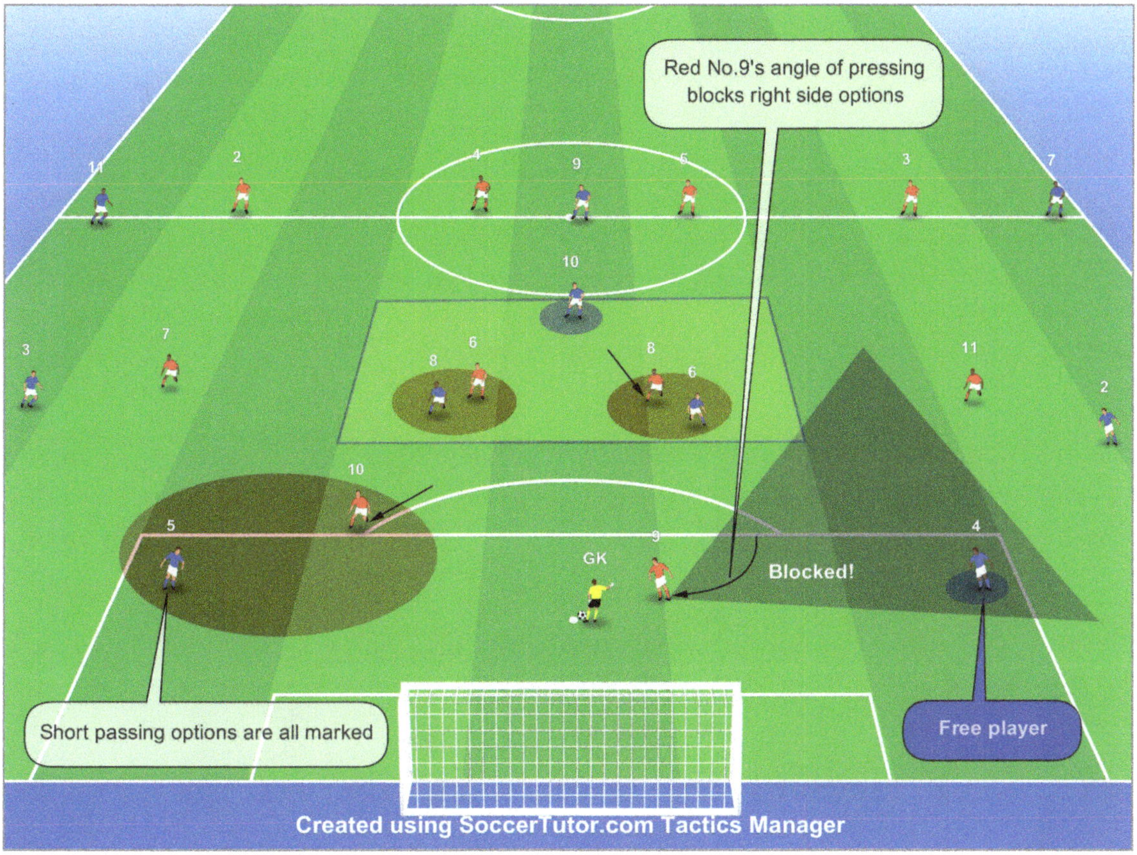

When playing against ultra-aggressive pressing with zonal defending and man marking, **as soon as the opposing forward (Nº9 in diagram) decides to press the goalkeeper (GK), a red central midfielder (Nº8) must move forward to mark the defensive midfielder (Nº6)**.

The other red forward (Nº10) reduces his distance to the blue centre back (Nº5), so that he is able to put him under pressure immediately if he receives.

Red Nº9 presses in a way that blocks a direct pass to his direct opponent (blue centre back Nº4).

All potential receivers of a short pass are either marked or passing lanes towards them are blocked.

However, in this situation there are **2 free players**:

1. **Centre back (Nº4)** who is in the shadow of red Nº9's pressing.

2. **Attacking midfielder (Nº10)**, who after the forward movement of red No8 stays completely free of marking and is in a dangerous position to receive between the lines.

BEAT THE PRESS WITH SINGLE & DOUBLE PIVOTS

Build Up: Against Ultra-Aggressive Pressing with Zonal Defending and Man Marking

3. Using the Link Players Closest to the Goalkeeper to Move the Ball to the Free Centre Back (4-2-3-1)

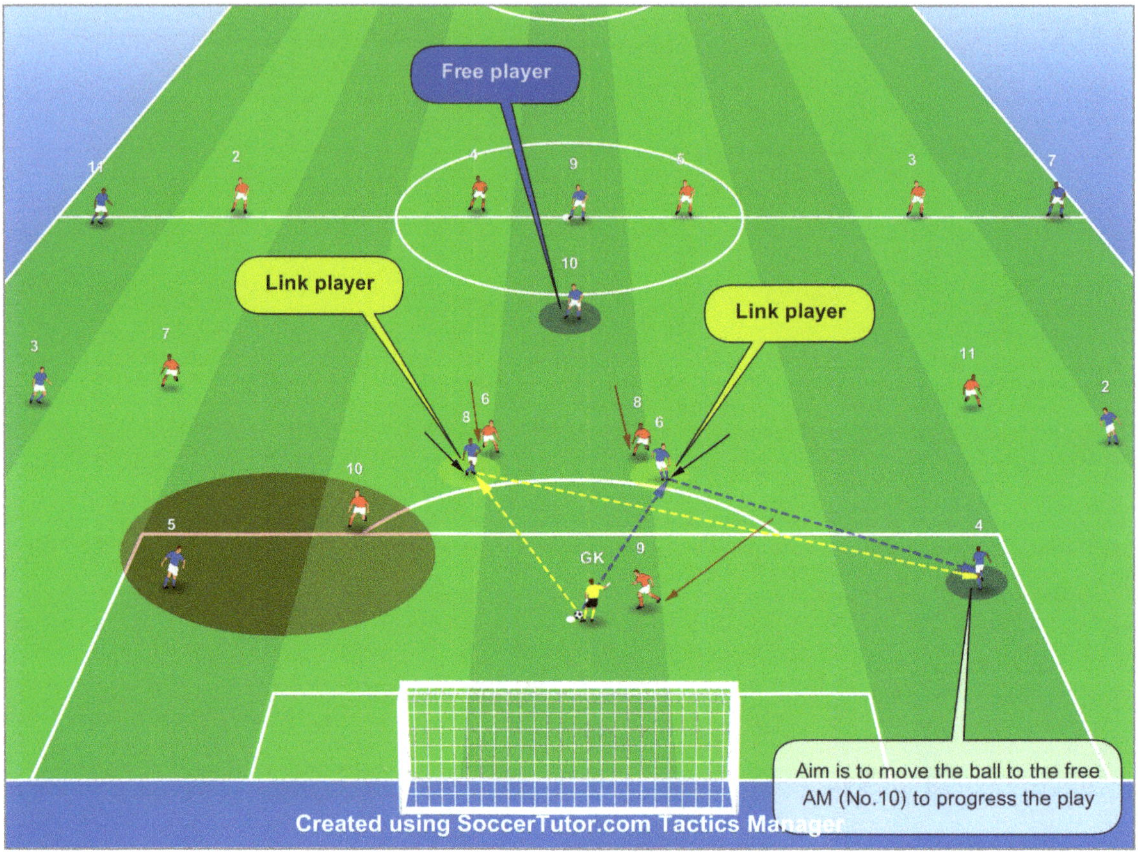

The key principle to achieving effective build up play in this situation is to **use link players near the goalkeeper (GK) to move the ball to the free centre back (N°4)**, who red N°9 has blocked the direct pass to.

A key advantage of a double pivot midfield over a single pivot is the presence of 2 potential link players near the ball (N°6 and N°8 - 2 defensive midfielders), both capable of directing play to **N°4**.

Once **N°4** receives, he will likely find space ahead and a **potential 2v1 advantage on that side** with the **full back (N°2)** against the red winger (N°11).

Note 1: It is essential that N°6 and N°8 apply the link player principles effectively, as detailed on page 129.

Note 2: Between the 2 options, N°6 is the better link player for this action because his potential pass to N°4 is shorter (blue arrows), giving the red winger N°11 less time to try and intercept the ball.

©SOCCERTUTOR.COM

BEAT THE PRESS WITH SINGLE & DOUBLE PIVOTS

Build Up: Against Ultra-Aggressive Pressing with Zonal Defending and Man Marking

4. Potential Options to Move the Ball Directly to the Free Attacking Midfielder when the Goalkeeper is Pressed (4-2-3-1)

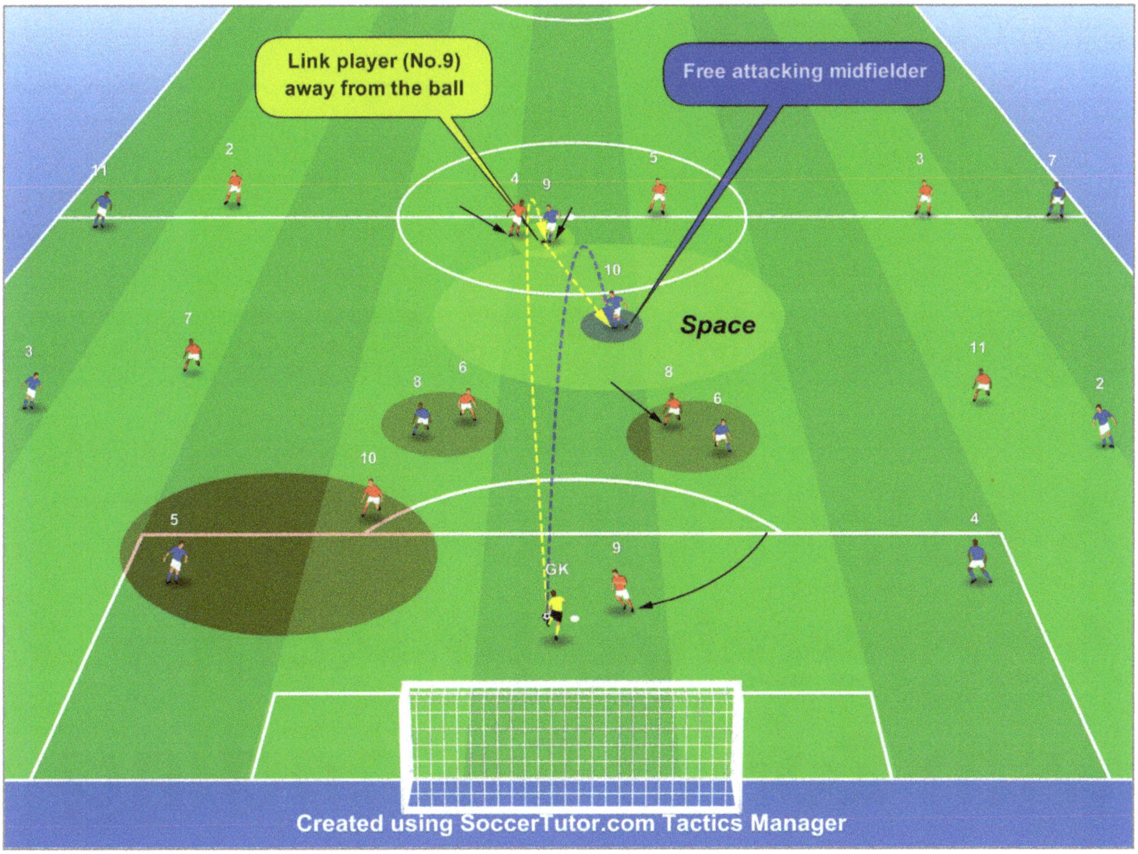

As explained previously, as the **red central midfielder (N°8) steps forward to mark the blue defensive midfielder (N°6)**, extra space is created between the lines.

The attacking midfielder (N°10) becomes the second unmarked player alongside the centre back (N°4).

This positional shift opens a valuable opportunity for the team to exploit centrally, especially if **N°10** has already adjusted his position to stay away from nearby markers. **N°10 is the key target player**, as he is positioned in the most dangerous zone, between the opposition's midfield and defensive lines.

This situation can be capitalised on with a direct pass from the **goalkeeper (GK)** to **N°10** (blue arrow), assuming the **GK** has enough time and space to scan the pitch and execute the pass accurately.

If direct access is blocked or the **GK** is under too much pressure, the ball can instead be played to the **forward (N°9)**, who then acts as a link player to set the ball back for **N°10** (yellow arrows). This indirect route still breaks lines and maintains momentum through the central channel.

©SOCCERTUTOR.COM BEAT THE PRESS WITH SINGLE & DOUBLE PIVOTS

BUILD UP TO BEAT THE PRESS

Training Session 7 (5 Practices)

Against Ultra-Aggressive Pressing with Zonal Defending and Man Marking

Based on Flick, Klopp, and Emery build up patterns

Training Session 7: Build Up to Beat the Press Against Ultra-Aggressive Pressing

TRAINING SESSION (5 PRACTICES)

1. Functional Build Up Patterns vs Ultra-Aggressive Pressing to Play Through or Over

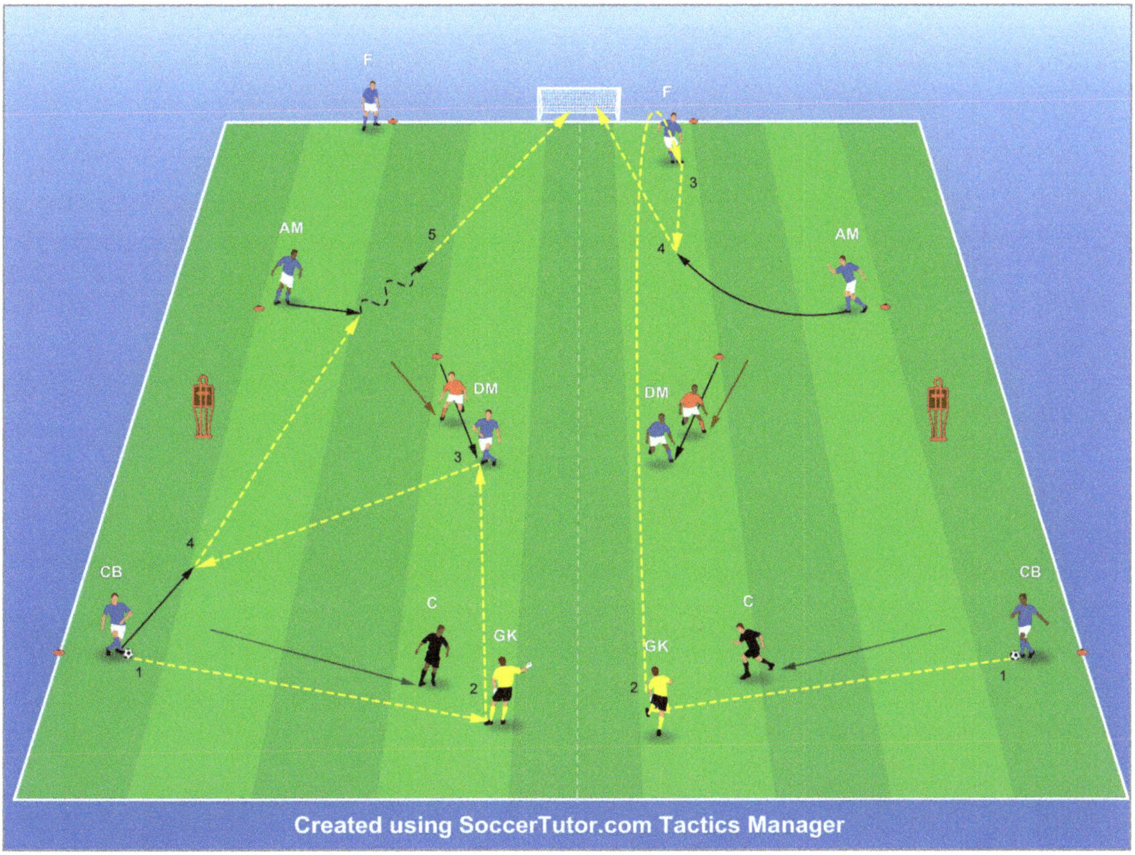

Practice Description

- Play on both sides simultaneously. The **centre back** (**CB**) passes to the **GK**, who is immediately pressed by the coach.
- The GK has 2 options to be effective.
- **Option 1 (Left Side):** Use the **defensive midfielder** (**DM**) as a link player to move the ball to the free **CB**.
- **CB** must quickly pass to the **attacking midfielder** (**AM**) before the red player can move across to block the passing lane. **AM** receives and scores.

- **Option 2 (Right Side):** Long aerial pass to the **forward** (**F**), who lays the ball off to the **AM**, who has moved inside to receive and score.
- **Note:** There can be 2 players in each position who switch after each repetition to speed up the practice.

Coaching Points

1. Synchronised, well-timed runs.
2. Offer support at the right moment.
3. Quick combination play.

BEAT THE PRESS WITH SINGLE & DOUBLE PIVOTS

Training Session 7: Build Up to Beat the Press Against Ultra-Aggressive Pressing

PROGRESSION
2. Build Up Patterns with Link Player Principles vs Ultra-Aggressive Pressing and Man Marking

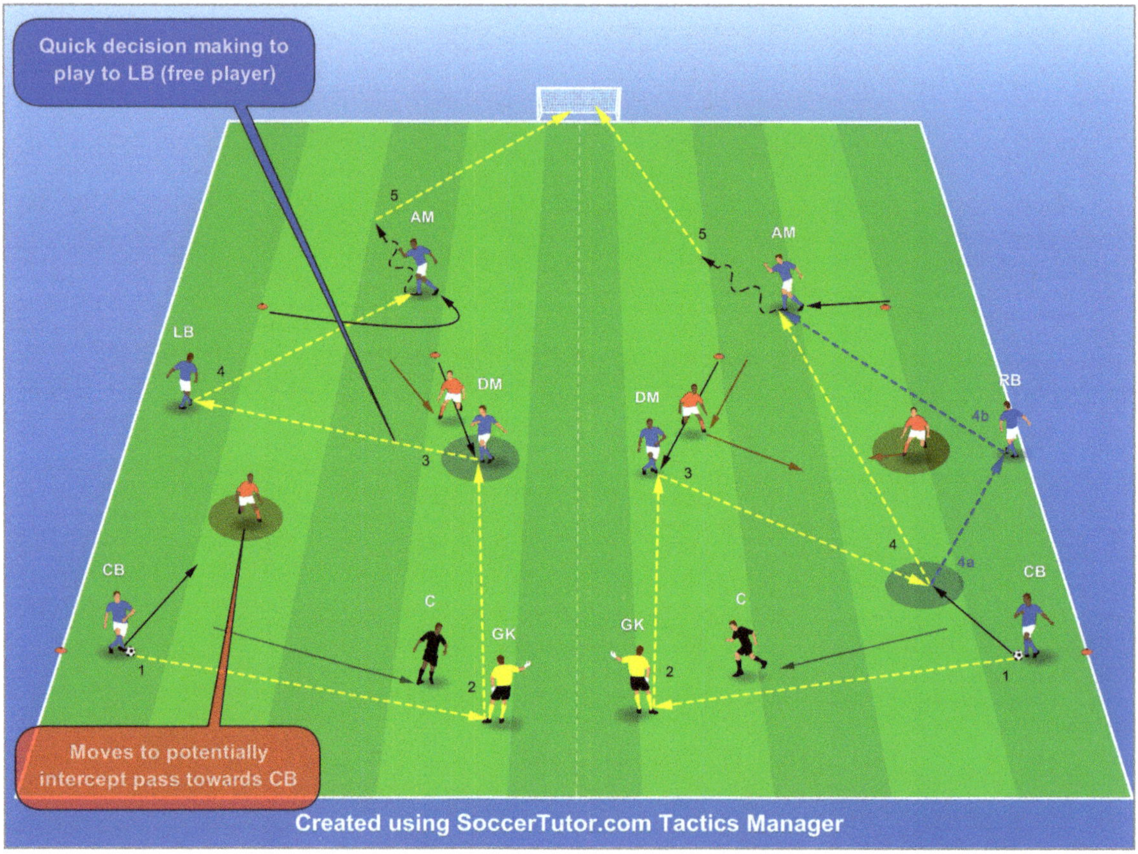

Practice Description

- Progressing from the previous practice, 2 blue full backs (in place of 2 forwards) and 2 red wide players are added. The focus is on link player principles - **see analysis pages in this section for full details and explanation**.

- The link player should be aware of their positioning to make the right decisions and direct the ball to the correct player.

- **Option 1 (Left Side):** The red wide player is advanced, so **DM** passes to the **full back** (**LB**), who is in space to receive.

- The next pass is to the **AM**, who receives, turns, and scores.

- **Option 2 (Right Side):** The red wide player is deeper, so **DM** passes back to the free centre back (**CB**).

- **CB** passes directly to **AM** (yellow arrow) or via the **link player** (**RB** - blue arrows) depending on the positioning of the red wide player and the width of the available passing lane.

BEAT THE PRESS WITH SINGLE & DOUBLE PIVOTS

Training Session 7: Build Up to Beat the Press Against Ultra-Aggressive Pressing

PROGRESSION

3. Using the Link Player to Move the Ball to the Free Player 8 v 8 (+GKs) Conditioned Game

Variation 1: Find the Free Player through Deep Link Player (DM)

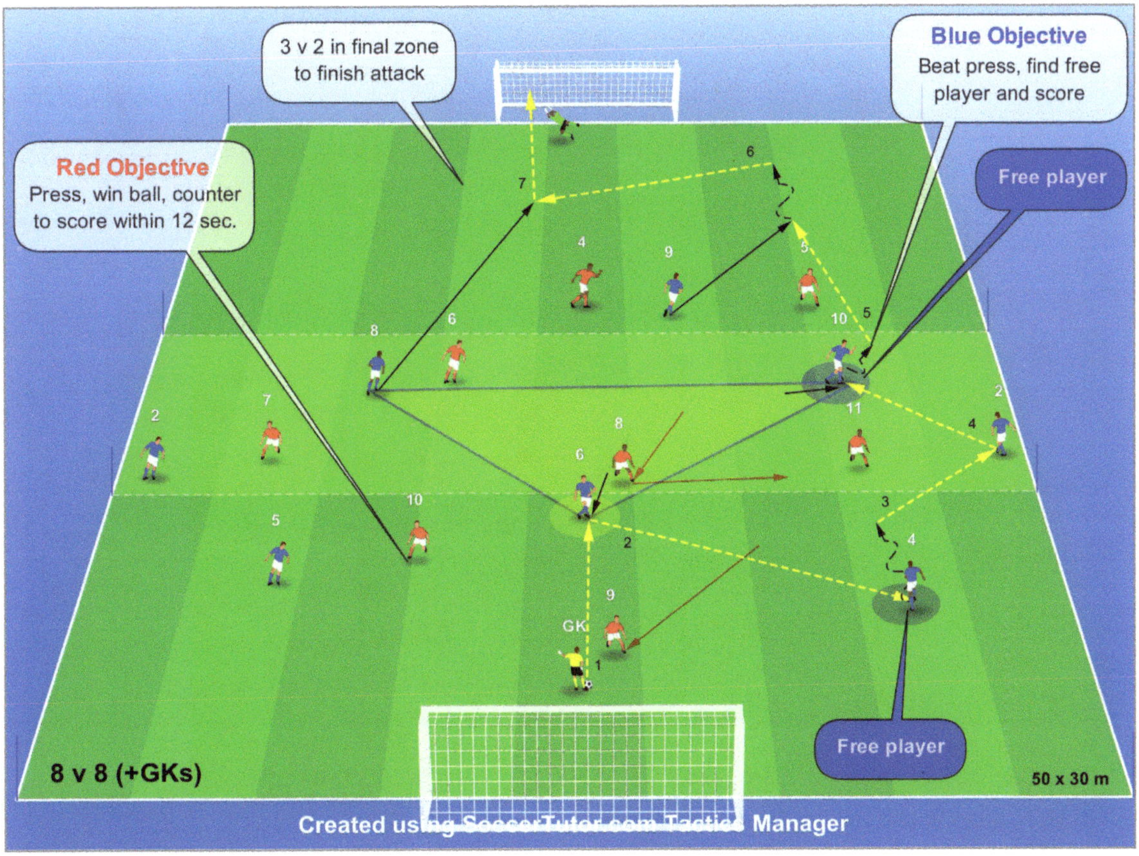

Practice Description (Variation 1)

- The blue attacking team have 2 centre backs, 2 full backs, 3 central midfielders, and 1 forward (**4-3-1 from 4-3-3**).
- The red defending team have 2 centre backs, their midfield 4, and 2 forwards from the 4-4-2.
- The pitch is split into 3 zones. The low zone starts with an initial 2 (+GK) v 2 situation. The middle zone starts with 5v4 and the high zone is 1v2.

- **Red Objective:** Apply ultra-aggressive pressing to win the ball and counter to score within 8-12 seconds.
- **Blue Objective:** Build up through thirds and score (find free player with direct pass or via link player using **link player principles** - *see page 129*).
- **The Variation 1 diagram shows the DM (N°6) as the link player**. Once **N°10** (**free player**) receives, it can be 3v2 or 3v3 to finish the attack. Restart from blue **GK**.

BEAT THE PRESS WITH SINGLE & DOUBLE PIVOTS

Training Session 7: Build Up to Beat the Press Against Ultra-Aggressive Pressing

Variation 2: Defensive Midfielder Plays Direct to Full Back as Opposing Winger Steps Forward to Intercept

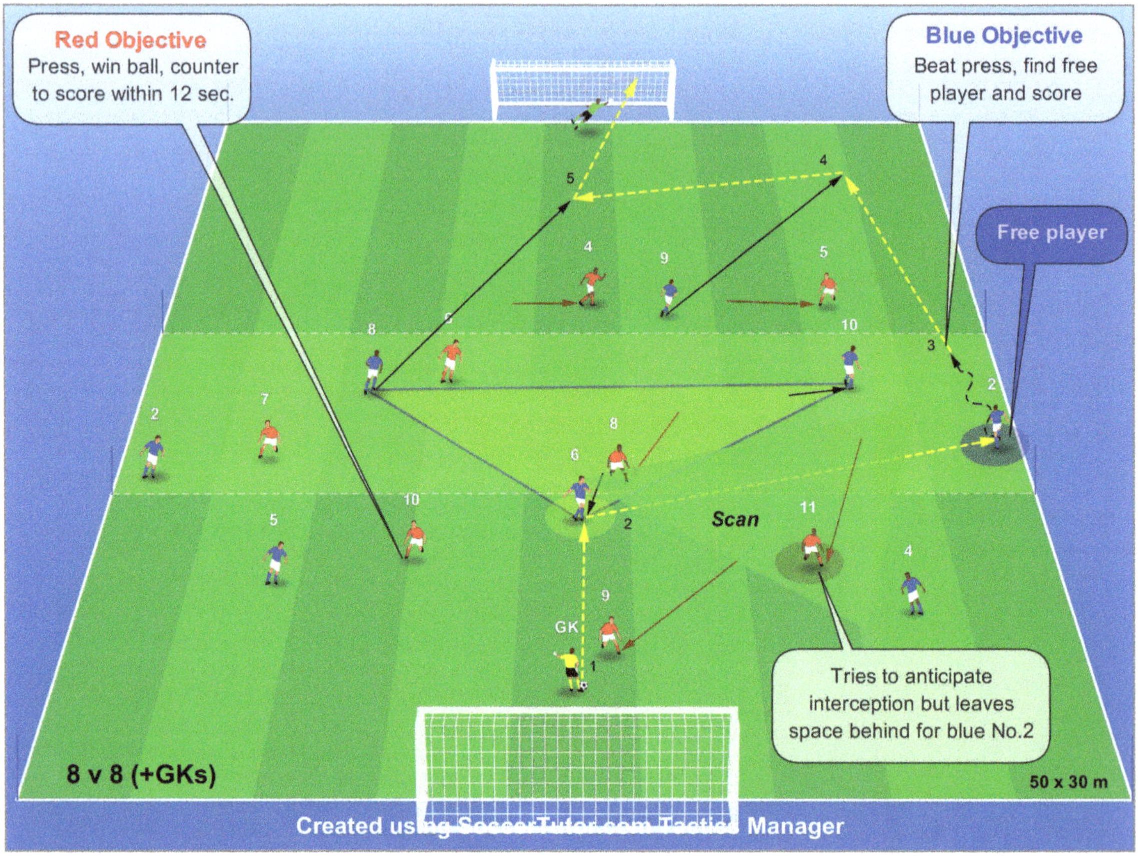

Red Objective
Press, win ball, counter to score within 12 sec.

Blue Objective
Beat press, find free player and score

Free player

Scan

Tries to anticipate interception but leaves space behind for blue No.2

8 v 8 (+GKs)

50 x 30 m

Practice Description (Variation 2)

- In **Variation 2**, the defensive midfielder (**N°6**) scans and sees the opposing winger (red N°11) in an advanced position anticipating an opportunity to intercept a pass towards the centre back (**N°4**).

- Instead of playing to **N°4**, **N°6** plays an intelligent pass directly to the **full back (N°2)**, who is in available space because the opposing winger (red N°11) has moved forward and out of a good defensive position.

- The blues then aim to play into the end zone and score.

- If the red defending team win the ball, they again look to counter quickly.

BEAT THE PRESS WITH SINGLE & DOUBLE PIVOTS

Training Session 7: Build Up to Beat the Press Against Ultra-Aggressive Pressing

Variation 3: Find the Free Player through Advanced Link Player (Forward)

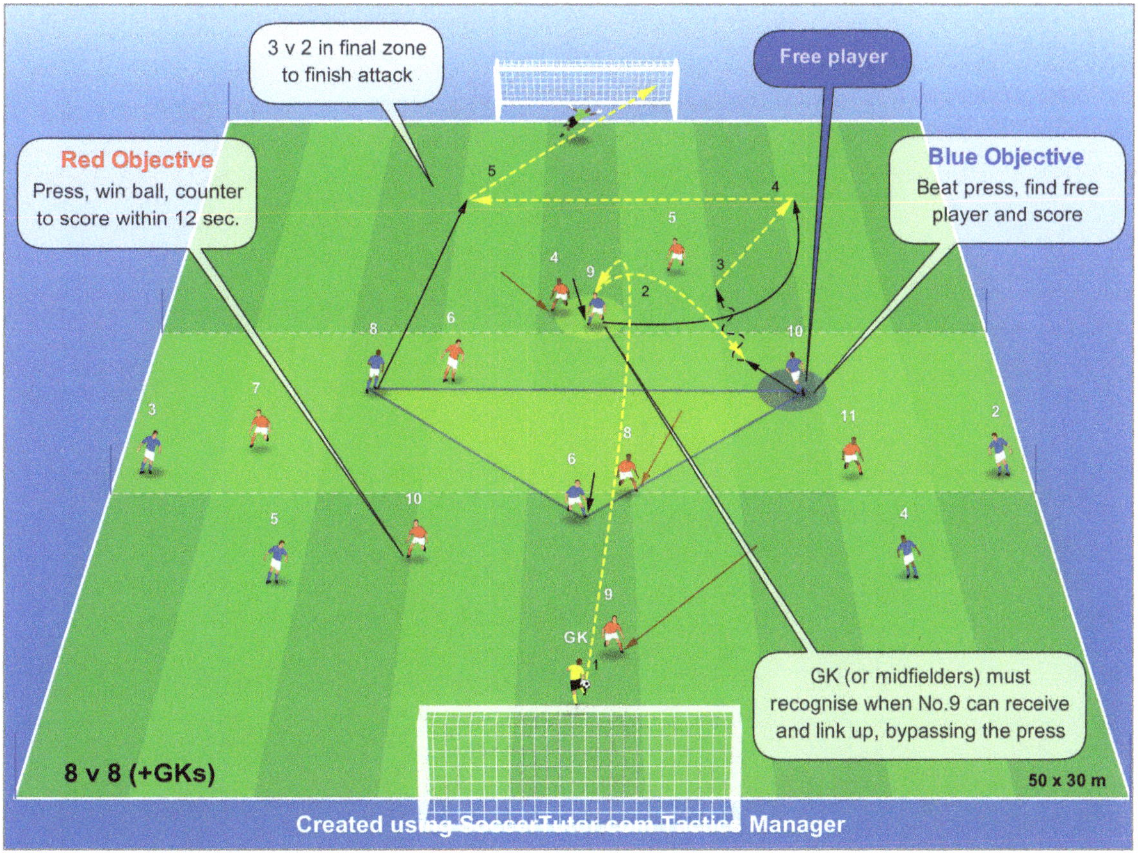

Practice Description (Variation 3)

- In **Variation 3**, the blues move the ball to the free player (**attacking midfielder - N°10**) using the forward (N°9) as the link player instead of the defensive midfielder (N°6).

- **The goalkeeper (GK) or midfielders must recognise when N°9 is positioned effectively to receive and link play**, allowing the ball to bypass the midfield pressure.

- If the pass successfully reaches **N°9**, the blues create a 3v2 or 3v3 attack in the high zone to try and score. If the red defending team wins the ball, they again look to counter quickly.

- **Restrictions:** All midfielders start inside the middle zone but can move freely after play begins. Red centre backs cannot enter the middle zone unless a blue player receives inside it.

- **Note:** *This game can be easily adapted to a double pivot (4-2-3-1) formation.*

Coaching Points

1. *Apply the link player principles (see page 129 for more full explanation).*
2. Synchronised movements.
3. Accurate and quick passing.
4. Read the situation (decision making).
5. High speed of play.

BEAT THE PRESS WITH SINGLE & DOUBLE PIVOTS

Training Session 7: Build Up to Beat the Press Against Ultra-Aggressive Pressing

PROGRESSION

4. Finding Free Player Against Ultra-Aggressive Pressing Half Pitch Game

Variation 1: Find the Free Player through Deep Link Player (DM)

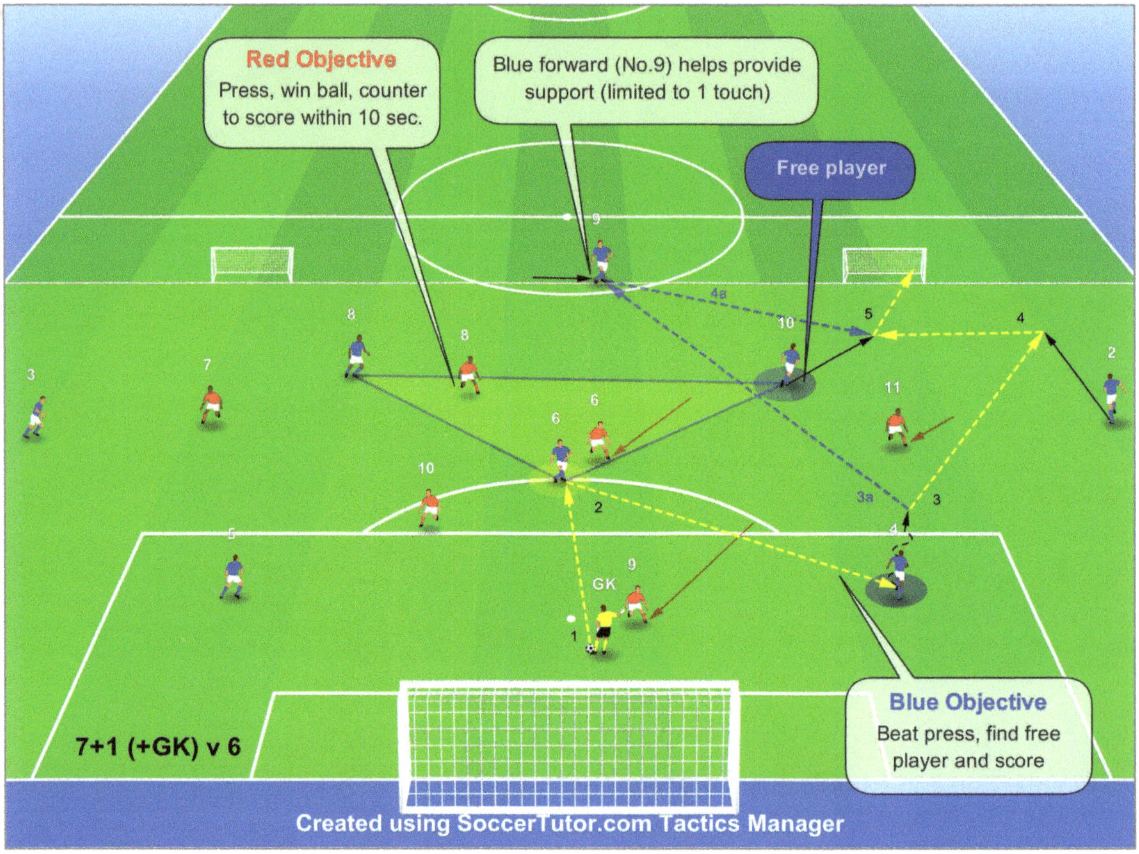

Practice Description (Variation 1)

- **Blue Objective:** Progress ball from the **GK** and score. *See previous practices + analysis pages for solutions.* The diagram shows an example with the **defensive midfielder (N°6)** is the link player. They have a **numerical advantage of 9v6 including the goalkeeper (GK) and outside forward (N°9)**.

- **Red Objective:** Apply ultra-aggressive pressing and force blues to find the free player with a direct pass or via a link player. Win the ball and counter to score within 8-10 seconds.

Restrictions

1. A red player must press **GK** immediately.
2. The blue **forward (N°9)** can help provide support but is limited to playing 1 touch passes back into the area.
3. If the ball goes out of play, the coach restarts with a pass to the red team.

Training Session 7: Build Up to Beat the Press Against Ultra-Aggressive Pressing

Variation 2: Find the Free Player through Advanced Link Player (Forward)

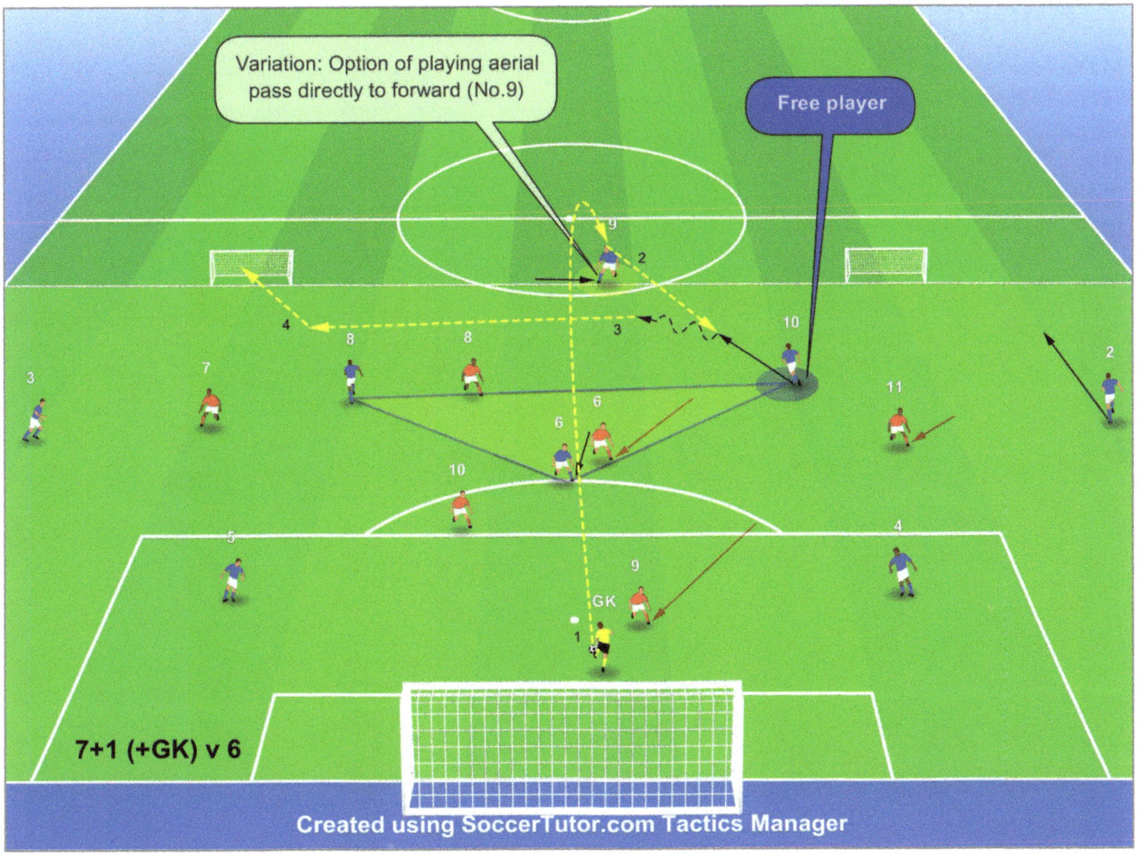

[Diagram: 7+1 (+GK) v 6. Variation: Option of playing aerial pass directly to forward (No.9). Free player indicated.]

Practice Description (Variation 2)

- In **Variation 2**, the blues move the ball to the free player (**attacking midfielder - Nº10**) using the forward (**Nº9**) as the link player instead of the defensive midfielder (**Nº6**).

- **The goalkeeper (GK) or midfielders must recognise when Nº9 is positioned effectively to receive and link play,** allowing the ball to bypass the midfield pressure.

- **Restrictions:** The same rules and restrictions apply, ensuring tactical continuity while allowing the players to experience a key variation to the build up structure.

- **Note 1:** The link players have to apply the appropriate **link player principles** to avoid mistakes (see page 129).

- **Note 2:** *This game can be easily adapted to a double pivot (4-2-3-1) formation.*

BEAT THE PRESS WITH SINGLE & DOUBLE PIVOTS

Training Session 7: Build Up to Beat the Press Against Ultra-Aggressive Pressing

PROGRESSION

5. Finding the Free Player Against Ultra-Aggressive Pressing 11v11 Game

Practice Description

- We play an 11v11 game with the reds applying ultra-aggressive high pressing (up to goalkeeper) with man marking.

- **Note:** See previous practices (+ analysis pages) for build up solutions/principles.

- **Blue Objective:** Build up play and score (1 goal). If they successfully find the free player with a direct pass or via a link player before scoring = 2 goals.

- **Red Objective:** Ultra-aggressive press to win the ball, counter, and score.

- Play always restarts with the blue **GK**. Team roles are reversed after a set time.

Coaching Points

1. **Synchronised off-the-ball movements** to maintain structure and passing options.
2. **Decision making under pressure** - when to use link player or direct option.
3. **The link player principles should be applied** (*see page 129*).

Note: *This game can be easily adapted to a single pivot (4-3-3) formation.*

BUILD UP TO BEAT THE PRESS

Tactical Analysis

Exploit Space Out Wide to Bypass Midfield Marking

Build up play patterns from Flick, Klopp, and Emery's teams

Build Up to Exploit Space Out Wide and Bypass Midfield Marking (Single Pivot)

1. Opposition's Man Marking Across the Pitch Against a 4-3-3 Build Up Shape

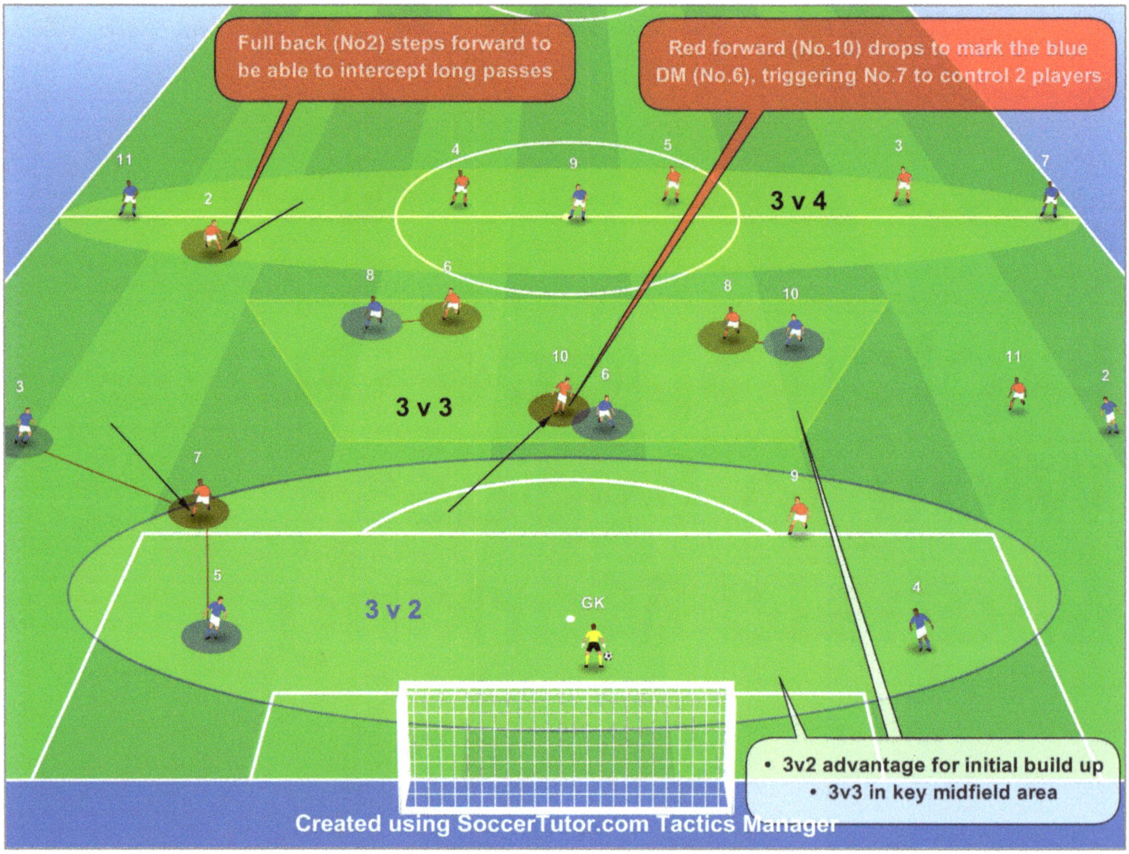

Full back (No2) steps forward to be able to intercept long passes

Red forward (No.10) drops to mark the blue DM (No.6), triggering No.7 to control 2 players

- 3v2 advantage for initial build up
- 3v3 in key midfield area

Here we analyse the opposition's (reds) tactics when pressing with man marking while keeping a numerical advantage at the back, such as a 4v3 (as shown in the diagram).

The blue team has a 7 (+GK) v 6 advantage in the rest of the pitch, so the red team use 5 direct markers while 1 player (N°7) covers 2 opponents. This helps them avoid leaving any player completely free.

In this setup, **red N°10 drops into midfield to mark blue N°6, prompting red N°7 to push forward between blue N°3 and N°5.**

Red N°2 steps up slightly to be ready to intercept aerial passes towards blue N°3.

This defensive structure keeps midfield coverage tight for the reds, secures their right flank, and allows them to press both blue centre backs.

Build Up to Beat the Press: Exploit Space Out Wide to Bypass Midfield Marking

2. Effective Positioning of Wide Players to Maximise the Available Space to Play Out from the Back (4-3-3)

CB (No.5) drops deeper to create larger distances between wide teammates → *More difficult for red No.2 and No.7 to control 3 blue opponents*

The first principle the (blue) build up team must apply to disrupt the reds is effective positioning of the wide players, especially on the weak side, where red Nº7 is responsible for 2 opponents. The blue players on this side begin by increasing their distances between each other.

Since the **winger (Nº11)** is unable to move further forward without being offside, the **centre back (Nº5) must drop deeper to lengthen the distance**.

At the same time, all 3 blue players on the left should **make sure they are equally spaced**.

These movements make it more difficult for red Nº2 and Nº7 to control 3 players on their side.

BEAT THE PRESS WITH SINGLE & DOUBLE PIVOTS

Build Up to Beat the Press: Exploit Space Out Wide to Bypass Midfield Marking

3a (Variation 1). Full Back Receives Unmarked Directly from the Goalkeeper in Between the Lines (4-3-3)

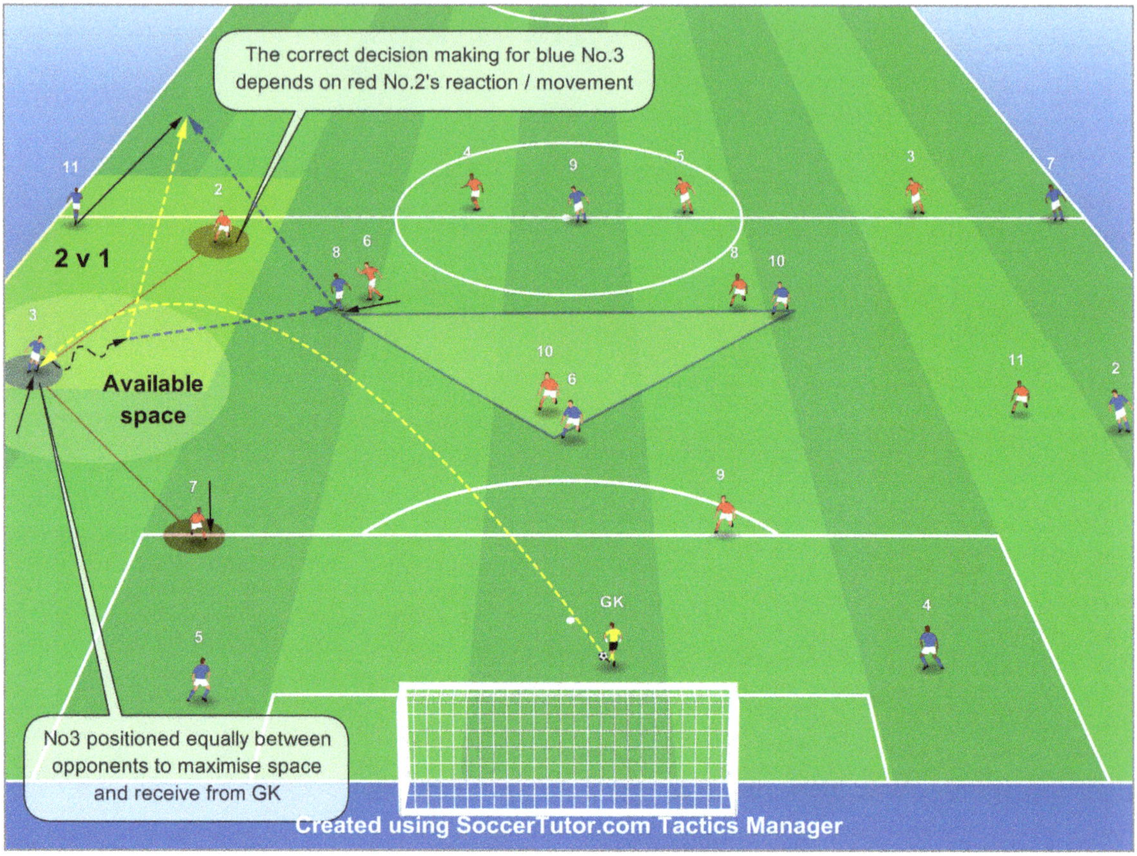

Once effective positioning is achieved, the next step for the blue players on the left (especially the **full back - N°3**) is to read the positioning of red N°2 and N°7.

In this example, the **red winger (N°7) moves into an advanced position to limit space for the blue centre back (N°5)**.

N°3 should position himself at an equal distance from both of his teammates, maximising available space to receive a pass from the **goalkeeper (GK)**.

If the pass is accurate, it can neutralise 3 or even 4 defenders, creating a 2v1 situation that can be exploited.

If red N°2 steps out to press N°3, then the **winger (N°11)** is free and can be reached either directly (yellow arrow) or via the **attacking midfielder (N°8 -** blue arrows).

If red N°2 instead drops back to mark N°11, **N°3** will have space to drive forward and find the next pass.

BEAT THE PRESS WITH SINGLE & DOUBLE PIVOTS

Build Up to Beat the Press: Exploit Space Out Wide to Bypass Midfield Marking

3b (Variation 2). Full Back Plays First Time Pass or Header to Winger when the Opposing Full Back Moves Out of Position to Press (4-3-3)

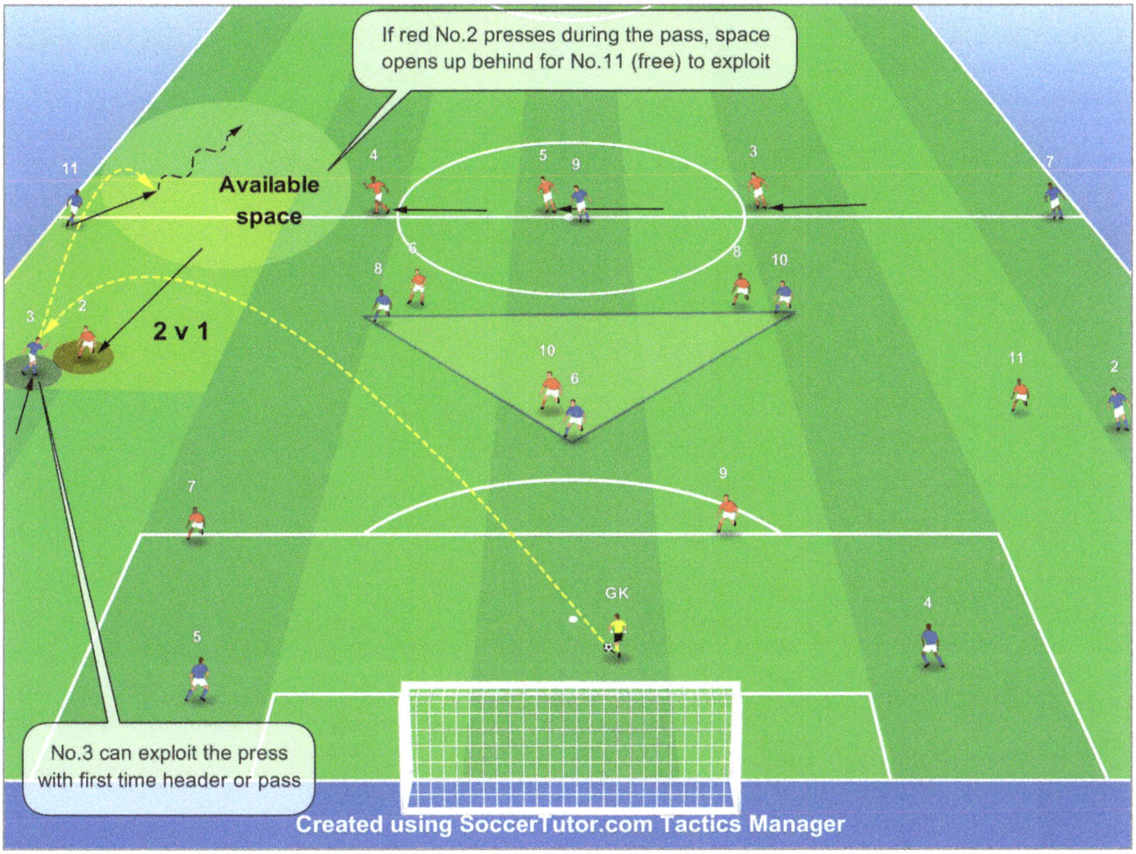

In this second variation, if the red full back N°2 decides to take advantage of the transmission phase (the time the ball takes to travel) to step out and apply pressure, the space he leaves behind can be exploited immediately.

As red N°2 pushes forward, he abandons his original position in the defensive line, which opens up a clear lane behind him.

This space can be used effectively if the blue full back (N°3) anticipates the press and plays a first-time pass or header into the path of the winger (N°11), who will be completely free of marking.

N°11, starting from a higher position, is now in an ideal zone to receive in behind the defensive line and attack the space at speed.

Note: This quick combination bypasses the pressing player and moves the ball directly into the final third, potentially creating a goal-scoring opportunity. Timing, awareness, and the quality of the delivery from N°3 are crucial to ensure the opposing team cannot recover in time.

BEAT THE PRESS WITH SINGLE & DOUBLE PIVOTS

Build Up to Beat the Press: Exploit Space Out Wide to Bypass Midfield Marking

3c (Variation 3). Winger Receives Unmarked from GK in Between Lines when the Opposing Full Back Moves Out of Position (4-3-3)

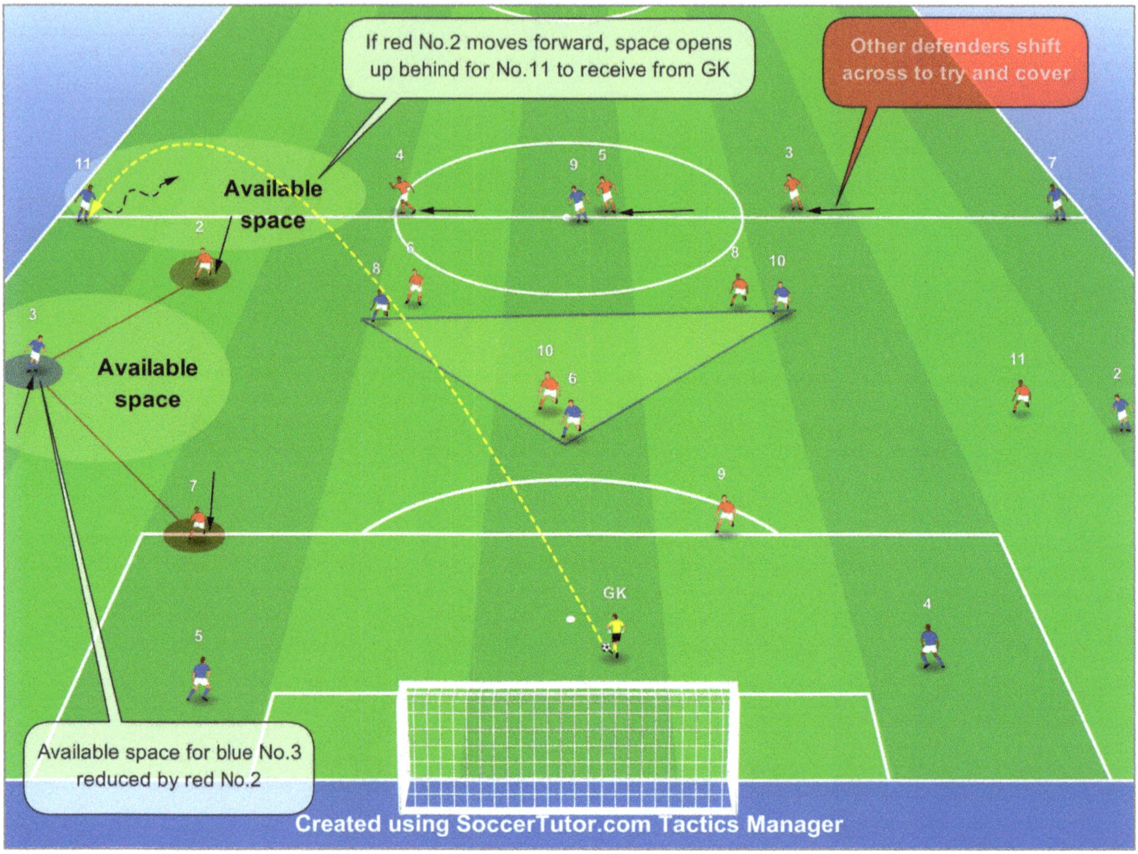

In this third variation, if the red full back Nº2 decides to shift early into a more advanced position to limit the **blue full back's (Nº3)** space and prepare to intercept a potential long pass, the rest of the red defensive line must also shift across to maintain horizontal compactness.

In response, **Nº3 should adjust his positioning to remain in between red Nº2 and Nº7**, ensuring he stays in the most available space to receive. Meanwhile, the **winger (Nº11) must stay as far as possible from nearby defenders and be prepared to receive** a direct long pass from the goalkeeper.

As shown in the diagram, there is clear available space behind red Nº2, which can be exploited before the red defence has time to recover.

If the goalkeeper (GK) delivers an accurate long pass, it can bypass 7 red players and move the ball into a dangerous area near the opponents' goal.

Build Up to Beat the Press: Exploit Space Out Wide to Bypass Midfield Marking

4a. The Opposing Wide Players Prevent the Wide Passing Lanes Leaving the Centre Back Free to Receive from the GK (4-3-3)

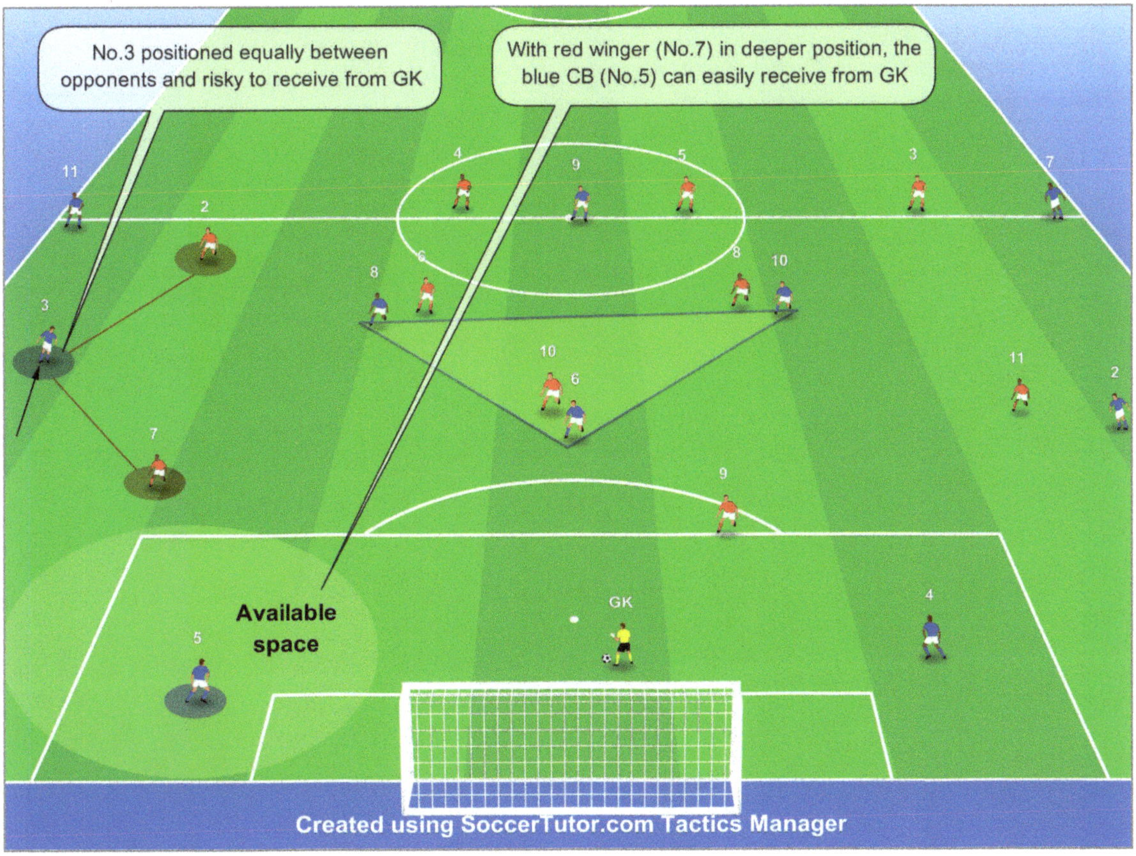

![Diagram: No.3 positioned equally between opponents and risky to receive from GK. With red winger (No.7) in deeper position, the blue CB (No.5) can easily receive from GK. Available space marked near No.5.]

If both the red N°2 and N°7 decide to stay in deeper positions to restrict space for the **blue winger (N°11)** and **full back (N°3)**, this adjustment shifts the dynamic of the build up play.

As shown in the diagram, **enough space is created for the centre back (N°5) to receive a short pass from the goalkeeper (GK) without any pressure**.

N°5 can take time on the ball, scan the pitch and decide how best to progress play either by carrying the ball forward or connecting with a midfielder. This situation demonstrates how **dropping deep defensively may neutralise direct threats out wide but can open up space centrally**, offering the possession team a new route to build up play effectively.

BEAT THE PRESS WITH SINGLE & DOUBLE PIVOTS

Build Up to Beat the Press: Exploit Space Out Wide to Bypass Midfield Marking

4b. Moving the Ball to the Advanced Full Back (Free Out Wide) via Link Players (4-3-3)

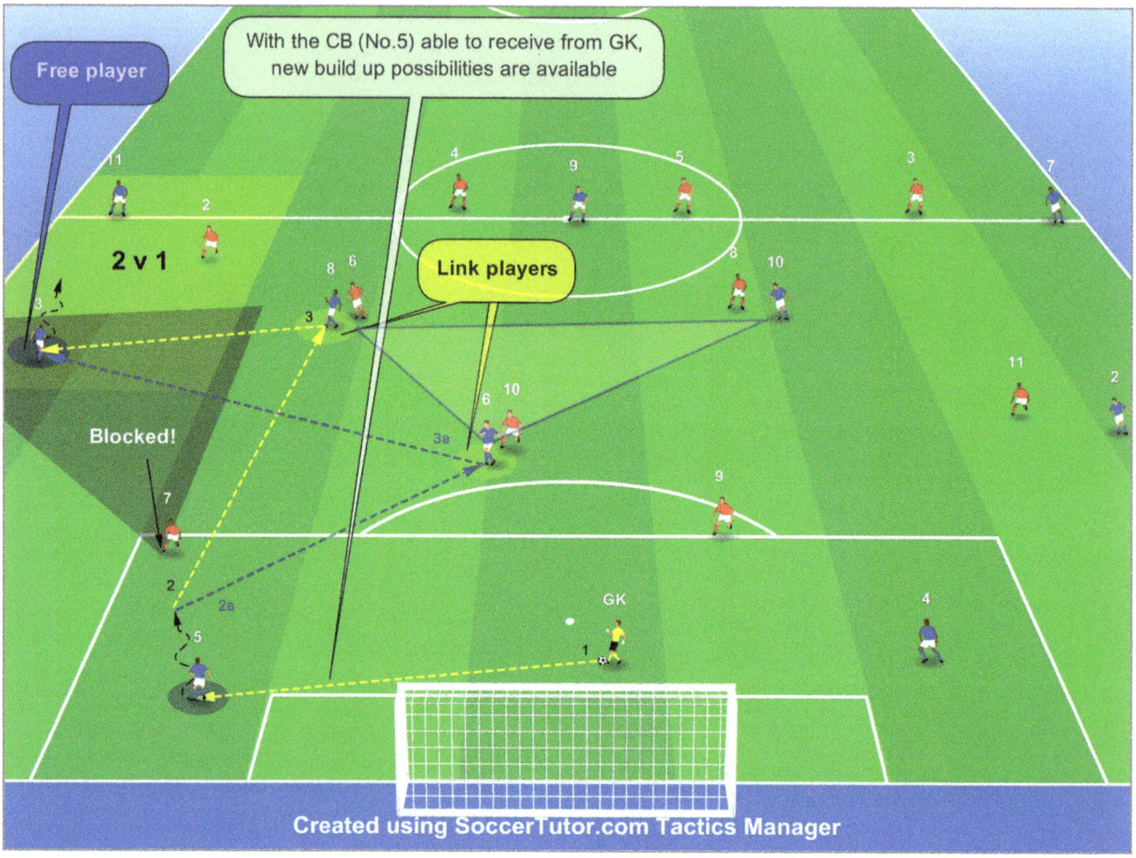

As soon as the **goalkeeper (GK)** plays the pass to the **centre back (N°5)**, **the red winger N°7 applies pressure in a way that blocks the path to the full back (N°3)**, making him unavailable for a direct pass despite being free.

To solve this, the blues must apply the principle of using link players positioned near the ball.

When using a single pivot (4-3-3 formation), the typical link players are the defensive midfielder (N°6) and the attacking midfielder closest to the ball (N°8 in diagram example).

N°6 is ideally positioned to redirect the ball to the free **N°3** (blue arrows) due to a wide visual field which enables him to notice all the potential players who can get involved.

However, **N°8** can also offer an effective solution, especially if he positions himself well and executes the pass quickly (yellow arrows). Since the combination takes place higher up the pitch, the overall risk is lower, but **N°8 must still follow the key link player principles outlined on page 129.**

Once the ball reaches N°3, a 2v1 situation is created, allowing the blues to progress their attack with a clear advantage.

Build Up to Beat the Press: Exploit Space Out Wide to Bypass Midfield Marking

5. Positioning of Wide Players when Opposition Apply Ultra-Aggressive Pressing (4-3-3)

This defensive setup (opposing red team) combines man marking in midfield with a high press, while maintaining a numerical advantage at the back. The red N°10 drops to mark the blue defensive midfielder, while the wide players push forward between the full backs and centre backs.

The red forward (N°9) presses centrally to limit the goalkeeper's passing options, creating a potential 3v3 situation up front. The red full backs step up slightly to cover the blue wingers and full backs, preserving the red team's 4v3 advantage at the back.

While the blue team's build up principles remain similar to earlier examples, they now apply on both sides of the pitch. This setup is well-suited to play against ultra-aggressive pressing (up to the goalkeeper), but it **demands quicker decision-making as the time available is reduced**.

The diagram shows the effective positioning of the attacking players. Their **decisions depend on the red opposing team's shifts and positioning**, helping them identify available spaces and the players who can exploit them.

Note: A similar structure is used when playing against teams playing and defending with a 4-2-3-1 formation.

Build Up to Beat the Press: Exploit Space Out Wide to Bypass Midfield Marking

Build Up to Exploit Space Out Wide and Bypass Midfield Marking (Double Pivot)

1. Opposition's Man Marking Across the Pitch Against a 4-2-3-1 Build Up Shape

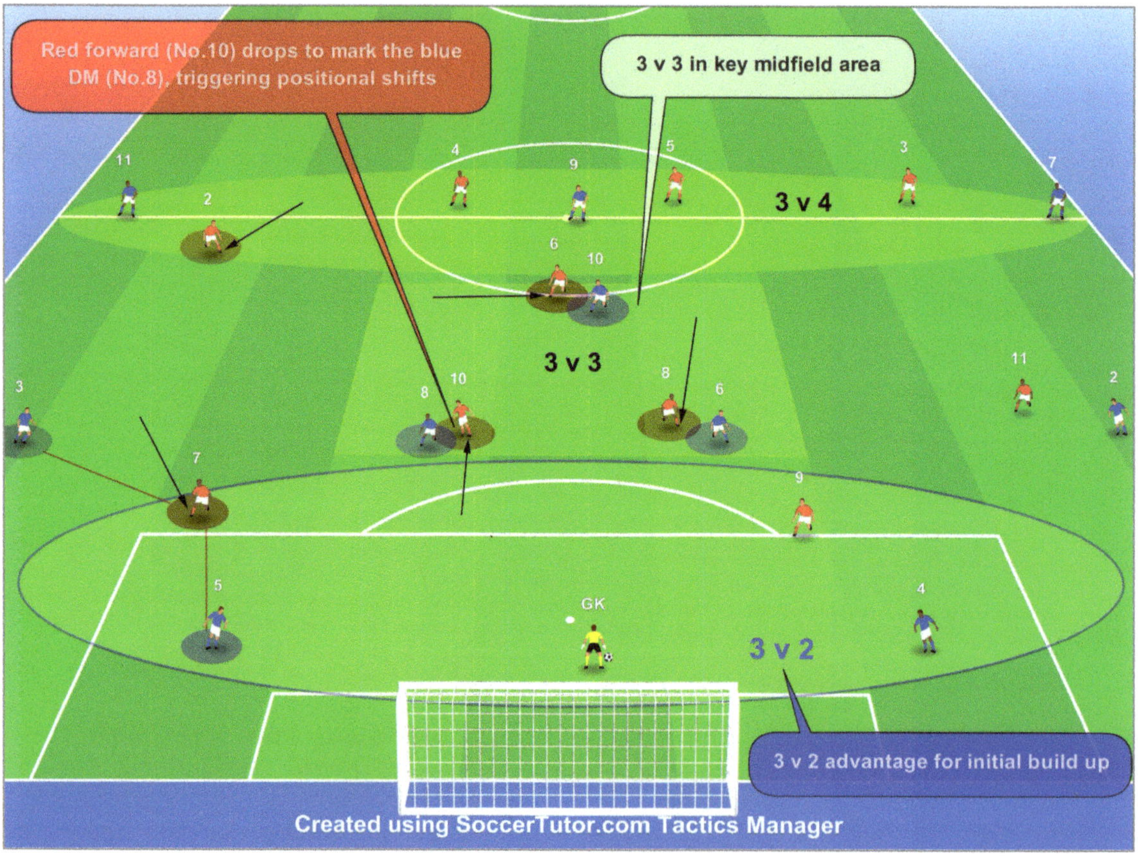

When using the 4-2-3-1 formation, the opposition adjusts similarly as they do to facing the 4-3-3.

Red N°10 drops into midfield to mark blue N°6, prompting red N°7 to push forward between blue N°3 and N°5. Red N°2 also steps up slightly to be ready to intercept aerial passes towards blue N°3 while staying close to the back line to keep numerical superiority (and compactness).

These movements allow the reds to apply man marking in midfield. As a result, the **blue build up team has a 3 v 2 advantage in the low zone**, while the red defending team keeps a 4 v 3 advantage in their defence.

Note: The attacking team's solutions mirror those previously shown for the single pivot midfield (4-3-3), and the goalkeeper's (GK) decision depends on the actions of red N°2 and N°7.

BEAT THE PRESS WITH SINGLE & DOUBLE PIVOTS

Build Up to Beat the Press: Exploit Space Out Wide to Bypass Midfield Marking

2. Moving the Ball to the Advanced Full Back (Free Out Wide) via Link Players (4-2-3-1)

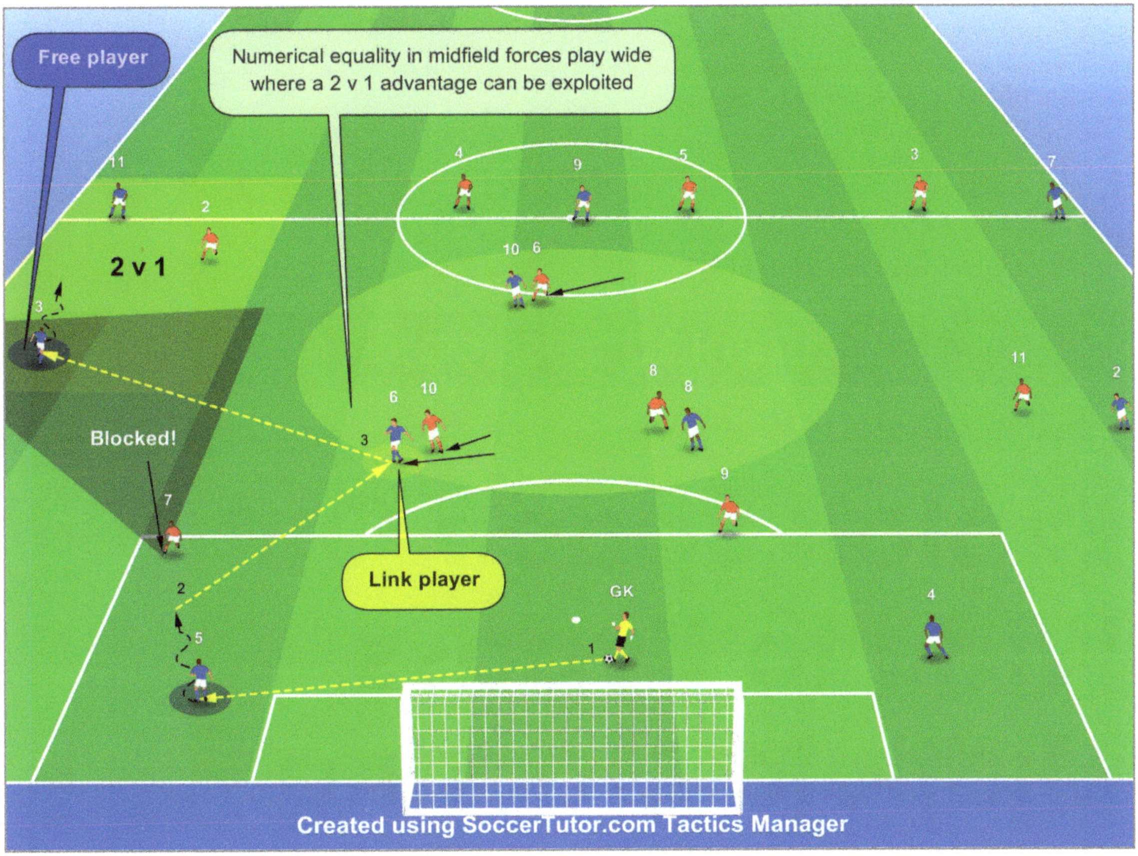

If the ball is played from the goalkeeper (**GK**) to a centre back (**N°5 in diagram**), the closest defensive midfielder (**N°8**) acts as the link player to move the ball to the full back (**N°3**).

N°3 is free but is blocked off by the pressing of the red winger N°11.

If this link play is successful and the ball reaches **N°3**, the blues will create a **favourable 2v1 situation near the ball area**, providing an excellent opportunity to progress into an effective attack

BUILD UP TO BEAT THE PRESS

Training Session 8 (4 Practices)

Exploit Space Out Wide to Bypass Midfield Marking

Based on Flick, Klopp, and Emery build up patterns

Training Session 8: Exploit Space Out Wide to Bypass Midfield Marking

TRAINING SESSION (4 PRACTICES)
1. Decision Making to Break Lines in Wide Areas Depending on Opposition Pressing

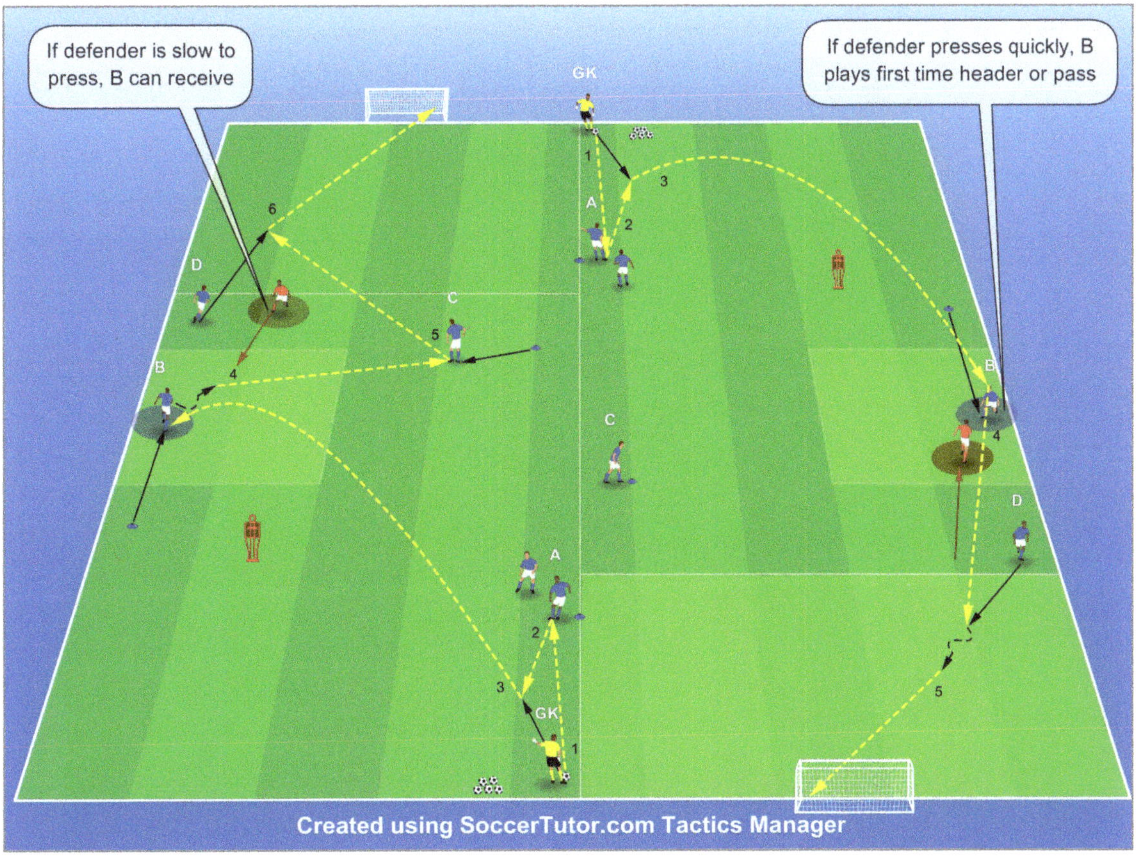

If defender is slow to press, B can receive

If defender presses quickly, B plays first time header or pass

Practice Description

- In a total area of 60x40 metres, divide into 2 halves and play on both sides simultaneously. Each half includes an 8x6 metre area near the sideline.
- Blue players **A**, **B**, and **C** are positioned on cones, while **D** and a red defender start near the end zone line.
- It begins with the **goalkeeper's** (**GK**) pass to **A**, who returns the ball back (one-two). **GK** delivers a long pass to **B**, targeting the area between the red defender and the mannequin.
- As the ball travels, the red defender must decide whether to intervene. **If the defender initially holds their position (left side)**, **B** receives and looks to find **D** directly or via the link player (**C**). **D** then passes into the small goal.
- **If the defender moves forward to intercept the pass (right side)**, **B** plays into space for **D**, who runs onto the pass.
- After each repetition, the players rotate positions (**A → B → C → D**). Change the defenders after a set number of repetitions or replace with coaches.

BEAT THE PRESS WITH SINGLE & DOUBLE PIVOTS

Training Session 8: Exploit Space Out Wide to Bypass Midfield Marking

PROGRESSION
2. Decision Making to Break Lines in Wide Areas Depending on Opposition Pressing Small Sided Game

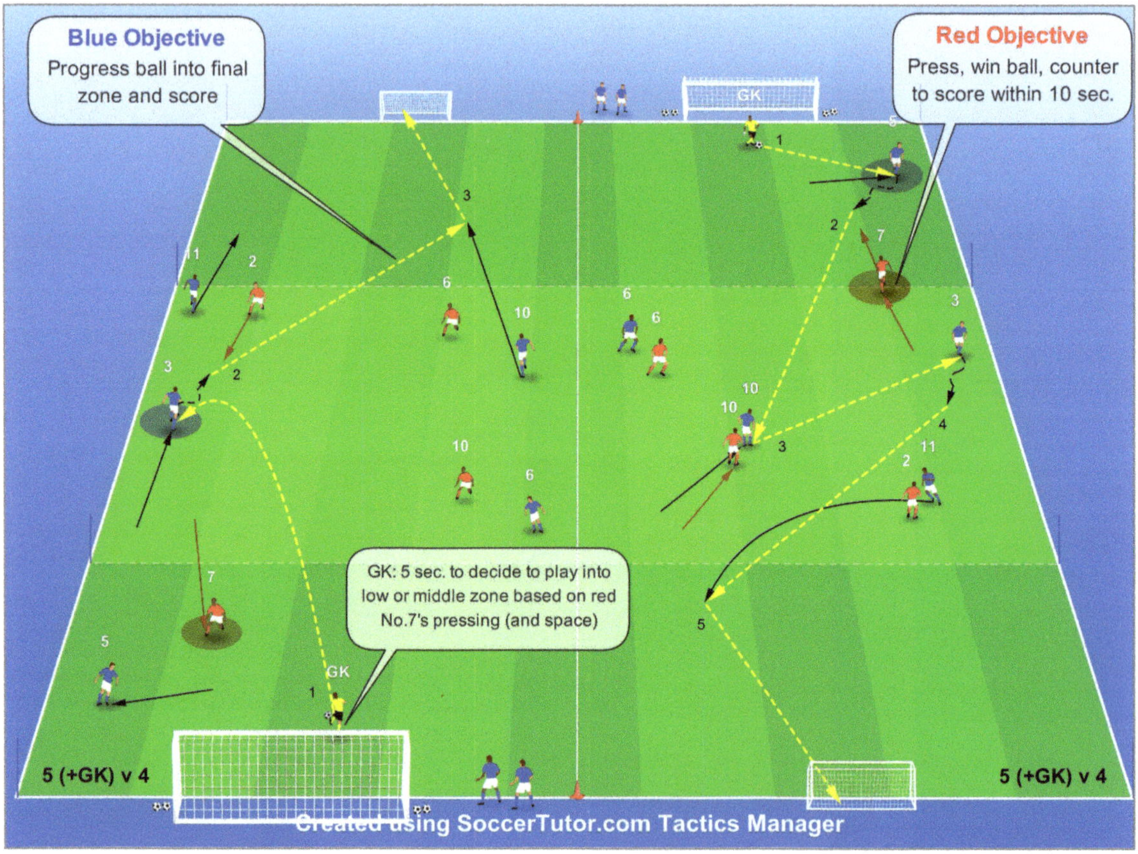

Blue Objective: Progress ball into final zone and score

Red Objective: Press, win ball, counter to score within 10 sec.

GK: 5 sec. to decide to play into low or middle zone based on red No.7's pressing (and space)

5 (+GK) v 4   5 (+GK) v 4

Practice Description

- This progression uses the same 60 x 40 metre area from the previous practice. The middle zone is 30 metres. Both sides run simultaneously.

- At the start, there is a blue **GK + centre back (N°5)** in the low zone and a 4v4 situation in the middle zone.

- **GK** starts and **N°5** shifts to the left. The nearest red player (N°7) moves into a balanced position to cover **blue N°5** and **N°3**. Based on this, **GK** decides to pass into the middle zone or the low zone.

- The blues move the ball to **N°3** directly (**left side**) or via a link player (**N°10**) based on red **N°7's pressing action**. Once **N°3** receives, the aim is to play into the high zone and score in the small goal.

- **Defending Objective:** Press, win the ball, and counter to score in 10 seconds.

- **Restrictions:** Only 1 red player can leave the middle zone at any time. No reds allowed in the end (final) zone. **The blue GK has 5 seconds to decide and pass**.

- Make sure to train right flank also (switch the small/large goals round at each end).

BEAT THE PRESS WITH SINGLE & DOUBLE PIVOTS

Training Session 8: Exploit Space Out Wide to Bypass Midfield Marking

PROGRESSION

3. Split-Pitch Read the Game Situation Build Up Play Tactical Game to Beat the Press (4-3-3)

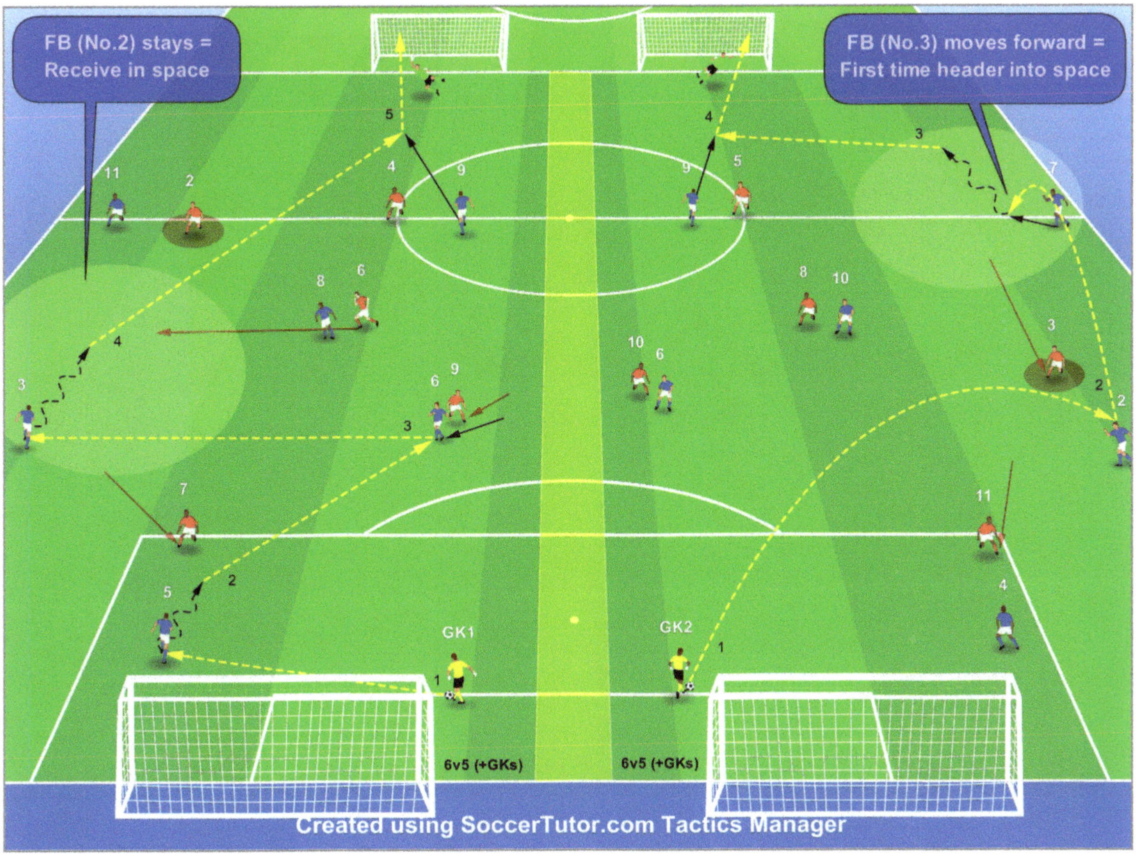

Practice Description

- The pitch is split into 2 halves, with both 6v5 (+GKs) games active at the same time. This is so the players do more repetitions than normal.

- The blues have a **defensive midfielder** (**N°6**) and **forward** (**N°9**) on both sides.

- The red wingers (N°7 and N°11) must cover 2 players (blue full backs and centre backs), while the blue midfielders are man-marked.

- The **GK starts and must choose the** passing option with the most space - see analysis pages for full details.

- The blues' decision-making after the initial pass is also key to successfully progressing and scoring - **see diagram for 2 different solutions based on red full back's actions**.

- **Restrictions:** After receiving a new ball, the GK has 5 seconds to decide where to direct the ball.

- **Defending Objective:** Press first receiver (after first pass), win the ball and counter to score within 10-12 seconds.

BEAT THE PRESS WITH SINGLE & DOUBLE PIVOTS

Training Session 8: Exploit Space Out Wide to Bypass Midfield Marking

VARIATION

4. Split-Pitch Read the Game Situation Build Up Play Tactical Game to Beat the Press (4-2-3-1)

Practice Description

- **This variation of the previous game (4-3-3) is adjusted to build up play with the 4-2-3-1 formation (double pivot).**

- In this setup, the **blue team have an attacking midfielder (N°10) and forward (N°9) on both sides** due to the structure of the 4-2-3-1 system.

- The same workings, rules, and restrictions from the previous practice are applied without any changes. The format and objectives also remain the same.

- The diagram shows 2 options based on the red winger's pressing action to move the ball to the free full back (N°3 or N°2) - the left shows a direct pass and the right shows the use of a link player (N°10).

- **Defending Objective:** Press first receiver (after first pass), win the ball and counter to score within 10-12 seconds.

- **Progression:** 11v11 game in ¾ of a full pitch with the red team applying a high or ultra-aggressive high press with man marking in midfield.

BEAT THE PRESS WITH SINGLE & DOUBLE PIVOTS

BUILD UP TO BEAT THE PRESS

Tactical Analysis

Against Full Pitch Man Marking

Build up play patterns from Flick, Klopp, and Emery's teams

Build Up Solutions Against Full Pitch Man Marking (Single Pivot)

1. Opposition's Man Marking Across the Pitch Against a 4-3-3 Build Up Shape

Man marking can be applied across the entire pitch, including during high pressing (on first receiver) and ultra-aggressive pressing (up to the goalkeeper).

In this setup, an opposing (red) centre back steps into midfield to mark the free player. In the diagram example, **red N°4 moves forward to mark the blue attacking midfielder (N°8), allowing red N°10 to stay high rather than dropping back**.

This adjustment creates numerical equality in midfield (3v3) and in defence for the red team (3v3).

In such situations, the **attacking (blue) team must rely on the individual quality of their players to overcome direct opponents and progress**.

Build Up to Beat the Press: Against Full Pitch Man Marking

2. Utilising a Target Player with Goalkeeper's Long Pass and Support Play Movements (4-3-3)

![Diagram showing target player with lay-off outlets and available space]

If the possession (attacking) team have a **forward who can play effectively as a target player** - tall, strong, and capable of shielding the ball, then a long aerial pass becomes a valuable option. Players like **Haaland** or **Lukaku** are good examples of this profile.

To maximise this, nearby teammates must coordinate their movements to make sure the target player has a 1v1 situation and is not double marked.

In the diagram example, the ball is with the **goalkeeper** (**GK**), so the **blue midfielders drop back, forcing their red markers to follow**.

This creates more space for blue the forward (N°9), preventing any of the red midfielders from applying additional pressure. With only his direct opponent (red N°5) to contend with, **N°9 has a better chance to control a long pass, shield it effectively, and retain possession**.

At the same time, the blue midfielders can make quick directional movement changes once the long pass is played, attacking the space highlighted. This movement can allow them to receive a lay-off from **N°9**, potentially **bypassing up to 7 opponents and the first 2 pressing lines**.

Build Up to Beat the Press: Against Full Pitch Man Marking

3. Utilising a Target Player with Goalkeeper's Long Pass and Support Runs in Behind the Defensive Line (4-3-3)

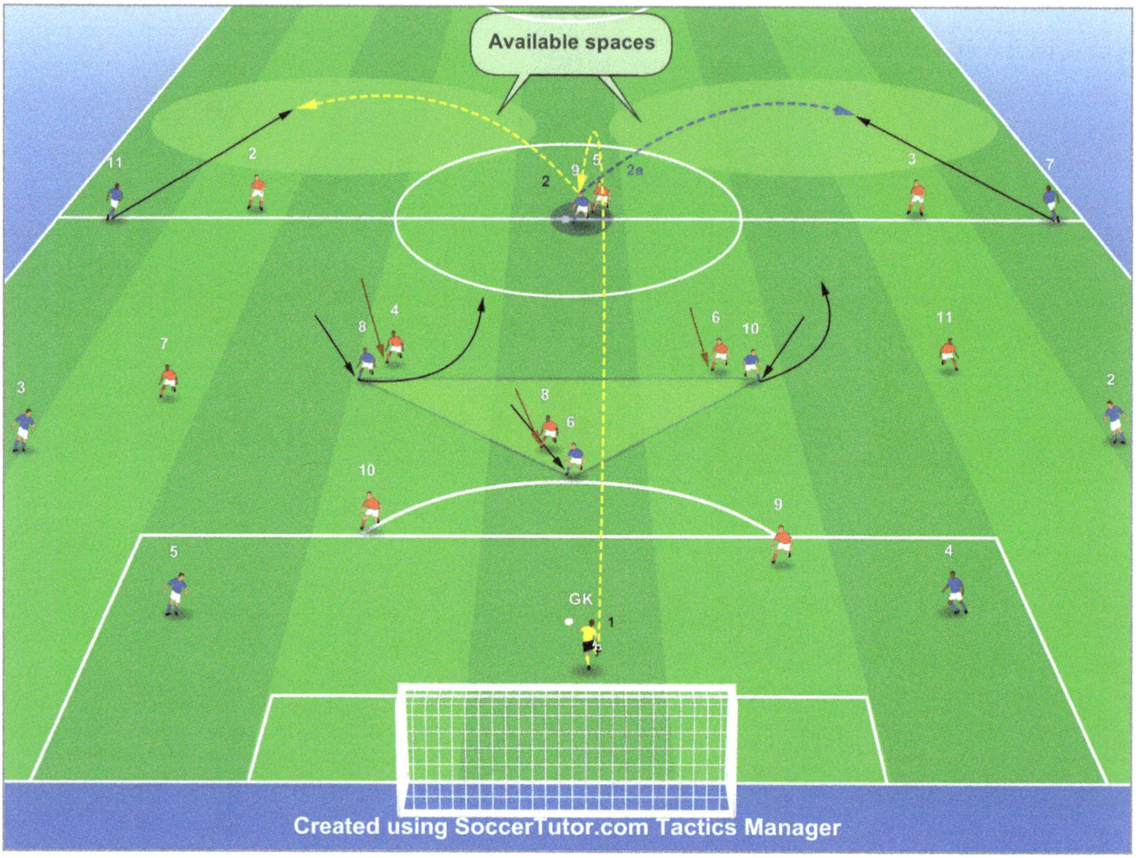

An effective target player can also be used to exploit space behind the defensive line with a long pass followed by well-timed supporting runs.

As shown in the diagram, once the long pass is played towards the **forward (N°9)**, the **wingers (N°11 and N°7)** must time their runs to arrive just as he challenges for the ball.

This gives N°9 2 main options:

1. Lay the ball back to a supporting teammate (see previous page).
2. Head the ball it into the space in behind the defensive line (diagram above).

Note: This approach increases N°9's effectiveness, allowing him to either retain possession or play into space for onrushing teammates, thereby stretching the defensive line and creating attacking opportunities.

BEAT THE PRESS WITH SINGLE & DOUBLE PIVOTS

Build Up to Beat the Press: Against Full Pitch Man Marking

4. Exploiting a Forward's Speed with the Goalkeeper's Long Pass into Available Space in Behind (4-3-3)

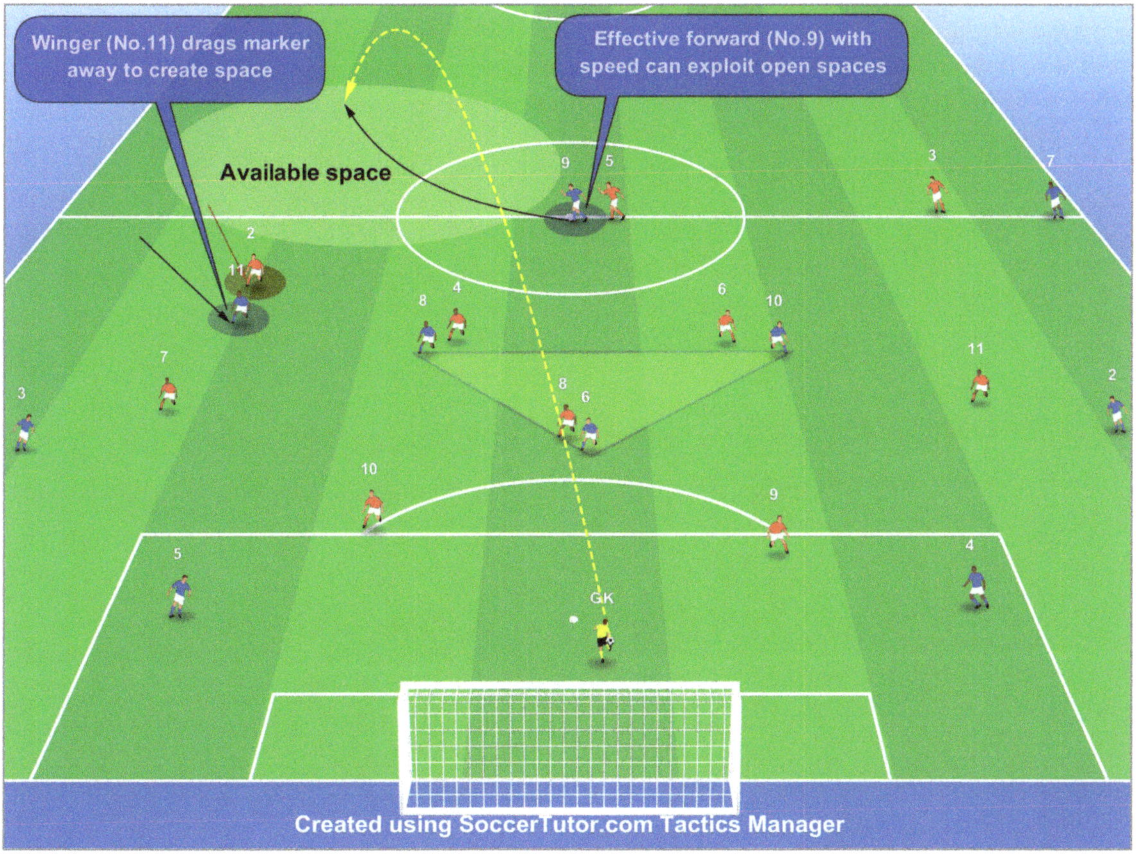

If the forward is not a target man but rather a fast, dynamic player who thrives in space (a "runner" type), then the team should create conditions that allow them to exploit these qualities effectively.

One common strategy is to use decoy movements from nearby teammates to open up space in the defensive line.

In the diagram example, the **goalkeeper (GK) is in possession and the winger (N°11) drops back and moves inside, prompting his direct opponent (red N°2) to follow**. This coordinated movement pulls the red full back out of position, creating available space behind him on the left side.

This space becomes an ideal zone for the forward (N°9) to run into. With the space created, **GK** can deliver a long pass into the highlighted available space. If the timing is right, **N°9** can:

1. Use speed to receive the ball in stride.
2. Bypass his marker (red centre back N°5).
3. Engage in a favourable 1v1.
4. Provide the team with a high-quality opportunity based on individual player strengths.

Build Up to Beat the Press: Against Full Pitch Man Marking

5. Exploiting the Wingers' Ability to Make Runs in Behind Defensive Line and Receive Long Passes from the Goalkeeper (4-3-3)

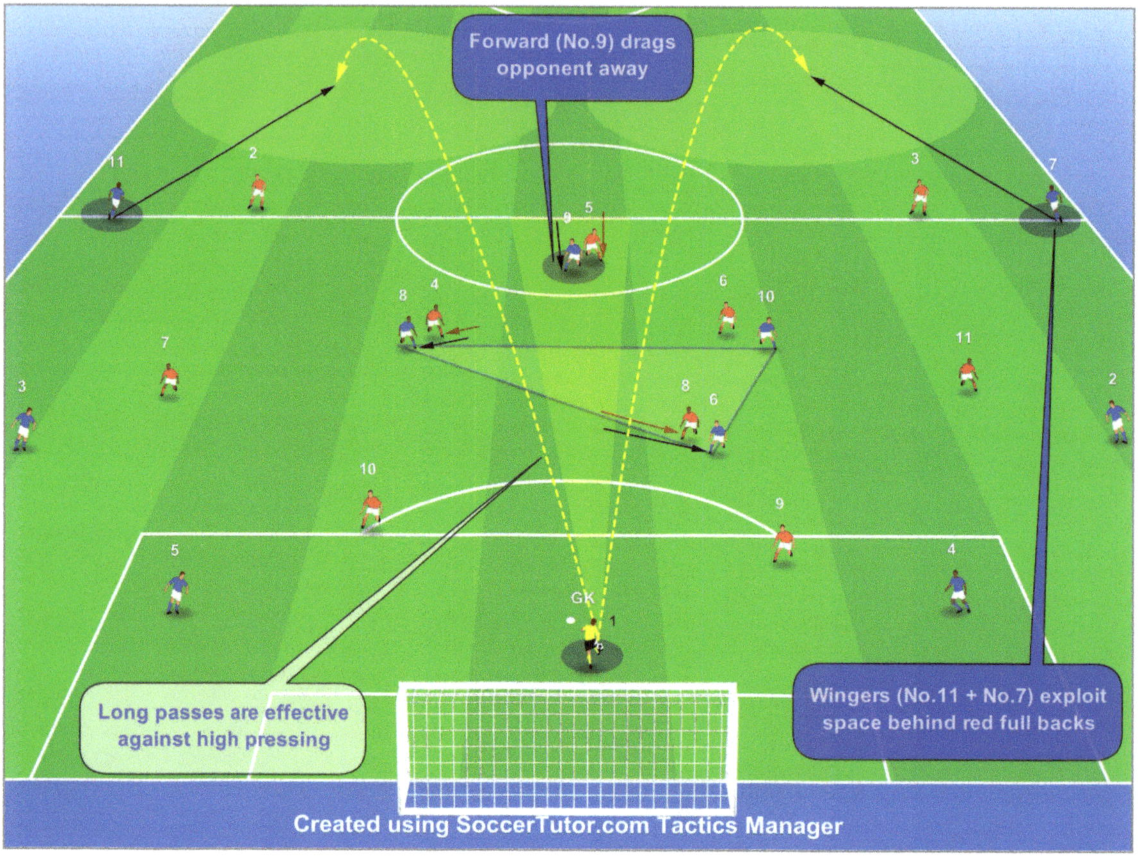

If the attacking team has fast and effective wingers, another strategy is to **target the space behind the opposition's full backs**. This becomes more effective when the forward makes a well-timed movement into midfield to draw a centre back out of position.

In the diagram example, the **goalkeeper (GK)** is in possession and 2 of the **central midfielders (N°6 and N°8)** help create a wider passing lane towards the **forward (N°9)**. When **N°9 drops a few metres to offer a passing option, the red centre back (N°5) is forced to follow**, which removes his ability to support and cover the red full backs (N°2 and N°3).

This opens up the opportunity for the **GK** to play a pass behind either of the red full backs and into space for the **wingers (N°11 or N°7)** to run onto.

If the pass is accurate and well-weighted, it can result in a favourable attacking situation.

Note: These build-up options can be used against high pressing (on first receiver) and ultra-aggressive pressing (up to the goalkeeper). However, under ultra-aggressive pressing, the available time for the goalkeeper and players to read the situation and execute their movements is significantly reduced.

Build Up to Beat the Press: Against Full Pitch Man Marking

6. Using Link Players to Find the Free Player Near the Ball with GK in Possession Against Ultra-Aggressive High Pressing (4-3-3)

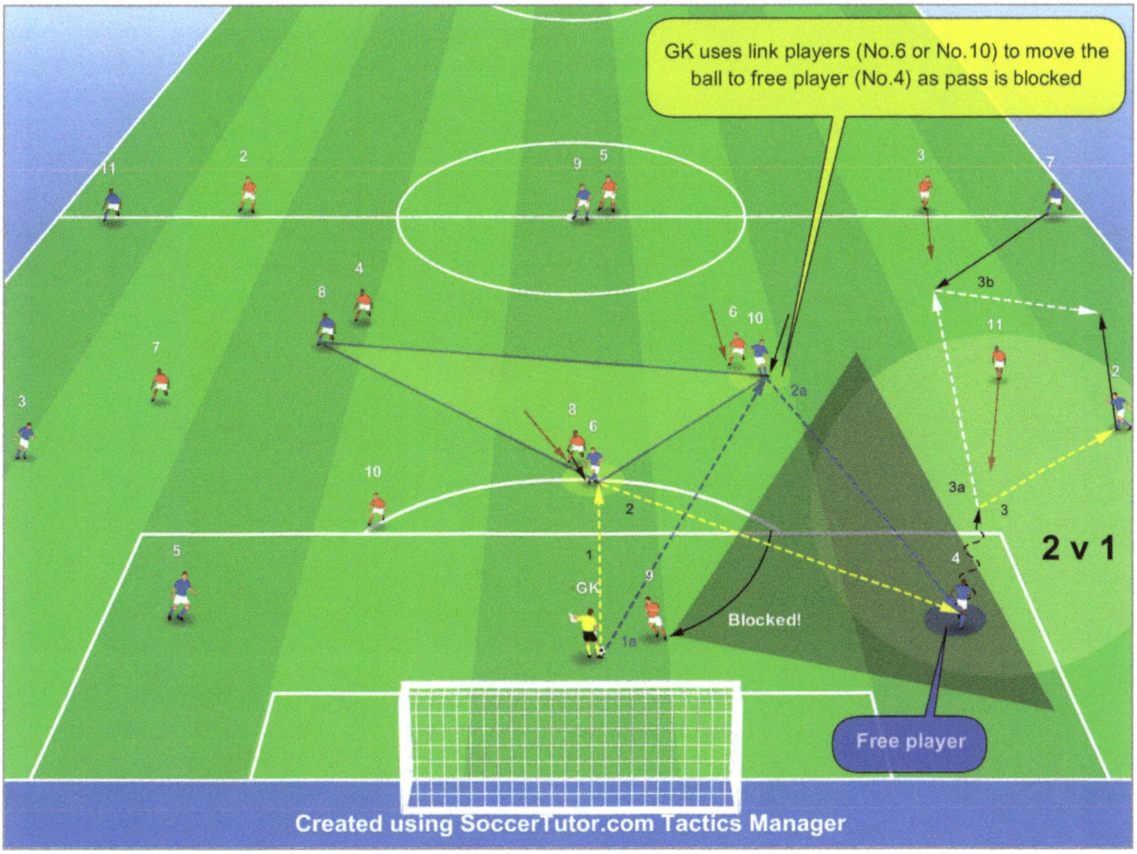

When ultra-aggressive pressing (up to the goalkeeper) is applied, an opposing forward or midfielder presses the goalkeeper in possession. As this happens, their direct opponent is left unmarked but is often put in the shadow of the pressing player (passing lane blocked).

To exploit this, the team should **apply the principle of using nearby link players to move the ball to the free teammate**.

In the diagram example, once red N°9 presses the **goalkeeper (GK)**, the **centre back (N°4) becomes the free player**. Using a single pivot, the **potential link players are the defensive midfielder (N°6) and the attacking midfielder on the strong side (N°10)**.

The relevant players must apply the link player principles (see page 129).

When the ball reaches N°4, a 2v1 situation can develop - the next decision depends on how the red winger presses:

- If the red winger (N°11) steps up to press N°4, the full back (N°2) becomes the free option (yellow arrow).
- If a direct pass to N°2 is blocked, the ball can go via the winger (N°7 - white arrows), who acts as a link player.

BEAT THE PRESS WITH SINGLE & DOUBLE PIVOTS

Build Up to Beat the Press: Against Full Pitch Man Marking

7. Moving the Ball to the Free Attacking Midfielder Directly or via a Link Player when the Pass is Blocked (4-3-3)

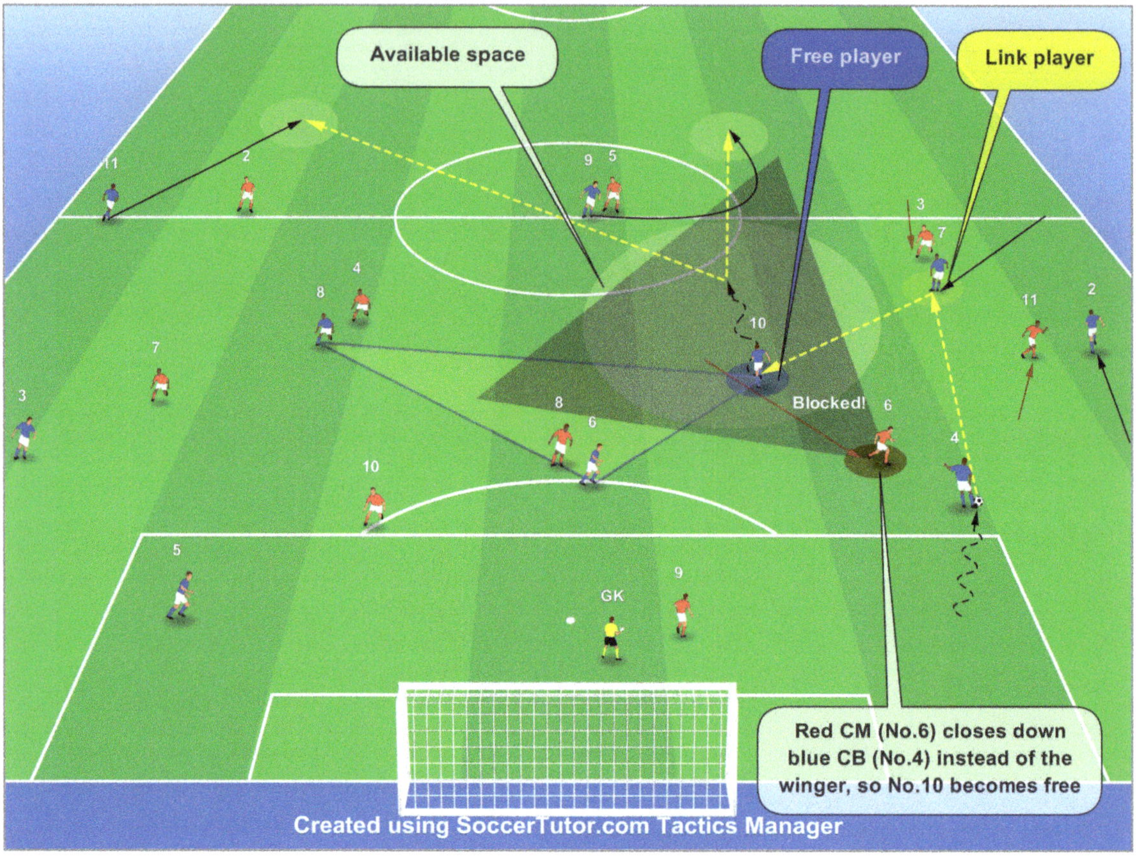

Red CM (No.6) closes down blue CB (No.4) instead of the winger, so No.10 becomes free

In this variation of the previous example, the reaction of the red team is different.

The red central midfielder (N°6) moves forward to close down the centre back (N°4) this time, so the attacking midfielder (N°10) will become the free player between the lines.

The ball can be directed to **N°10** directly *if the passing lane is clear*.

If the direct pass is blocked as shown in the diagram, a link player is used (**winger N°7**), who can help bypass the pressure and deliver the ball to **N°10** in the available space in the centre, as highlighted.

Note: When facing ultra-aggressive pressing with man marking applied across the full pitch, **successfully moving the ball to the free player in the early phase is crucial**. Doing so can allow the team to continue advancing play by applying the same build up principles in subsequent phases. This is especially effective if the link players consistently position and time their movements well.

BEAT THE PRESS WITH SINGLE & DOUBLE PIVOTS

Build Up to Beat the Press: Against Full Pitch Man Marking

8. Using Link Player Close to Ball to Find Free Defensive Midfielder when Opposing Central Midfielder Presses the Goalkeeper (4-3-3)

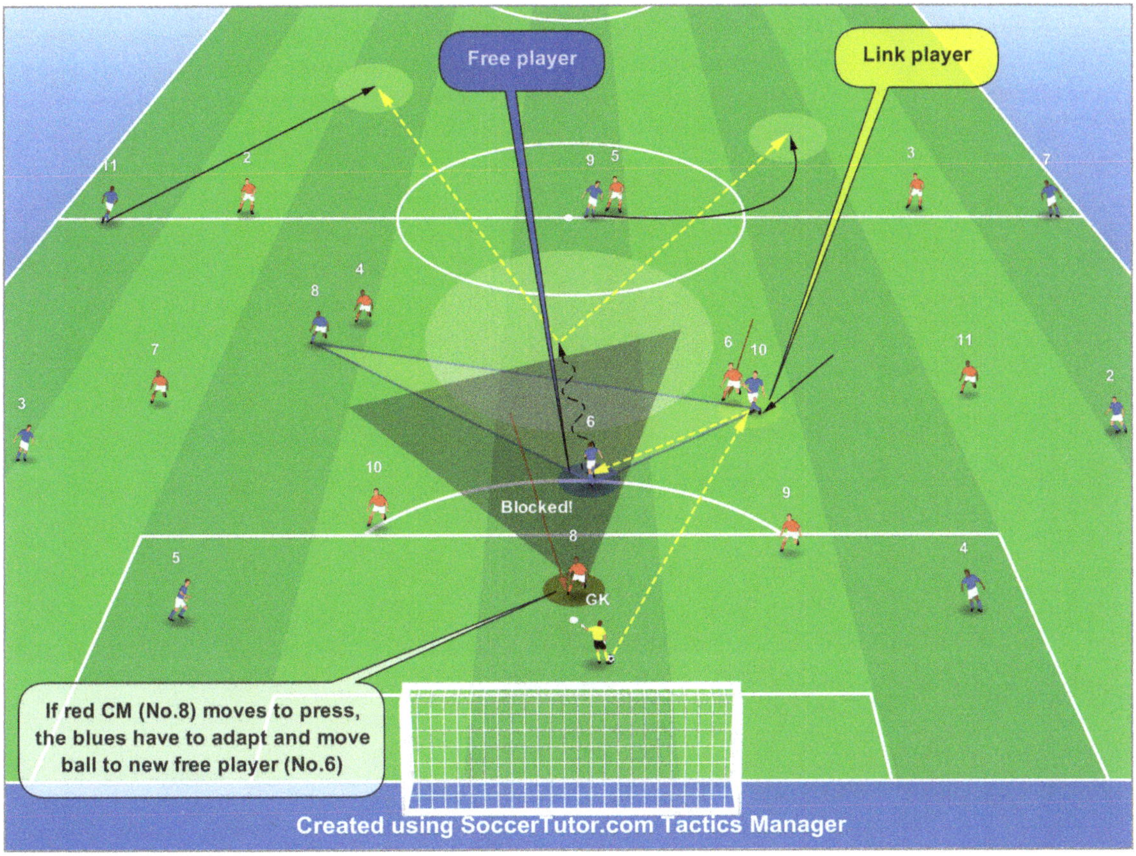

If one of the opposing central midfielders (Nº8 in diagram example) moves forward to press the goalkeeper (GK), the blue defensive midfielder (Nº6) will be left completely free of marking in the centre, although the direct pass to him will be blocked.

The blue team must quickly read this situation and look to find the new free player as quickly as possible.

The ball can be moved to Nº6 via a link player (e.g. attacking midfielder Nº10), depending on the positioning and pressure from the red team.

Note: The speed of execution is key to taking advantage before the red team recovers.

Build Up to Beat the Press: Against Full Pitch Man Marking

Build Up Solutions Against Full Pitch Man Marking (Double Pivot)

1. Opposition's Man Marking Across the Pitch Against a 4-2-3-1 Build Up Shape

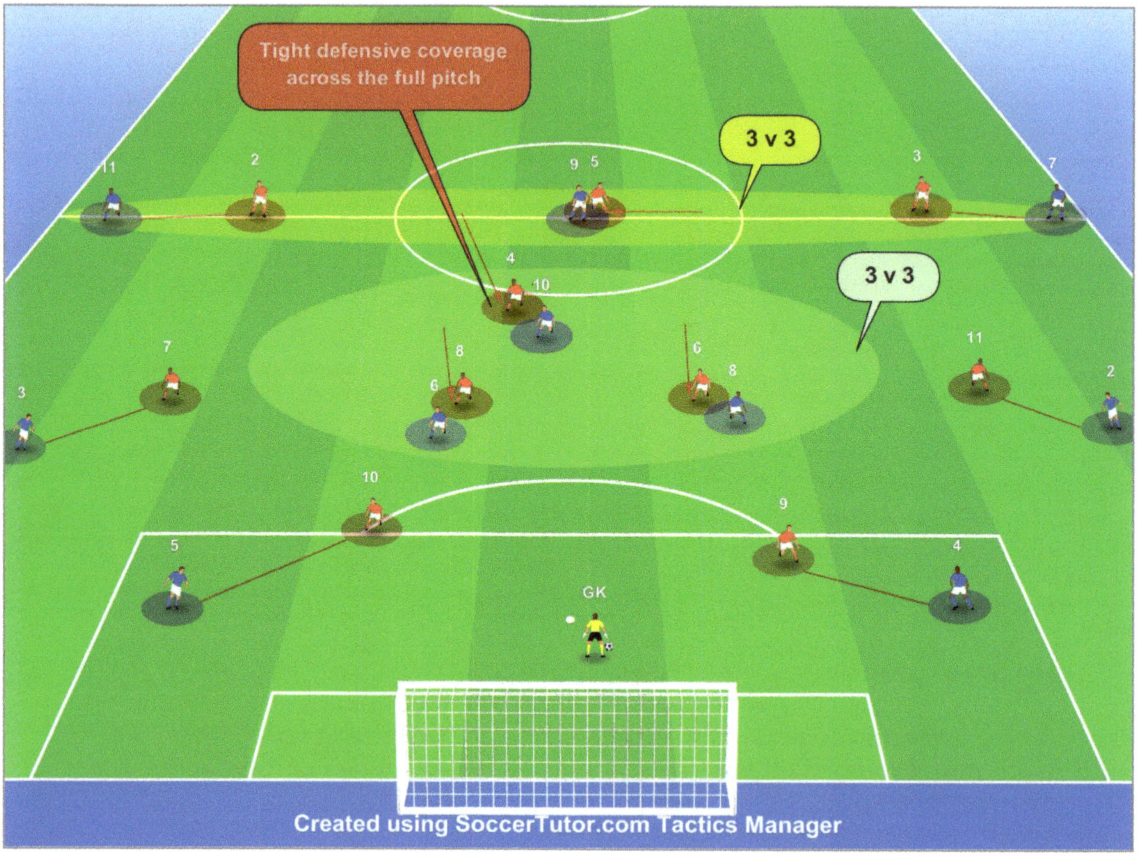

When using a double pivot (4-2-3-1), the defending team (red opposition) adjusts in a similar way to how they would against the 4-3-3.

A red centre back steps into midfield to mark the free player (Nº10 - attacking midfielder). As a result, both red forwards (Nº9 and Nº10) remain high. This creates numerical equality in midfield (3v3) and in defence for the red team (3v3).

The opposition (reds) are able to maintain aggressive pressing while covering key zones. The following pages will show how to deal with this situation using the 4-2-3-1 formation (double pivot).

Build Up to Beat the Press: Against Full Pitch Man Marking

2. Utilising a Target Player with Goalkeeper's Long Pass and Support Play Movements (4-2-3-1)

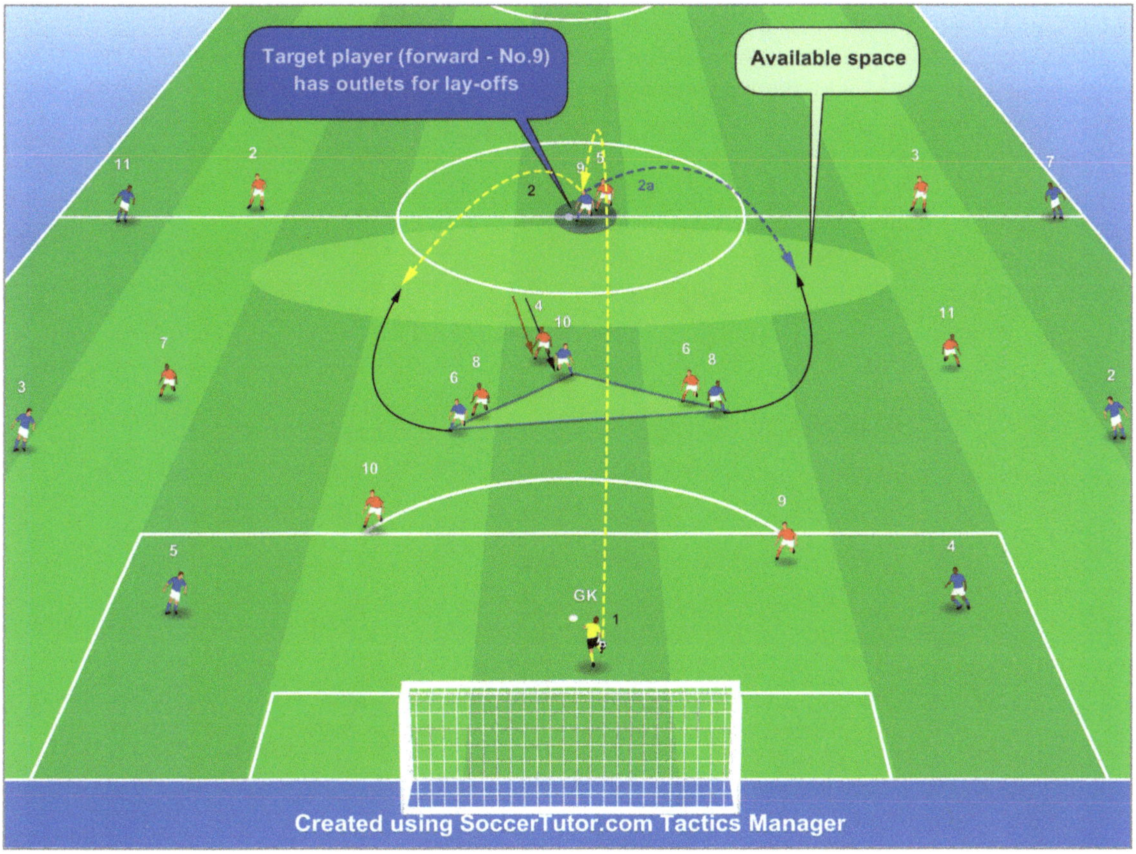

The objectives depend on the individual qualities of the attacking players. **If the forward (Nº9) is an effective target player, it is crucial to create space for him to receive under pressure from his direct marker (centre back)**.

To achieve this, **the attacking midfielder (Nº10) drops deeper, drawing the other centre back (Nº4) with him**. This movement opens up space for **Nº9**, which can also be exploited by the **defensive midfielders (Nº6 and Nº8)**.

As the long pass from the **goalkeeper (GK)** is played, **Nº6** and **Nº8** make quick curved movements to attack the space.

If **Nº9** successfully receives and holds the ball under pressure, he can then lay it off to one of the supporting players, **potentially neutralising up to 7 opponents and the first 2 pressing lines**.

Note: The earlier options presented for the single pivot (4-3-3 formation) against high pressing can be adapted to this specific formation easily as there are no differences (e.g. the "runner" type forward or the fast wingers capable of exploiting spaces in behind) - see pages 166 to 168.

BEAT THE PRESS WITH SINGLE & DOUBLE PIVOTS

Build Up to Beat the Press: Against Full Pitch Man Marking

3. Using Link Players to Find Free Player Near the Ball with the GK in Possession Against Ultra-Aggressive High Pressing (4-2-3-1)

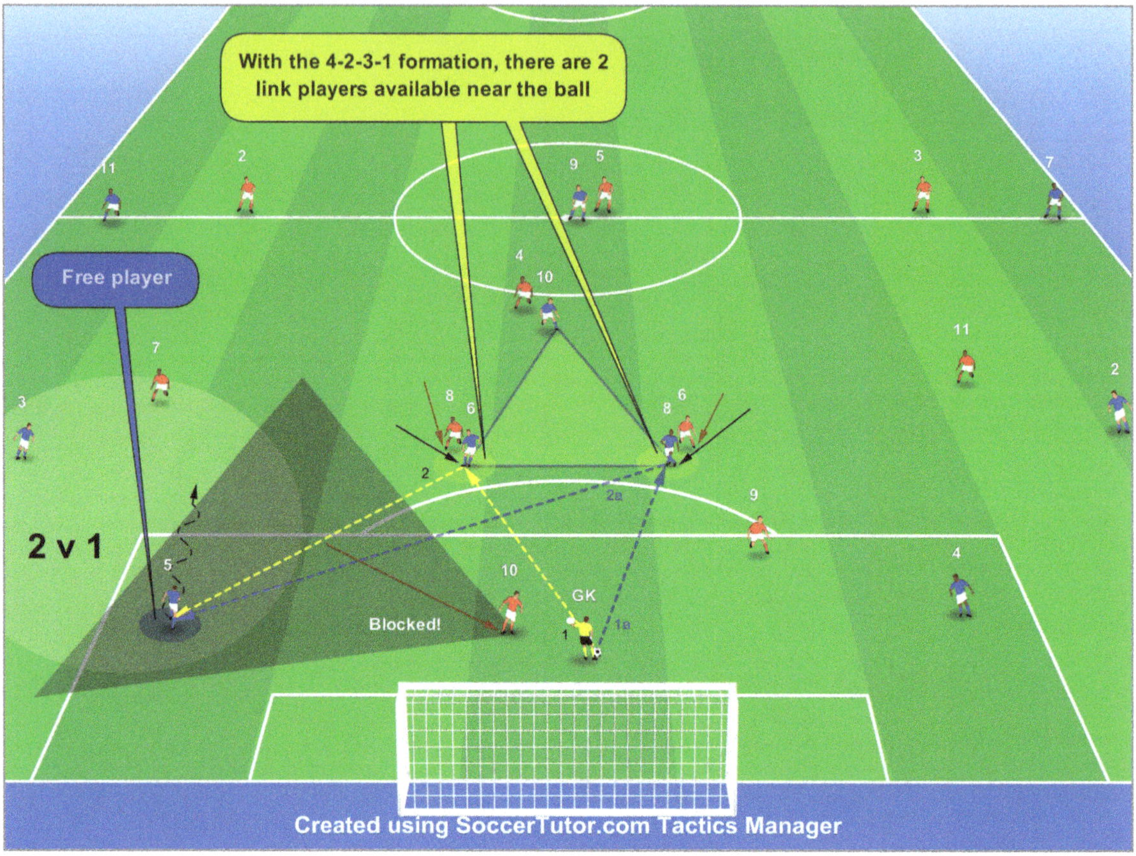

When ultra-aggressive pressing (up to the goalkeeper) is applied, an opposing forward or midfielder presses the goalkeeper in possession. As this happens, their direct opponent is left unmarked but often put in the shadow of the pressing player (passing lane blocked).

The team should apply the principle of using nearby link players to move the ball to the free teammate.

In the diagram example, once red Nº10 presses the **goalkeeper (GK)**, the **centre back (Nº5) becomes the free player**. Using a double pivot, the **potential link players are 2 defensive midfielder (Nº6 and Nº8)**.

These players must apply the established link player principles (see page 129).

When the ball reaches Nº5, a 2v1 situation can develop - the next decision depends on how the red winger presses:

- If the red winger (Nº7) steps up to press Nº5, the full back (Nº3) becomes the free player and option.

- If a direct pass to Nº3 is blocked, the ball can go via the winger (Nº11), who can act as a link player after shifting inside.

BEAT THE PRESS WITH SINGLE & DOUBLE PIVOTS

BUILD UP TO BEAT THE PRESS

Training Session 9 (5 Practices)

Against Full Pitch Man Marking

Based on Flick, Klopp, and Emery build up patterns

Training Session 9: Build Up to Beat the Press Against Full Pitch Man Marking

TRAINING SESSION (5 PRACTICES)
1. Beating a Full Pitch Man Marking Press by Finding Free Player Support Play Zones

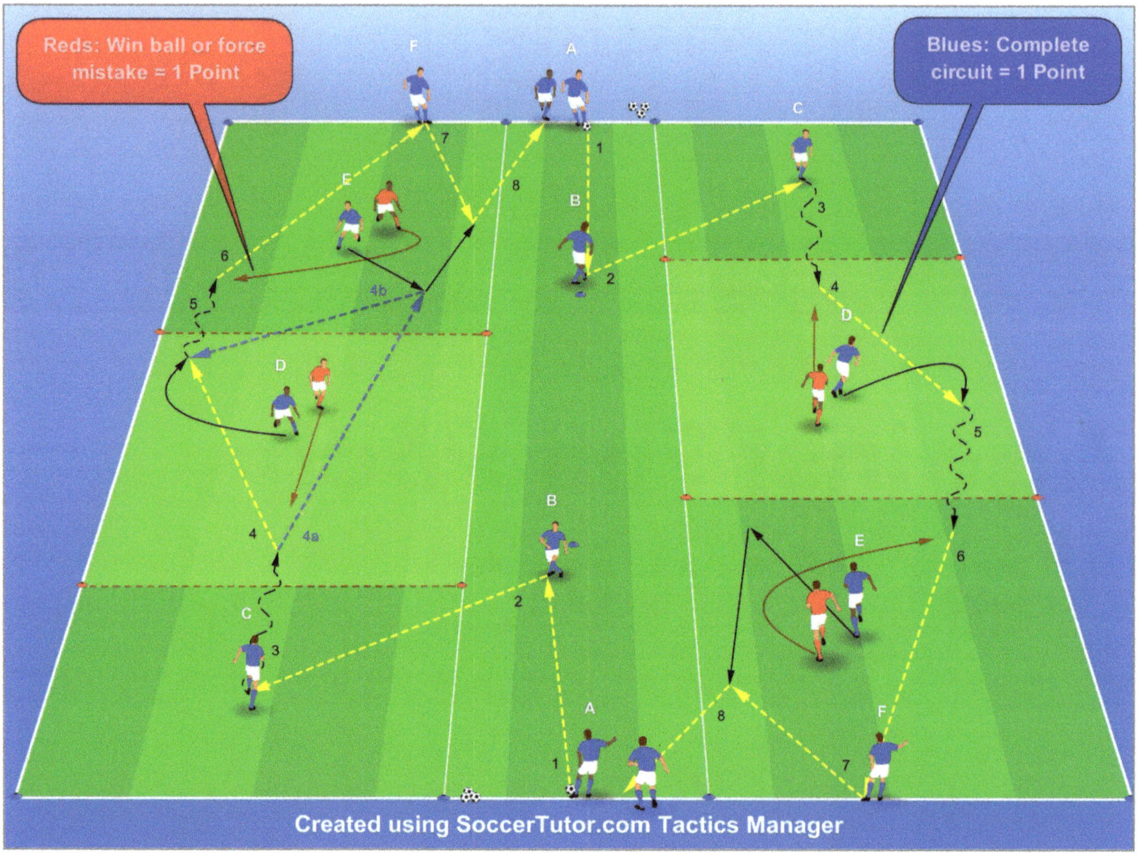

Practice Description

NOTE: *This practice also appears in the "Beat the Press with a Box Midfield" book. It is included again here due to its importance to this specific training session.*

- This practice is played simultaneously on both sides. There is 1 low zone (8x5m) and 2 larger zones (8x8m). The sequence starts with **A** passing to **B**, who plays it diagonally back to **C**.
- **C** dribbles from **Zone 1** into **Zone 2**, triggering the red player to press.
- **D** moves into a passing lane to become the free player, with **E** mirroring this movement on the opposite side to provide **C** with 2 passing options.
- **C** can pass directly to **D** (yellow arrow) or play to **E**, who acts as a link player to move the ball to **D** (blue arrows).
- Once **D** receives, they dribble into **Zone 3**. **E** moves to offer a passing option. As the red player presses the ball, the pass is directed to **E** (free player) either directly or via **F** (as shown). **E** passes to the start (1 point). All blues rotate to the next position and the sequence repeats.

BEAT THE PRESS WITH SINGLE & DOUBLE PIVOTS

Training Session 9: Build Up to Beat the Press Against Full Pitch Man Marking

PROGRESSION
2. Beating a Full Pitch Man Marking Press with a Long Pass and Support Runs Functional Combinations

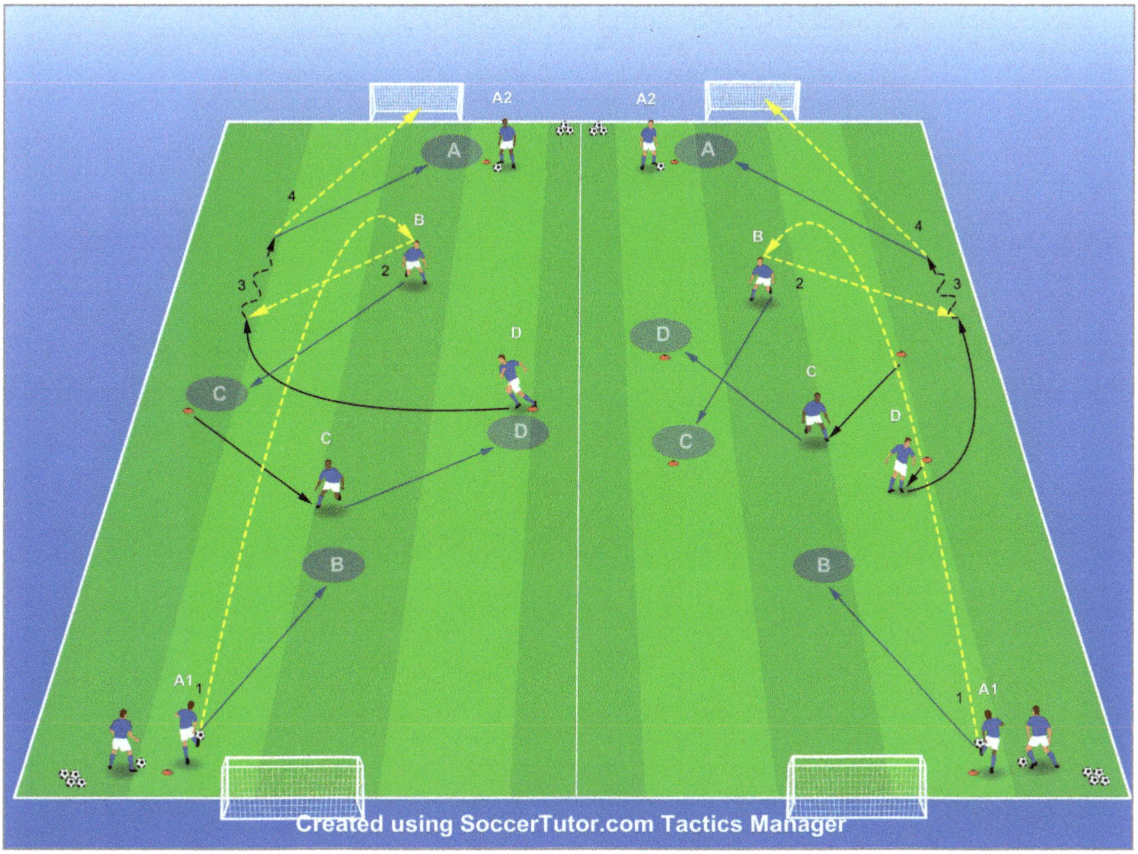

Practice Description

NOTE: *This practice also appears in the "Beat the Press with a Box Midfield" book. It is included again here due to its importance to this specific training session.*

- This practice is played simultaneously on both sides and each player has a defined role. **A1** = Long passer. **B** = Receiver. **C** = Create space. **D** = Exploit space.
- **On the left**, **C** drops back as if to draw an opponent out of position, while **D** makes a run into the vacated space.
- **A1** plays a long pass to **B**, who directs the ball into **D's** path. **D** finishes the sequence by dribbling forward, passing into the small goal, and moving to **A2**.
- **On the right**, **C** drops back while **D** makes an overlapping run into the vacated space. **D** receives, passes into the small goal, and moves to **A2**.
- **Player Rotations:** A1 → B → C → D → A2.
- → Repeat sequence in opposite direction.
- **Coaching Point:** Intelligent well-timed movement to disrupt man marking.

Training Session 9: Build Up to Beat the Press Against Full Pitch Man Marking

PROGRESSION

3. Beating a Full Pitch Man Marking Press with a Single Pivot Build Up Shape in a Half Pitch Game

Variation 1: Against High Pressing (7 +GK vs 7)

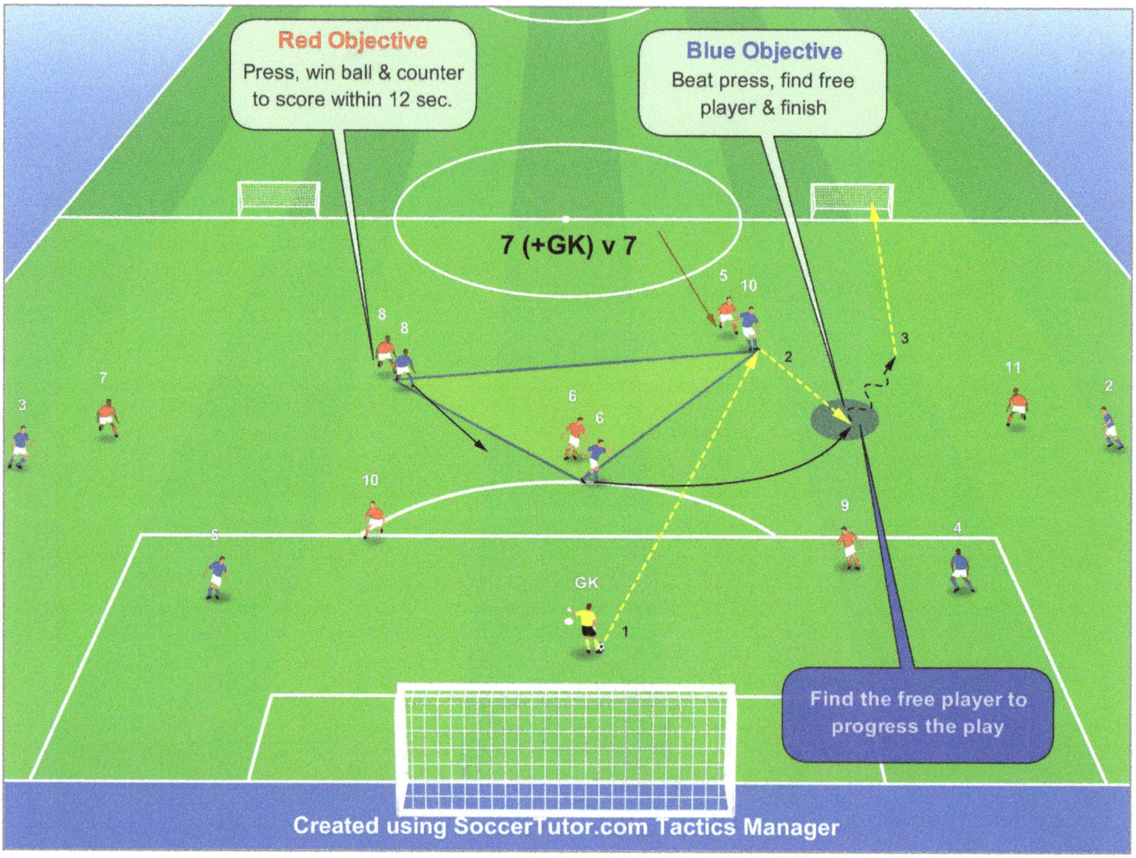

Practice Description (Variation 1)

- This 7v7 (+GK) game is played in the low half of the pitch. The blues use a 4-3 shape from the 4-3-3 formation. The 2 wingers and forward are not involved.

- **Blue Team Objective: Find the free player to progress play against high pressing with full pitch man marking** and use any numerical advantages to break forward and score in either of the 2 small goals.

- **Red Team Objective:** Apply a full pitch man marking press to force the blues into quick decisions. Win the ball and counter to score within 10-12 seconds.

- **Note:** This practice sharpens quick decision making, movement, passing to break through high pressing, and exploiting numerical advantages in match-like conditions.

BEAT THE PRESS WITH SINGLE & DOUBLE PIVOTS

Training Session 9: Build Up to Beat the Press Against Full Pitch Man Marking

Variation 2: Against Ultra-Aggressive High Pressing (7 +GK vs 7)

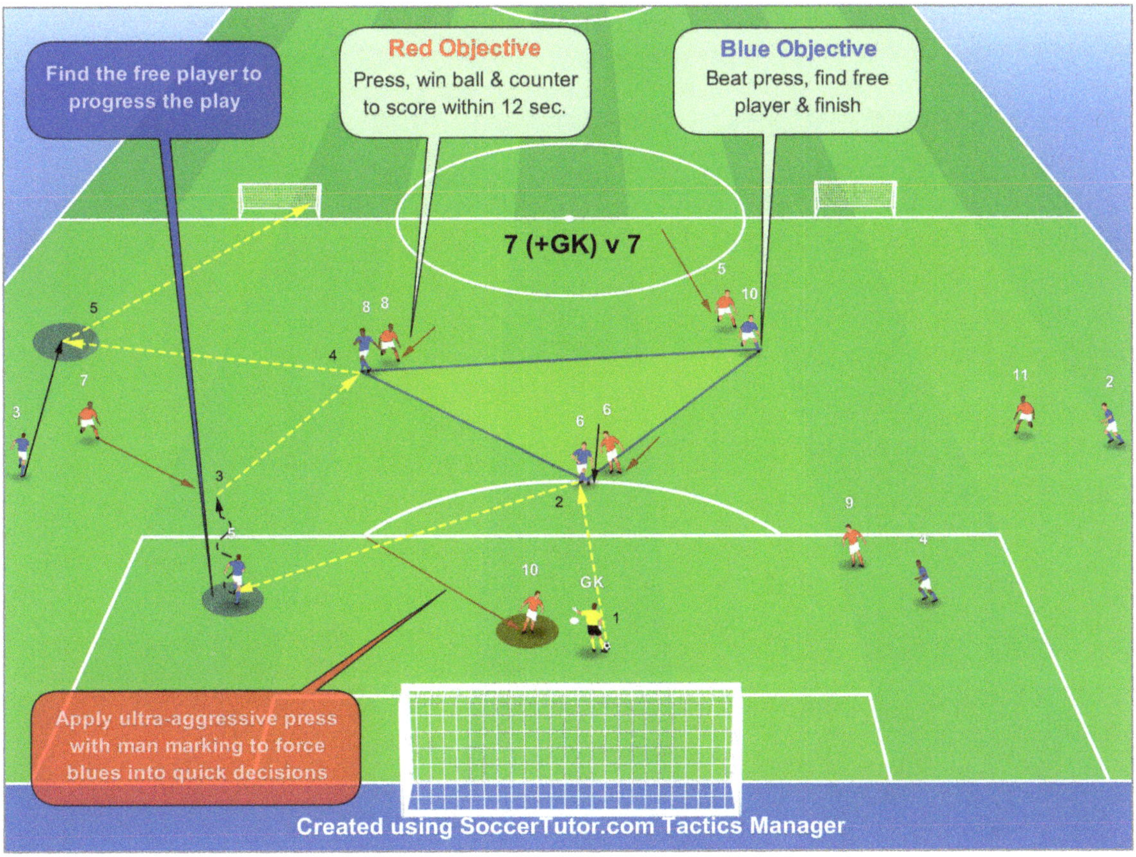

![Diagram showing 7(+GK) v 7 practice setup with blue and red teams, annotations: "Find the free player to progress the play", "Red Objective: Press, win ball & counter to score within 12 sec.", "Blue Objective: Beat press, find free player & finish", "Apply ultra-aggressive press with man marking to force blues into quick decisions"]

Practice Description (Variation 2)

- The structure remains the same, but the **red team now apply ultra-aggressive pressing** (up to the GK with red Nº10).
- All blue players are tightly marked except **free player (Nº5)** - *see analysis pages in this section for full details*.
- **Blue Team Objective:** Find the free player, use link players, break pressing lines and create/exploit available spaces to progress the ball forward and score in the small goals.
- **Red Team Objective:** Press to win the ball and counter to score within 10–12 seconds, just like in Variation 1.

Coaching Points

1. **Intelligent off-ball movements** to lose markers.
2. **Timing and synchronisation** of supporting runs.
3. **Accuracy in passing** to ensure effective ball circulation (well-weighted under pressure).
4. **Reading the pressing cues** to identify the free player.
5. **Using the link player principles (see page 129) effectively** to connect lines and beat the press.

Training Session 9: Build Up to Beat the Press Against Full Pitch Man Marking

PROGRESSION
4. Beating a Full Pitch Man Marking Press with the Goalkeeper's Long Pass 6v6 (+GKs) Game
Variation 1: Forward (Target Player) Uses Hold Up/Link Play

Red Objective
High press, win ball & counter to score 2 small goals within 12 sec.

Blue Objective
Create and expoit space (No.9) from long pass

Practice Description (Variation 1)

- This practice simulates **build up play against full pitch man marking**, focusing on **creating and exploiting space using the goalkeeper's (GK) long pass**.

- In this 6v6 (+GKs) game, the blues set up with a **3-3 shape from 4-3-3 formation**. The reds defend with a 4-2 shape.

- We start with the coach's pass to the blue **GK**. The centre backs and full backs are not involved.

- **Blue Team Objective:** Create space through off-ball movement, **play a long pass from the GK to the forward (Nº9) or wingers (Nº11 and Nº7), and score**.

- Note: *See analysis pages in this section for the full explanation of the tactics in this situation.*

- **Red Team Objective:** Apply high press man marking across the whole area. Win the ball and counter to score in the small goals within 10-12 seconds.

©SOCCERTUTOR.COM

BEAT THE PRESS WITH SINGLE & DOUBLE PIVOTS

Training Session 9: Build Up to Beat the Press Against Full Pitch Man Marking

Variation 2: Forward (Target Player) Uses Speed to Receive Directly

[Diagram: 6 v 6 (+GKs)]

Red Objective
High press, win ball & counter to score 2 small goals within 12 sec.

Blue Objective
Create and exploit space (No.9) from long pass

Practice Description (Variation 2)

- The previous page (**Variation 1**) showed the forward (**N°9**) staying close to his marker (**1v1**) and receiving the long pass from the goalkeeper (**GK**).
- Using link play, **N°9** is able to set the ball back for an oncoming teammate (**attacking midfielder N°8** in diagram).
- In **Variation 2**, N°9 utilises his speed to get away from his marker and receive directly from GK in behind. Players support the attack.
- **Restriction:** GK must pass within 4–5 seconds of receiving from the coach to maintain game intensity and practice decision making under pressure.

- **Note 1:** The practice can easily be adjusted to practice with a double pivot midfield (4-2-3-1 formation).
- **Note 2:** *See analysis pages in this section for the full explanation of the tactics in this situation.*

BEAT THE PRESS WITH SINGLE & DOUBLE PIVOTS

Training Session 9: Build Up to Beat the Press Against Full Pitch Man Marking

PROGRESSION

5. Reading Tactical Triggers to Beat the Press Against Full Pitch Man Marking Game

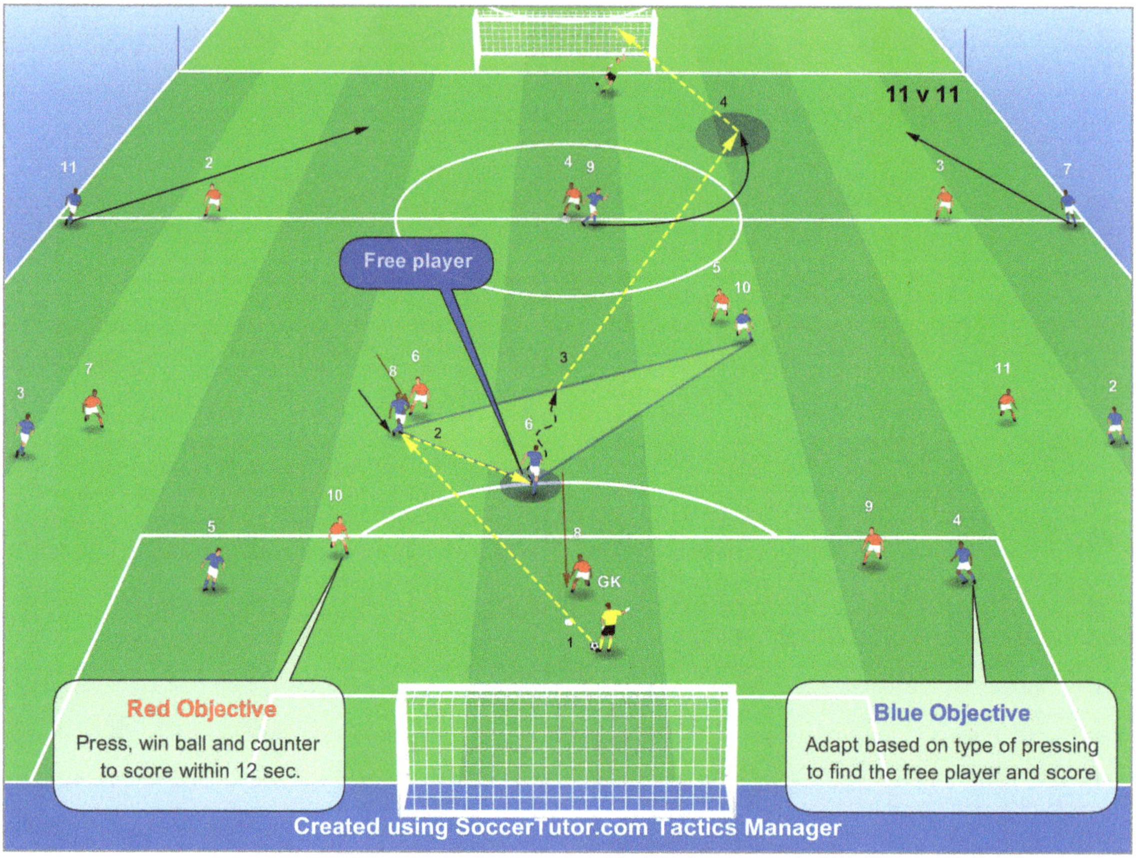

Red Objective
Press, win ball and counter to score within 12 sec.

Blue Objective
Adapt based on type of pressing to find the free player and score

Practice Description

- **Tactical Objective:** Find the free player against ultra-aggressive pressing (up to GK) or create and exploit space against high pressing (on first receiver). In 3/4 of a full pitch, we play an 11v11 game.

- The reds apply full pitch man marking using ultra-aggressive pressing or high pressing (**see previous practices + analysis pages**).

- **Blue Team Objective:** Adapt based on the type of pressing applied and progress the ball forward to score.

- **Against ultra-aggressive pressing (up to goalkeeper)**, the blues must find and use the free player to beat the press.

- **In the diagram example, the defensive midfielder (N°6) is free as his direct opponent (red N°8) moves to press GK.**

- **Against high pressing (on first receiver)**, they must coordinate synchronised movements to create and exploit space.

- **Red Team Objective:** Win the ball and counter to score within 10-12 seconds.

FINAL MESSAGE FOR COACHES

Athanasios Terzis

- Football Tactics Expert
- Award Winning Author
- PAOK U23 Assistant Coach
- UEFA 'A' Coaching Licence
- Greek Football Federation Instructor

- Building up from the back **must be developed step by step** for success.

- The **risk factor is high** since the build up play happens near your team's goal.

- Losing possession in this area **can lead to dangerous situations**, including goal scoring opportunities for the opposition.

- Players need to **gradually gain confidence** in the process to become more effective.

- Coaches must **introduce build up play progressively** to ensure players are comfortable and limit costly mistakes.

Free Trial

Football Coaching Specialists Since 2001

Tactics Manager

Create your own Practices, Tactics & Plan Sessions!

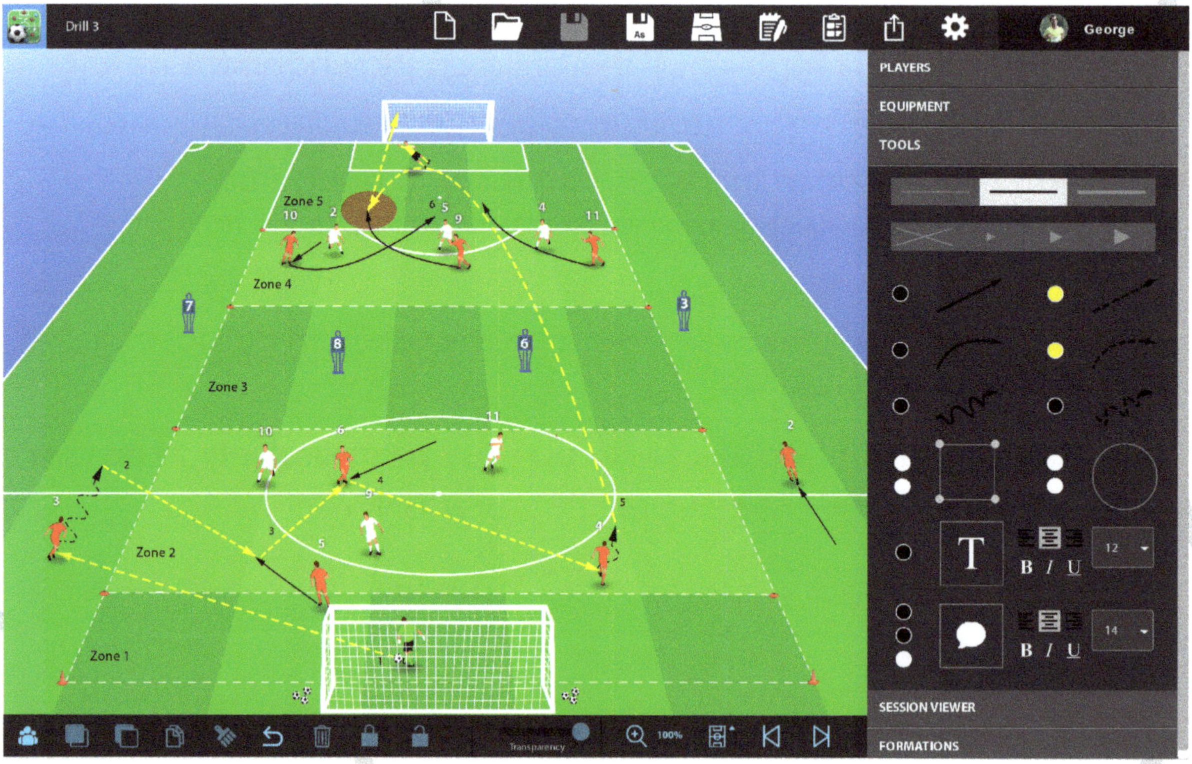

Tactics Manager App

SoccerTutor.com

Football Coaching Specialists Since 2001

BEAT THE PRESS WITH A BOX MIDFIELD

Build Up Play and Sessions from Guardiola, Alonso and Arteta's Tactics

Terzis Athanasios

SoccerTutor.com - Football Coaching Specialists Since 2001

Coaching Books Available in Full Colour Print and eBook
PC | Mac | iPhone | iPad | Android Phone / Tablet | Chromebook

FREE Coach Viewer **APP**

SoccerTutor.com

Football Coaching Specialists Since 2001

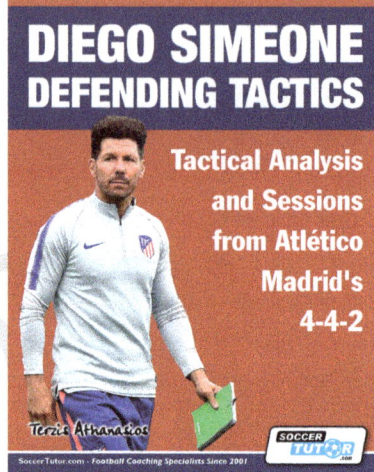

More Coaching Books Available from Athanasios Terzis

PC | Mac | iPhone | iPad | Android Phone / Tablet | Chromebook

 **FREE** Coach Viewer **APP**

SoccerTutor.com

Football Coaching Specialists Since 2001

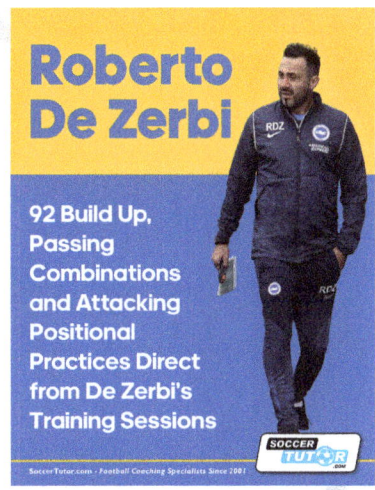

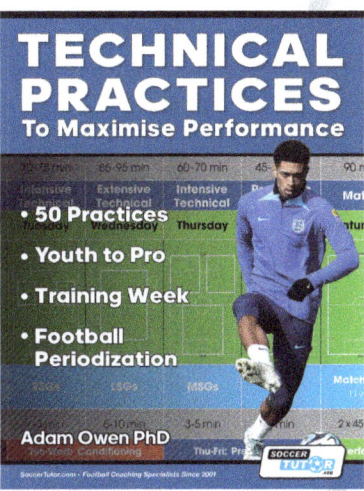

More Coaching Books Available in Full Colour Print and eBook
PC | Mac | iPhone | iPad | Android Phone / Tablet | Chromebook

 **FREE** Coach Viewer **APP**

SoccerTutor.com

www.ingramcontent.com/pod-product-compliance
Lightning Source LLC
Chambersburg PA
CBHW040932240426
43673CB00051B/1957